DELIVERANCE DEFINED

DON DICKERMAN

CHARISMA HOUSE

DELIVERANCE DEFINED by Don Dickerman
Published by Charisma House, an imprint of Charisma Media
1150 Greenwood Blvd., Lake Mary, Florida 32746

Unless otherwise noted, all Scripture quotations are taken from the King James Version of the Bible.

Scripture quotations marked AMPC are from the Amplified® Bible (AMPC), Copyright © 1954, 1958, 1962, 1964, 1965, 1987 by The Lockman Foundation. Used by permission. www.Lockman.org

Scripture quotations marked ESV are from The ESV® Bible (The Holy Bible, English Standard Version®), copyright © 2001 by Crossway, a publishing ministry of Good News Publishers. Used by permission. All rights reserved.

Scripture quotations marked MEV are from the Modern English Version. Copyright © 2014 by Military Bible Association. Used by permission. All rights reserved.

Scripture quotations marked MSG are from *The Message: The Bible in Contemporary English*, copyright © 1993, 1994, 1995, 1996, 2000, 2001, 2002. Used by permission of NavPress Publishing Group.

Scripture quotations marked NIV are taken from the Holy Bible, New International Version®, NIV®. Copyright © 1973, 1978, 1984, 2011 by Biblica, Inc.® Used by permission of Zondervan. All rights reserved worldwide. www.zondervan.com. The "NIV" and "New International Version" are trademarks registered in the United States Patent and Trademark Office by Biblica, Inc.®

Scripture quotations marked NKJV are taken from the New King James Version®. Copyright © 1982 by Thomas Nelson. Used by permission. All rights reserved.

Scripture quotations marked NLT are taken from the *Holy Bible*, New Living Translation, copyright ©1996, 2004, 2015 by Tyndale House Foundation. Used by permission of Tyndale House Publishers, Carol Stream, Illinois 60188. All rights reserved.

Deliverance Defined is an outstanding resource for anyone seeking to understand and engage in deliverance ministry. Don Dickerman's decades of experience in spiritual warfare are evident throughout the book, providing practical, biblical insights on how to recognize and defeat demonic forces. His teachings on closing the doorways through which demons enter and walking in complete freedom have been a profound blessing in my life and ministry, enhancing my understanding of spiritual warfare and deliverance.

—Vladimir Savchuk
Senior Pastor, Hungry Generation
Author, *Break Free* and *Host the Holy Ghost*

Don Dickerman has devoted his life to liberating captives through the power of Jesus Christ. His ministry has helped thousands around the world. He is a fantastic resource for the body of Christ. You will definitely want to read his book *Deliverance Defined*!

—Frank Harber PhD, JD
CEO and Chief Legal Counsel, Defending The Faith Alliance

Don Dickerman is fulfilling Isaiah 61 by healing the brokenhearted and setting the captives free. He knows salvation is not enough for the church and that freedom is equally important. He has been an instrument in setting thousands of prisoners free, both behind bars and on the other side. I have experienced this freedom through his work. He exposes the lies and the demonic forces that hold Christians back from experiencing freedom, the joy-filled life, their identity in Christ, and their destiny.

—Bill Noble
Dallas Businessman

I see Don Dickerman as this generation's general and forerunner for deliverance ministry. I have recommended his original book, *When Pigs Move In*, thousands of times. His new book, *Deliverance Defined*, takes things to the next level. Whether you are new to deliverance ministry or advanced, the book has so much to offer.

This is one of those books that a hundred years from now people will still be using to teach deliverance. If you are ready to get activated in deliverance ministry, this is a must-read!

—Isaiah Saldivar
Author, *How to Cast Out Demons*

Over the years my respect for Pastor Don Dickerman has grown due to his unwavering focus on helping Christians exercise the freedom of Jesus Christ's suffering on the cross of Calvary. A prolific writer around spiritual liberty with a strong anointing for deliverance, he has now written a new book, *Deliverance Defined: How to Lock Up and Lock Out Demons*.

This detailed guide is a profound investigation into the often-misunderstood realm of spiritual deliverance. It exhibits Pastor Dickerman's extensive experience in man's liberation with both theological insights and practical guidance for the Christian in the battle for his soul, teaching readers how to cast evil out and receive a total and unreserved freedom from spiritual oppression. This resource is grounded in a deep understanding of the Bible and sheds light on the reality of demonic oppression in modern life, how to discern the signs of demonic activity, shut entryways through which demons enter, and walk in complete freedom.

Whether you're a minister, a counselor, or someone seeking personal freedom, this book serves as a comprehensive guide to recognizing and defeating evil spirits. Pastor Dickerman's ability to demystify deliverance while maintaining a strong biblical foundation makes *Deliverance Defined* a must-read for anyone serious about understanding spiritual warfare and walking in true freedom.

—Prophet Nanasei Opoku-Sarkodie
The Potters City, Accra, Ghana

For more resources like this, visit MyCharismaShop.com and the author's website at liberatedliving.info.

Cataloging-in-Publication Data is on file with the Library of Congress.

International Standard Book Number: 978-1-63641-469-0
E-book ISBN: 978-1-63641-470-6

1 2024
Printed in the United States of America

Most Charisma Media products are available at special quantity discounts for bulk purchase for sales promotions, premiums, fund-raising, and educational needs. For details, call us at (407) 333-0600 or visit our website at charismamedia.com.

CONTENTS

SPECIAL THANKS

THIS BOOK IS the result of much prayer and seeking from God's Holy Spirit. I dedicate this book in the memory of my deceased wife, Peggy, who stood faithfully with me through many years of travel to more than 850 prisons and for deliverance ministry. She traveled with me to visit David Berkowitz in New York. It is also dedicated to our great sons, Donnie and Dr. Rob.

I am thankful for a staff of dedicated people, and they all have contributed to the information we have gathered through literally thousands of deliverance sessions:

Cherie Flowers, our office administrator (she's the one you talk to if you call our office).

Bill Morgan, who I call the world's smartest man, in spite of being an Aggie. Since I am a huge Texas Longhorn fan, we have to put that aside while ministering. Bill will be my successor.

Ronnie and Jeannie Cummings, who have been with me the longest. They have traveled all over the country to minister with me.

Robert Sullivan, a former Texas Longhorn linebacker. Sometimes we have to double-team Bill.

Pat Muhney, a carpenter/builder/handyman, who is also one of our faithful and humble ministers.

Jonathan Smith, an IT specialist and our newest minister.

Mark Burgin, Jim Pierce, Rosalie Escobedo, Gary Davis, Bill Morgan, and Robert Sullivan, who all serve as our board of directors.

THE CALL TO DELIVERANCE

MANY YEARS AGO I felt God leading me to find out everything I could about demons and to pass it on to others in deliverance ministry, to see an army of men and women who would understand who they are in Christ. The church is building up audiences, not armies. I believe Jesus gave us marching orders and told us to *stand* our ground.

There is so much to say. Some of what you will read are my personal revelations about deliverance. Jesus called demons *devils, deaf and dumb spirits*, and *foul, unclean spirits*—and He told us to cast them out.

If you're holding this book, I believe it's no accident. You've likely sensed a call to go deeper in your walk with Christ, to learn how to protect yourself and those you love from spiritual darkness, and to understand and wield the authority given to you by Jesus. In a world where demonic forces are often misunderstood or dismissed, this book aims to equip you with the truth and the tools needed to lock up and lock out the enemy's influence.

Deliverance isn't reserved for an elite few; it's a gift given to all believers by the authority of Jesus Christ. Over the past forty years I've had the privilege of seeing deliverance transform countless lives. People once bound by fear, addiction, sickness, and torment have found freedom through Jesus. In these pages I'll share insights gained through these experiences, not just to encourage you but to empower you to become a warrior in this battle against darkness.

So what are demons? They are not spirits of dead people or

wandering souls without a home. They are fallen angels, organized in a sophisticated, structured hierarchy—a copycat of God's holy order—and they are at war with God and His people. They have specific ranks and assignments, and they enter the soulish area of human beings through unconfessed sin, generational permissions, or other open doors. Their aim? To torment, deceive, kill, steal, and destroy. The power of the demon is the lie, plain and simple—twisted truth, tainted truth, partial truth. The father of lies and deception is Satan. His demons are like him.

Deliverance is how we deal with demons, but it is probably not what you have heard that it is. It is not like the movies. It is not like Hollywood—it is like the Holy Word! It is for believers! It is nothing to be afraid of and is totally nonthreatening to the individual. It is simply breaking the permission that has allowed the enemy to operate in our lives. Remember what Acts 10:38 says? "God anointed Jesus of Nazareth with the Holy Ghost and with power: who went about doing good, and healing all that were oppressed of the devil." That is what deliverance is, breaking the oppressing power of the enemy!

Deliverance is freedom from the presence of demon powers that abide in the soul or flesh, or that are attached to a believer's life. While deliverance is not "the" ministry, it is important to understand that it is certainly part of "the" ministry.

Deliverance is so amazing. It is a truth encounter. The Holy Spirit so wonderfully brings truth to us and forces the demons to react in obedience to commands in the authority of the Lord Jesus Christ. Scriptural deliverance is relieving spiritual oppression!

Deliverance is like being in a courtroom where Jehovah God is seated at the judge's bench. He is the judge of all truth and righteousness. It is His legal system. Law is what He has spoken! Whatever God speaks becomes law. You can't see His face, just His glory. Holy angels encircle the bench and proclaim His holiness. He is the righteous judge.

Henceforth there is laid up for me a crown of righteousness, which the Lord, the *righteous judge*, shall give me at that day: and not to me only, but unto all them also that love his appearing.

—2 TIMOTHY 4:8, EMPHASIS ADDED

God's courtroom is no ordinary courtroom; only truth will be recognized here. You see, deliverance is not about power, and it is not just about authority, though we certainly have it in Jesus Christ's name. Deliverance is about the truth.

One particular scripture about deliverance resounds in my spirit: "Behold, I give unto you power to tread on serpents and scorpions, and over all the power of the enemy: and nothing shall by any means hurt you" (Luke 10:19). Who gave us power and authority over the kingdom of darkness? Jesus! We have been given power of attorney, legal authority, to act in Jesus' name! The authority was and is His name, and He commissioned you and me to act in the authority of His name. As blood-washed children of God, we can take authority over evil spirits and command them to go. With great power and authority in the name of Jesus, we are to speak freedom!

That's what this book is about—speaking freedom by the authority and power of Jesus' name and bringing deliverance to the captives.

In the pages ahead you'll discover how to identify demonic forces and protect yourself and your loved ones from spiritual attacks. I've also included a list of demon names and their demonic functions—a reference guide that will help you better understand the enemy's strategies and dismantle them through the authority in Jesus' name.

You were created to walk in victory not in fear. Jesus defeated darkness on the cross, giving you authority over every demonic power that seeks to harm or control you. As you read, I pray you'll be equipped, strengthened, and emboldened, knowing that no power of hell can stand against the name of Jesus.

Let this book be your guide as you learn to lock up and lock out the forces of darkness and walk in the freedom God has for you.

PART I

RESTORING DELIVERANCE TO THE CHURCH

CHAPTER 1

HOW CAN A CHRISTIAN HAVE A DEMON?

AFTER FORTY YEARS in deliverance ministry, the number one question I get is, How can a Christian have a demon? It is an example of the spiritual blindness and willing ignorance purported by small-minded pastors. I'm a Christian, so I couldn't have a demon.

Perhaps the simplest way to answer this question is with another question: How can a Christian get sick, get a disease or emotional wound, have an evil thought, or battle with anger? You see, if the premise of the question is "I have the Holy Spirit; therefore, I could not have a demon spirit," then that is flawed spiritual logic. The Holy Spirit does not fight for us to prevent evil; if He did, you would have no problems.

It is scripturally clear that a believer can "quench" the Spirit (1 Thess. 5:19). A believer can "grieve" the Holy Spirit (Eph. 4:30). A believer can ignore the Spirit's leading and directing. The Holy Spirit does not force Himself against our will. We are tripartite beings, a trinity of spirit, soul, and body. Demon spirits cannot enter the spirit of a believer, for that is where the Holy Spirit dwells. However, they certainly can and do get into our flesh and soul. Some ask, How can light have fellowship with darkness? It is not fellowship; it is war. It is oppression.

It is not demonic possession, for that implies ownership. We are owned, purchased, and bought with a price—we are owned by the Father, bought by the Son, and indwelt by the Spirit. So we are talking about demonic oppression, not possession. A common and correct term is *demonized.*

Deliverance is not for lost people. What would be the point of casting demons from those who are eternally doomed Christ rejecters? Look at the people Jesus ministered to. Virtually all were "children of Abraham," meaning they were people of faith: "Know ye therefore that they which are of faith, the same are the children of Abraham" (Gal. 3:7).

Believers are the ones who qualify for deliverance. Galatians 3:29 tells us, "And if ye be Christ's then are ye Abraham's seed, and heirs according to the promise." Jesus ministered deliverance to believers. He even disqualified those who were not believers. Remember the story of the Canaanite woman who begged Jesus for help for her daughter? The woman was not a believer. She was not one of the "children of Abraham." It was only after she expressed great faith that her "grievously vexed" daughter was delivered (Matt. 15:22).

Deliverance is for believers. As a believer with a free will, you can open any door you want. *Deliverance is not the door to salvation; salvation is the door to deliverance.*

TORMENTED BY DEMONS

When I started in ministry, supernaturally God began to place people in my life. Inmates would seek me out, tell me they had demons, and ask me to help them. These were always believers, and I had always been taught that Christians could not have demons. I now believe this is the biggest lie Satan has perpetrated on the body of Christ. The deception is so great that most believers will not even consider that they may be demonically oppressed.

Christians can, and often do, have demons in their souls and flesh working great oppression in their lives. We are possessed by the Holy Spirit, who lives in our spirits. Possession implies ownership. We are owned, purchased, and bought with a price by the Lord Jesus. It is correct, possibly, to say that a demon may possess an *area* of a Christian's life but never can they own us. A well-known pastor in Atlanta refers to this as "demonic control" in particular areas of a believer's life where legal rights have been surrendered.

I was preaching at a prison when I was first introduced to the reality of demon powers living in Christians. I was really not open to discussion that evil spirits could actually dwell within a believer because I was born in a Baptist home, saved in a Baptist church, ordained as a Baptist deacon, licensed and ordained as a Baptist minister, and graduated from a Baptist seminary. Never in any of my years of seminary training at nondenominational seminaries and two Baptist seminaries did I hear that this was a possibility. I don't recall ever hearing any discussion about demons or spiritual warfare taking place within believers. It was a foreign concept to me. I only recall one professor ever even mentioning demon powers.

However, while at this prison, I encountered a believer who had demons! It happened at a prison for women. I was accompanied by my wife, Peggy, and a few others from our Texas-based ministry. My host was the director of Prison Fellowship. By this time I had been preaching in prisons for many years, and I had encountered many inmates who had told me about demons in their lives, but this experience was different.

I preached to a group of about thirty-five women in a small chapel area. After the service, a young woman came up to me and said, "You are the one! I don't know why I am telling you this. I just feel drawn to you. I feel like you will understand, and I feel like you will help me."

What she told me would forever change my life and ministry.

"Brother Don," she said, "I know I am saved, and I know Jesus lives in my heart, but I am tormented by demons! Will you help me?"

Remember, I had always been taught this was not possible. However, I was looking into the eyes of a young lady who was desperate for deliverance. She began to tell me things I never thought I would hear. She told me with pleading eyes, "My parents were Satan worshippers, and I was dedicated to Satan as a baby. I was raised to become the bride of Lucifer." She began to tell me of ritualistic abuse from the time she was born, some of which I cannot even repeat. She explained that she was being groomed to become the highest-ranking female in this satanic group.

She told me of her parents and others urging demon spirits to come into her. This was all part of a plan to fill her with demons so that she could one day become Lucifer's bride.

I listened, and even as I was listening, I wondered how I could help her. She told me many times, "I know I'm saved. I know Jesus lives in my heart, but I am tormented by demons." Again, man's theology must come into agreement with genuine experience. I was looking into the eyes of a desperate, born-again child of God. My mind raced through Scripture and accounts of Jesus commanding evil spirits to leave, but I didn't know how to do it. I didn't know I could do it!

God had been preparing me for several years, but I did not know it. Now I began to see some of His preparation. Stories from other inmates filled my mind. There was one deliverance session I had on videotape. The person on the tape experienced incredible freedom from demons in a county jail. I had met and had great respect for the minister who walked this man through deliverance. Suddenly I had a plan.

I told the young woman I knew a man who had a ministry of setting captives free and that I would contact him and try to make arrangements with the prison for him to come there and minister to her. "You will be free!" I told her.

Over the next several months I corresponded with the inmate. I learned more about the strongholds and the torment she was experiencing. I was able to lead her to forgive her parents through our many letters. She would eventually forgive all those who had deceived her and taken advantage of her.

As you might imagine, it's not easy to make arrangements with a prison for something like this, but the prison officials were very cooperative, and arrangements were made. Actually, in retrospect, it was probably easier than making such arrangements in a church.

We were given a private conference room, and there would be no officers present. The only people present would be the inmate, the pastor who would minister deliverance, and me. I was going to be the one who prayed as the pastor commanded evil spirits to leave.

When the time came for the deliverance session, there was just one hitch in the plan: The pastor did not show up! Something had come up. I thought, "Are you kidding me? This woman is expecting deliverance, and I'm the only one here. God set me up!" I'm glad He did. It was clear to me then, but it's even more plain now as I look back over the years. God put me in a situation where I had to act; I had to use the faith He had given to me.

I will never forget that first deliverance experience. It was by far the most dramatic of the thousands I have had since then. I walked up the stairs of this stately government building and presented my papers for clearance to the officer at the front gate. I remember her looking at me with some curiosity in her eyes. She knew why I was there, but I'm sure she didn't understand it. I felt as if she must have thought I didn't fit the part of an exorcist. I wasn't dressed in black. I didn't have a big wooden cross, and I was not a priest. As a matter of fact, I was in my blue jeans, tennis shoes, and golf shirt.

It's funny how being set free has been given such a dark, negative connotation. Hollywood has done a lot of damage to the concept of freedom from demon powers. *Exorcism* is not the word I would choose anyway. I like *oppression relief* or *oppression healing*. Acts 10:38 says, "God anointed Jesus of Nazareth with the Holy Ghost and with power: who went about doing good, and healing all that were oppressed of the devil; for God was with him." It is oppression healing!

I MADE A DECISION TO TAKE A STEP OF FAITH

A correctional officer escorted me up the inside stairs to the third floor of the prison and to the private conference room. I figured this was where prison staff meetings took place. Inside the room was a long table with three chairs on each side and a chair at each end. I had been praying with such intensity since I arrived in town the day before and realized the pastor was not going to be there. I had made a decision to take a step of faith. I took a seat with my back to the windows on the west wall and waited in prayer for the inmate to come in through a door to my right.

She arrived and greeted me with a hug, and then she sat directly across from me. The officer who escorted her in left, and we talked for several minutes before we prayed.

I thought, "What am I doing? Am I going to cast out demons? I am going to take on evil spirits, fallen angels that live in another human being? How did I get here? Am I crazy? Do I think I have authority over the kingdom of darkness?" I was bombarded with all kinds of doubts, but I kept rebuking those thoughts with Scripture that the Holy Spirit brought to my mind.

We'd had a word of prayer earlier to open the session, but the time had come. I told the woman what I was going to do. As I looked across the table, she had lowered her head, and her eyes peered up at me, almost covered by her eyelids. Never had I seen or sensed so much evil. Chills went through me. I trembled and felt fear try to overcome me, but I knew fear was a spirit, and I was not going to give in, "for God hath not given us the spirit of fear; but of power, and of love, and of a sound mind" (2 Tim. 1:7). I rebuked fear in the name of Jesus, and immediately it stopped.

I asked the inmate to pray a prayer after me, acknowledging Jesus Christ as her Savior and Lord. She confessed and repented of unforgiveness, hatred, bitterness, and anger, and she renounced all her involvement in satanism. It was very difficult for her to get the words out of her mouth. The demons did all they could to prevent her from speaking words that would break their power. She struggled through the prayer as she started to tremble, and her arms jerked. Her head dropped with her chin on her chest. I could not see her facial expression clearly, but her face began to contort and a growling sound, low and muffled, came from her lips.

I knew there was likely a demonic kingdom there, and if so, then some demon power would be in charge of the kingdom. I knew they were principalities and powers. After binding them with specific instructions, I commanded the prince demon, or the demon power that claimed to be in charge, to identify himself. I didn't know what to expect. The woman's voice changed; it became gruff and monotone, and the demons were speaking through her, just as they did through the man Jesus encountered in the Gadarenes.

"Identify yourself," I commanded. The demon immediately gave his name through the inmate. With each response, I commanded the demon to reveal if the answer would stand as truth before Jehovah God. The pastor who was supposed to be ministering to this woman had told me when I first met him that demons will not lie to Jehovah God. I commanded this demon power to reveal how many demons were present and how many were in his kingdom. After several lies, and after I called the evil spirit before the throne of God, the evil entity said, "We are too many; we are too powerful for you."

He was right; he was too powerful for me—but he was not dealing with me. He was dealing with my Savior. I reminded the evil spirit that this was not between us but between my Master and his master, and that his master had been soundly defeated. The demon spat out death threats aimed at my family and me. "No," I commanded him firmly, "you won't do anything but be obedient to the command in the name of the Lord Jesus." God had given me boldness beyond my understanding.

I commanded the spirit to reveal if he had any consent from this woman or from Jehovah God to stay there. There was silence. I repeated the question in the authority of Jesus' name and commanded a response. "No." There was no consent for the unclean spirit to be there. Her salvation, repentance, and renunciation of involvement had broken the power of the enemy.

I commanded the spirit to reveal if any demon power present had any permission to remain. More silence. More commands. Eventually there was a no. I said, "You know you must leave her, don't you? You and all of your kingdom are going to be cast to the abyss, to the pit!"

"No, no, no!" The woman's arms had been jerking the whole time. I had placed my hands on hers, and as I commanded the demons to leave, she jerked her hands away and began to strangle herself. She was gagging and coughing, and fluid was running from her mouth. I got up and tried to pull her hands loose. Her face was turning blue. I could not budge her hands or fingers from her throat. She had reared back in the chair, and her body was rigid.

I commanded the spirits to release her in the name of the Anointed One, Jesus Christ. Immediately her hands fell to her side, and she fell limply onto the table, facedown. I took her again by the hands and asked how she felt. "I feel so much lighter and much better," she said.

When I told her I thought there were more present, again her arms began to quiver and her head dropped on her chest. "Who are you?" I commanded. Again her voice changed, and a name was given. "Why didn't you leave when you were commanded to go?" I asked.

"She's mine!" the demon persisted angrily. "She's mine!"

"No! She's not yours," I said with boldness. "She belongs to Jesus Christ, and she has been bought with a price, purchased, redeemed, and born again! She is an heir of God and a joint heir with Jesus Christ. You have no right to her life, and you will leave her now in Jesus Christ's mighty name." The woman began to cough. She jerked and trembled and cleared her throat as the vile demon left.

Still, there was another, and this one seemed as violent as the first. This spirit threatened to kill me with a menacing growl.

I countered, "You'll do nothing but leave as you are commanded in Christ Jesus' name."

"She's mine. I want her body! Her body is mine!"

As I commanded this spirit to leave, the woman again pulled her hands away and grabbed herself. I stood up, and from behind her chair I placed my hands on her forearms and commanded the spirit to release her immediately and go to the abyss. The release was immediate.

She slumped in her chair and then looked up at me with the most peaceful look. "They're gone. They're gone!" She stood up and began to praise God; the praise just flowed from her lips. She jumped straight up and down like she was on a pogo stick, still praising God.

"Oh," she said, "they are gone. I really am free!"

And she was really free. The authority and power of Jesus' name brought freedom and deliverance to a captive.

When I left the prison that day, I paused on the top step of the prison. I held my Bible up into the air and shouted, "Yes! In the name of Jesus, yes!"

THE TEMPLE OF GOD

You may be just like many others who question deliverance. Perhaps you are one of the people who has asked, "How can I have demons since I'm a Christian?" I don't want to use the entire book for this issue, but you must get it settled in your mind and heart. Believers can and often do have demon spirits living in them.

It may be helpful to explain this in somewhat simplistic terms. The myth must be destroyed for the body of Christ to be free. The myth (a widely held but false belief) has given evil spirits an advantage and has kept the church in bondage. Plain and simple, it is spiritual ignorance that allows this bondage to continue. *Ignorance* is a strong word, but the Word of God declares, "Where there is no vision, the people perish" (Prov. 29:18), and "My people are destroyed for lack of knowledge" (Hos. 4:6). Lack of knowledge is ignorance. And in this case it is willing ignorance.

The presence of the Holy Spirit does not prevent evil spirits from dwelling in a believer's body or soul! Until a believer can recognize and understand how demonic bondage occurs, he cannot be free. You can be Spirit-filled; memorize the Word of God; sing in the choir; teach Sunday school; and be a deacon, teacher, or preacher and still have demons. I deal with this almost daily! That believers cannot have demons is a dangerous, widely held belief, but it is a false belief. It is a myth.

You may wonder how a demon spirit can enter a follower of Christ. Look at the apparent ease with which Satan entered into Judas. John 13:27 records, "As soon as Judas took the bread, Satan entered into him. So Jesus told him, 'What you are about to do, do quickly'" (NIV). The prince of darkness did personal battle with Jesus, and he used people to try to attain victory. He *entered* into Judas. Demons enter people today, and their goal is still the same— to war against us, to oppose everything of God. We can best understand this by knowing that it is not Satan himself we deal with but his legions of demon powers on assignment from his kingdom of darkness. Jesus said to cast them *out*—so they must be *in*.

It is the foot-soldier demons that get into the lives of people. People are demonized by evil spirits who are under the rule of higher-ranking spirits. When the demon on the inside of a person is confronted, he most likely represents a higher-ranking demon power in the heavenlies; most often he uses the name of that demon.

When permission is given—that is, when legal rights are granted, whether through ancestral transgressions or open doors of trauma, abuse, disobedience, and unconfessed sin—demons can enter the believer. This is demonization; it is spiritual oppression. Remember, the spirits dwell in the flesh and/or the soul but never in the spirit, for that is where the Holy Spirit lives.

Again, while the unclean spirits may possess an area of a person's life, genuine possession by demons cannot happen to a Christian for possession is ownership, and we are owned by the Lord Jesus. Don't forget, we are purchased, bought with a price!

FOUR TRUTHS ABOUT DELIVERANCE

Before one can understand deliverance, it is necessary to know at least four truths concerning the process.

1. Demons are simple.

Not everyone has demons, but many people do. Demons are not always the source of an individual's problem, but many times they are. So the first logical assessment is maybe you do have them, maybe you don't. Hence, my simple approach is when in doubt, cast them out. If it is determined that there are no oppressing spirits present, you will still be the same person as before the process.

2. Demons cannot simply enter a person against their will.

If demons are present, it is because a legal right was obtained through their ancestry or a variety of other legal permissions that might include trauma at or during birth; childhood abuse; sexual embarrassments including abuse; oaths, pledges, and vows including to fraternities and sororities; open doors through willing disobedience to God, anger, bitterness, resentment, unforgiveness, drug and/or alcohol abuse, criminal activity, occult involvement, believing and practicing false doctrine—the list is numerous.

3. However, a believer can confess and receive forgiveness.

"If we confess our sins, he is faithful and just to forgive us our sins, and to cleanse us from all unrighteousness" (1 John 1:9). Doorways, legal permissions, must be canceled. When that is done, genuine deliverance can take place.

4. At this point, when all legal permissions have been willingly confessed, renounced, and denounced, demons can be cast out in Jesus' name.

Jesus' name is absolute authority. It is never about the deliverance minister; the authority is in Jesus' name, for it was He who said, "In my name shall they cast out devils" (Mark 16:17). Jesus called it a miracle. His name is absolute authority!

POSSESSION VERSUS OPPRESSION, DELIVERANCE VERSUS EXORCISM

I was on a plane one day, going to Florida for some prison services and deliverance sessions. As almost always happens, the person sitting beside me struck up a conversation. In the course of my conversation with the woman seated next to me, she asked, "Are you coming or going?" This is a tough question because many times I ask myself the same thing. I told her I was going to Florida.

I anticipated the questions that would follow.

"Business?"

"Yes."

"What do you do?"

"I'm a prison evangelist."

She hesitated but then asked, "That's what you do?"

"That is not all I do." I told her a little about demons at work in the lives of people.

She said, "Oh, have you seen the movie *The Exorcist*?"

I said, "Ma'am, I am an exorcist."

Then for some reason she changed the subject!

Casting out demons is seldom referred to as deliverance but rather is referred to as exorcism in our culture. However, the word *exorcism* is not even in the Bible. The word *deliverance*, on the other hand, is mentioned many times, including in Luke 4:18, when Jesus read aloud from the scroll of Isaiah in the synagogue in Nazareth:

> The Spirit of the Lord is upon me, because he hath anointed me
> to preach the gospel to the poor; he hath sent me to heal the
> brokenhearted, to preach deliverance to the captives, and recovering of sight to the blind, to set at liberty them that are bruised.

Remember what I said earlier: As believers we are owned by the Lord Jesus. However, Christians can be and often are *oppressed* by demon powers. Because of that, the need for deliverance in the body of Christ is great.

But how do demons get inside us in the first place, you may ask. That's the subject of the next chapter.

CHAPTER 2

HOW DEMONS GAIN ACCESS

ONE DAY I was in discussion with my pastor, a Greek expert and former professor at the world's largest seminary. I asked him about the Greek work *nāšā'*, which means to beguile, because the Bible tells us that is what Satan did to Eve.

> And the LORD God said unto the woman, What is this that thou hast done? And the woman said, The serpent *beguiled* me, and I did eat.
>
> —GENESIS 3:13, EMPHASIS ADDED

The words *beguile* and *beguiled* appear in the King James Version only seven times. In addition to Genesis 3:13, it is used in:

- Genesis 29:25 (emphasis added): "And it came to pass, that in the morning, behold, it was Leah: and he said to Laban, What is this thou hast done unto me? did not I serve with thee for Rachel? wherefore then hast thou *beguiled* me?"

- Numbers 25:18 (emphasis added): "For they vex you with their wiles, wherewith they have *beguiled* you in the matter of Peor, and in the matter of Cozbi, the daughter of a prince of Midian, their sister, which was slain in the day of the plague for Peor's sake."

- Joshua 9:22 (emphasis added): "And Joshua called for them, and he spake unto them, saying, Wherefore

have ye *beguiled* us, saying, We are very far from you;
when ye dwell among us?"

- 2 Corinthians 11:3 (emphasis added): "But I fear, lest
  by any means, as the serpent *beguiled* Eve through
  his subtlety, so your minds should be corrupted from
  the simplicity that is in Christ."

- Colossians 2:4 (emphasis added): "And this I say, lest
  any man should *beguile* you with enticing words."

- Colossians 2:18 (emphasis added): "Let no man *beguile*
  you of your reward in a voluntary humility and worshipping of angels, intruding into those things which
  he hath not seen, vainly puffed up by his fleshly mind."

If you take a moment to read each of these passages, you will notice
that every time the word *beguiled* is used, it is defined as to charm,
enchant, deceive, or trick. That is what happened in the Garden of
Eden. Satan beguiled Eve into disobeying God's command, and
Adam and Eve's disobedience allowed sin to enter the world.

Still today, Satan and his minions use the same tactic the serpent
used in the garden: they *beguile*. They charm, enchant, deceive, and
trick people into opening the door to sin because *sin is how demons
gain entrance to people's lives*.

As my pastor and I discussed the word *beguile*, the Holy Spirit
brought a name to my mind, someone who may have been the first
to receive deliverance: Mary Magdalene. Remember that demons
must have a doorway, a legal permission to enter someone's life. So
how did they get into Mary's life? Exploring this will show you how
they get into anyone's life.

MARY MAGDALENE'S MYSTERY AND MYTH

Mary Magdalene was one of Jesus' most well-known followers. The Scriptures describe her as a woman who had been delivered from seven demons (Luke 8:2; Mark 16:9), and though the Word is silent on the subject, there is speculation that she may have been a prostitute.

According to Mark 16:9–10 and John 20:14–17, Mary Magdalene was the first person to see the resurrected Christ. All four Gospels indicate that she witnessed Jesus' crucifixion and burial. John 19:25 says she stood by the cross where Jesus was crucified: "Now there stood by the cross of Jesus his mother, and his mother's sister, Mary the wife of Cleophas, and Mary Magdalene."

She saw the garden tomb where Joseph of Arimathea placed Jesus' body after He died (Mark 15:47). She also went to the tomb with two other women on the morning of the third day to anoint Jesus' body with sweet spices (Mark 16:1). When she realized the tomb was empty, Mary ran to tell the disciples. She returned to the tomb with Peter and remained there after he left (John 20:1–11). Christ then appeared to Mary and, according to John 20:17, instructed her to tell the apostles He would soon ascend to God the Father.

Despite these established facts, mystery and myth surround Mary Magdalene, partially because we don't know much about her history. She has often been conflated with other figures, including a nameless sinner in Luke 7 who wept on Christ's feet, wiping them with her hair and anointing them with spikenard, and with Mary of Bethany, sister of Martha and Lazarus, in John 11–12.

Various traditions and speculations have added to her mystique. Some suggest that Mary was a wealthy widow because she was able to follow Jesus and support His ministry financially. Others, mostly in the Catholic tradition, attribute miraculous acts to her or claim she forgave sins. In contrast, other blasphemous theories suggest that she was Jesus' wife or mother to His child.

The truth about her past remains elusive, but the unchallenged facts about Mary Magdalene's life establish that Jesus cleansed her of seven demons (Luke 8:2; Mark 16:9), implying that she experienced deliverance, perhaps becoming the first person to be delivered of demons.

My question is, since demons *must* have a legal permission to enter someone, what legal rights did they have to her life? How was she beguiled? I think the answer can be found in the city where she was born.

MAGDALA UNEARTHED

Magdalene may be a surname, meaning she came from Magdala, a prosperous fishing town on the western shore of the Sea of Galilee. It was the largest city around the Sea of Galilee, so although "there is no archaeological evidence that Jesus visited Magdala, it is almost certain that He did."[1]

Matthew 4:23 says, "Jesus went about all Galilee, teaching in their synagogues, and preaching the gospel of the kingdom, and healing all manner of sickness and all manner of disease among the people." It could have been then that Jesus visited Magdala and cast the demons from her. But what happened to Mary to cause her to be so tormented? Was she molested as a child? Was she a victim of rape or sexual exploitation? Again, demons can't just invade someone's life; there must be a legal entryway, a legal permission. So what gave legal rights to those demons?

Biblical Archaeology Review reports that "Magdala was... destroyed by the Romans *because of the moral depravity of its inhabitants*."[2] This is an obvious clue that the demons that oppressed Mary Magdalene may have gained permission due to ancestral sin, indicating that she may have been born with demons.

Mary Magdalene likely had no idea doors had been opened to demonic oppression in her life. The same is true for many people today. Few truly understand how demons enter their lives or recognize the subtle ways they gain access.

HOW DEMONS GAIN ACCESS

Since we know that demons can't enter a person's life without permission, the key is in recognizing how they gain access and closing those doors.

Gateways

Gates are doorways, entry points. Spiritual access to our life comes only through a doorway that we control. No one else can open these doors—just the owner.

Demons cannot enter a person by choice. That is, they can't occupy anyone they choose. There must be some permission granted by the person. There must be a gate or doorway of opportunity. I've heard former Satan worshippers call these entryways "portals." It's important to recognize these entryways and keep them closed and guarded. Be on guard at all times and remain alert.

Proverbs 25:28 says, "He that hath no rule [self-control] over his own spirit is like a city that is broken down, and without walls." Unfortunately, the gateways to our lives are often controlled by other people and other circumstances prior to birth and in our early childhood.

The significance of gates is seen most often in terms of protection, holding in what is good and keeping out the enemy. In Isaiah 62:6, God appointed watchmen over the gates: "I have set watchmen upon thy walls, O Jerusalem, which shall never hold their peace day nor night: ye that make mention of the LORD, keep not silence." The obvious function of a gate is to keep something out or to allow something in. *Gates, doorways, entry points,* and *portals* are various terms that describe the same function. They are access points for demons to reach believers.

Demons are empowered when we believe a lie. The lie, of course, is generally wrapped in an attractive package filled with partial truths. My friend Sid Roth, whose ministry now spans the world, speaks about being entangled in a New Age lie that offered him supernatural power but was filled with darkness and disconnection. After Sid's salvation, he had to find a deliverance minister to cast out the evil spirits that had come through his New Age encounter.

Often the lie that demons use to gain access is nothing more than convincing you that a particular person or teaching is a better way than what is written in God's Word. It may involve coming into agreement with New Age thinking or some Eastern mystical religion, which, however sincere you might be, are doorways for demons.

Any teaching that denies the deity of God the Father, God the Son, and God the Holy Spirit is, when embraced, a doorway for demon powers. That is one gate that lets the demon spirits in. Secret orders and fraternities that point people to God but do so by bypassing the death, burial, and resurrection of Jesus Christ are absolute doorways to demon powers. These fraternal or sorority-type organizations generally boast of the good works they do in communities, but they will not proclaim Jesus Christ as Lord. Often they have good people as members, and their organizations do good works. But the important issue is that there is only one way to God, and that is through Jesus Christ.

False religions or false teachings within the church are always potential gateways for demons. Embracing any teaching that offers a way to God apart from Jesus Christ is a lie of demons. It is important to know that demons are liars—they kill, steal, and destroy. Remember, it is their objective to war against the saints. They are subtle and slick. They manipulate much through false gifts.

After many years of deliverance ministry and multitudes of personal experiences, I can tell you that it is not difficult to walk in freedom. It is simple, and it involves yielding your life to truth. In His prayer for the saints to His Father, Jesus said, "Your word is truth" (John 17:17, NIV). Jesus also told His disciples, "And you shall know the truth, and the truth shall make you free" (John 8:32). Virtually every doorway for demons is hinged upon a lie. These may be thinly veiled lies—and often are.

God always honors the will of man. Scripture is the legal rule book or contract that governs what access demon powers have to the lives of believers. The Holy Spirit will not come into a person unless He is invited, but He is quick to accept the invitation. Demon powers also cannot and will not come into an individual's soul or body without legal permission. They cannot do it. But there are numerous ways for an individual to open one of these entryways, and there could be subcategories for all the gateways I will mention. I'm going to list some common permissions that believers give demons to oppress them.

Generational curses/ancestry

Any human being alive in this world is a candidate for evil spirits to be passed by this scriptural permission found in Exodus 20:5. The generational curse is God-given consent for evil spirits to be passed to a child because of the sins of the forefathers. Some argue that this doesn't seem fair. *Fair* is not a word in the demon dictionary. This is a consequence of sin, and every father and mother bears responsibility for breaking this curse in the family. It is real, and it is by far the most common entryway I encounter.

Generational or ancestral curses are often recognized by the impairment of normal physiological functions. It will be helpful to read Deuteronomy 28 and cross-reference the various curses. They can be summarized generally as follows:

- Mental and emotional breakdown—This is a very common work of demon powers and is evidenced by the numbers in treatment.

- Barrenness and impotency together with miscarriages and related female complications

- Failure, or plans and projects that never mature— Many times I have encountered blocking spirits and hindering spirits whose purpose and assignment is to prevent blessings from coming.

- Poverty or perpetual financial insufficiency—This curse is often the result of robbing from God (see Malachi 3:8) and may also be a sin of the forefathers.

- Spiritual hindrance in hearing God's voice, sensing God's presence, understanding the Bible, concentration in prayer, and being devoid of spiritual gifts

- Life traumas, or going from one crisis to another. This seems to be a fairly common curse. Virtually everyone knows someone who falls in this category.

- Untimely and unnatural deaths

- Breakdown of family relationships, including divorce

- Sickness and diseases, especially chronic and hereditary diseases

> For I the Lord thy God am a jealous God, visiting the *iniquity of the fathers upon the children unto the third and fourth generation* of them that hate me.
> —Exodus 20:5, emphasis added

Spiritual blessing is also promised to those who obey the commandments of the Lord. The blessings are counterparts to the previously mentioned curses.

Deuteronomy 28:1–8 (nkjv) tells of the blessings promised to those who are set on high by God:

> Now it shall come to pass, if you diligently obey the voice of the Lord your God, to observe carefully all His commandments which I command you today, that the Lord your God will set you high above all nations of the earth. And all these blessings shall come upon you and overtake you, because you obey the voice of the Lord your God:

Blessed shall you be in the city, and blessed shall you be in the country.

Blessed shall be the fruit of your body, the produce of your ground and the increase of your herds, the increase of your cattle and the offspring of your flocks.

Blessed shall be your basket and your kneading bowl.

Blessed shall you be when you come in, and blessed shall you be when you go out.

The LORD will cause your enemies who rise against you to be defeated before your face; they shall come out against you one way and flee before you seven ways.

The LORD will command the blessing on you in your storehouses and in all to which you set your hand, and He will bless you in the land which the LORD your God is giving you.

Is your life characterized by fruitfulness? Do you prosper—coming and going? Are you free from the harassment of enemies both natural and spiritual? Is your life a success? Is your relationship with God gratifying? Are you recognizing and fulfilling His purposes? These are the earmarks of a blessed life. According to these scriptures, there is no middle ground.

Yet another way to determine if curses are in operation is to look for the effects of curses. Common effects of curses are poverty, barrenness, pestilence, chronic sickness, failure, defeat, humiliation, insanity, torment, perpetual traumas, spiritual hindrances, domination by others, and a sense of abandonment by God and others. (See Deuteronomy 28:20–68.)

Mental disorders

Mental disorders such as depression and bipolar disorders are most commonly a result of generational curses or early childhood abuse. Along with many other disorders of the mind, medical authorities attribute these generational curses to genetics. Therefore, good information about family history can be very beneficial in the deliverance process.

Alcoholism and addiction

If there is evidence of alcoholism or abuse of alcohol in the family history, it is almost certain you will find that an addictive spirit has been passed to the offspring. The addiction may manifest in other ways. It may not be to alcohol; it may be nicotine, drugs, food, or even sex. Addictive behavior in the ancestry will give you a clue to what spirits may be lurking in the temple.

Religious spirits

Religious spirits are often bondage spirits that keep a person bound to legalistic ways that dishonor God and cause the person to feel as if they can never please God. This is a very common spirit that I see passed by ancestral curse. Indian heritage should also be explored and may be a very good clue to possible occult or religious spirits. Virtually any type of demon spirit may be passed through generational permission. Background history can be very helpful.

Birth trauma

Many other doorways should be considered at birth or during the time a mother is carrying a child. Trauma that takes place while the child is in the womb and shortly after birth and even the birth process should be looked into. I have seen evil spirits attach to a life because of difficulties encountered during the birth process.

Early childhood trauma

Spoken words can become curses, granting permission to evil spirits by words from the mother, father, or doctor. Many times I have encountered spirits of rejection and abandonment from trauma after the child's conception. Remember, John the Baptist leaped in the womb when he heard of Jesus' coming through a conversation between his mother, Elizabeth, and Mary the mother of Jesus.

One powerful spirit of abandonment I encountered had gained access by a baby being in an incubator for six weeks. This thirty-five-year-old curled up in a fetal position and began to weep, "Oh,

I'm in a box. I want my mother..." He explained, after this tormenting spirit was commanded to leave, that he could see himself as a tiny baby in the incubator, separating him from everyone. This is always a place to explore for possible doorways.

The early life of any individual can be a source of demon entry. Remember that demons don't play fair. Fear of the dark, Mom and Dad arguing, fear of divorce, divorce itself, abuse, death, guilt, shame or embarrassment, nightmares—the list is long for doorways that can come through childhood trauma. Injuries and hospitalization may even be a source.

One of the most common spirits encountered in deliverance ministry is a demon of confusion. Often it has its doorway as Mom and Dad arguing, threatening to leave, perhaps even leaving, all the while telling the child how much they are loved and how important they are. The confusion spirit generally brings its friends of doubt, unbelief, skepticism, and disbelief. Many times these spirits function as blocking or hindering spirits.

It is almost certain that if a child is sexually abused, humiliated, or embarrassed sexually, they will receive a demonic spirit whose work is sexual perversion. This spirit can come in two forms, one of which is called incubus and the other, succubus. This spirit can also come from sexual trauma later in life. Generally, this spirit will drive the person to sexual extremes—promiscuity in one person and frigidity in another.

Sickness

This is a very common gate for evil spirits. Recently, I found a spirit that identified itself as "mononucleosis." The person suffered from fatigue and extreme lack of energy. When this spirit manifested, she grabbed her jaws on both sides at the lymph node area. They were hurting her. She had suffered this sickness as a child, but the spirit that caused the sickness stayed and plagued her with various difficulties for fifteen years. When commanded in the name of Jesus Christ, the spirit left and so did the symptoms she had been experiencing.

I have seen hearing problems healed when spirits that came through mumps, chicken pox, measles, high fever, and the like were identified and commanded to leave. Sickness is always a possible doorway for demon spirits. When Jesus ministered healing to deaf people, He spoke, "Deaf and dumb spirit, I command you, come out of him and enter him no more!" (Mark 9:25, NKJV). He called deafness a spirit!

Surgery

This one was a puzzle to me when I first began to encounter it. How could evil spirits gain access to a believer's life through surgery? Did they come in through the incision? No. Was it fear? Remember, fear is a spirit. Maybe ungodly doctors? Perhaps the anesthesia? I still can't give you a positive answer. Maybe it is all of those things. I took a doctor through deliverance in Oklahoma, and he asked me how that could happen. He said, "I pray with all my patients before surgery. What prayer do I pray to keep that from happening?"

We discussed it awhile, and he explained the information in medical terms, but basically he said this: When a person is under anesthesia, there is a brief window, a transfer state, where they are neither conscious nor unconscious. During this brief window they are in what is similar to a hypnotic state as they go from consciousness to unconsciousness, and the same thing happens when they come back out. Maybe that's when it happens. I believe it is. I have, however, found that words from doctors can become spoken curses, such as, "You'll never walk again," "You will gradually get worse and may never heal," or "There is no hope for you to recover fully." Surgery should always be looked at as a possible gate.

Ridicule/humiliation

I have also found that traumas in the school years can be doorways for demon spirits. One such common doorway is ridicule or being embarrassed by a teacher. You might be surprised to know how many times I have seen this be a source of poor self-image spirits, spirits of rejection, or spirits of condemnation. The same can occur by rejection from peers, not feeling accepted in certain circles, and the like.

Immorality

Periods of immorality in the candidate's life should always be explored as possible doorways or invitations to evil spirits. Many of those who come to me for freedom will tell of a period of sexual promiscuity or some drinking and drugs during their high school and/or college days. Sex outside of marriage can not only open doors for demons, but it can also create a soul tie that gives them permission to stay until that curse is broken. A soul tie may occur whenever there is an unhealthy relationship. The most common is sexual relations outside of marriage.

Unconfessed sin

Virtually any sin that is unconfessed can be an open door for demons to torment believers. Some sins do appear to be bigger doorways, however.

Anger

One particular verse that comes to mind is Ephesians 4:26: "Be ye angry and sin not: let not the sun go down upon your wrath: neither give place to the devil." This clearly shows that anger that lingers from one day to the next can give place to the devil. Just because there is a gate or entryway does not mean a demon always comes in. Probably more often than not, they don't come in; however, it is an invitation, and we are to keep our lives covered and cleansed by the blood of Jesus.

Pain

Both physical and emotional pain often invite spirits of pain to take up residence through the pain trauma and then remain in the person's life to torment with pain. I have found chronic pain spirits, and I have encountered nagging pain spirits. The pain spirit many times will invite an addictive spirit to cover the pain, resulting in more bondage.

Death

Death can open doors in more than one way. It is not just the trauma of someone who is close to us dying, but there is also another consideration. When a person dies, if they had evil spirits oppressing or possessing them, suddenly those spirits are without a home. They will seek another, and my experience is that they tend to stay in the family.

I preached at the funeral of the father of one of my best friends. The father was an alcoholic and barely held his home together through the years. His son (my friend) did not drink—that is, until a few months after his father's death. Now my friend is struggling to hold his home together and is becoming an alcoholic. His mother told him, "You are acting just like your father!" I have seen this play out many times in many different ways.

Pornography

This gate is being attempted in the life of virtually every healthy male in the world—and females as well. And the age at which this gate is opened is getting younger and younger. This gate can lead to a powerfully addictive spirit that is bent on your destruction. Pastors, teachers, political leaders, men in high office, and the guy who cleans the basement are often victims here and find this demon one of the most difficult to be rid of. Once this gate is opened, it often stays open. The destructive demons slowly go about their work of destroying families, self-image, health, churches, children, and so on. This is a much too common gate for demons today.

Criminal activity

Criminal activity is most certainly an invitation for demon spirits. Having ministered in prisons since 1974, I have recognized this to be a very common and consistent doorway for evil spirits. The demons don't miss this opportunity very often. This, probably more than anything else, explains the revolving doors to our nation's penitentiaries. Many men and women accept Christ as Savior while incarcerated but are still not able to function in society because they are free only from the penalty of sin—yet remain in bondage to the powers of darkness.

Spoken curses

The tongue can speak blessing or curses, and the words we speak or the words spoken to us or over us can lend opportunity for demons to enter. The power of death and life is in the tongue (Prov. 18:21). Words as simple as "We are never going to have anything" can invite a spirit of poverty to help ensure those spoken words come to pass. Visualize a big angel on your right and a big demon on your left, each of them acting upon the words that come out of your mouth, and you might have a fairly accurate picture of how this works. Angels react to the words of faith you speak, and demons respond to words of doubt and disbelief.

Lust

This includes lust for money and material things or for bodily appetites, such as food and sex. Envy, covetousness, and jealousy are certain doorways for evil spirits. Lust is a doorway that is present in many lives.

The mind

The mind is clearly the battlefield. What we allow in through our eyes and ears can be entryways for demon powers. It can be books we have read; something as simple as fascinations with Greek, Roman, or Egyptian mythology; and movies that induce fear or grossly depict sin, along with television programs and even cartoons. I've ministered to children who have received demons from cartoons. Creatures become their friends, and they fantasize. This can invite demons. The Harry Potter books and movies are among the absolute worst! Parents bear a heavy responsibility, and I see many simply turning their heads.

The occult

Remember, there can be almost as many divisions of doorways as you could imagine depending on the categories and subcategories.

Let me just say here that I don't think I can cover all the possible occult doorways. But I want to list some that may surprise you.

- Freemasonry
- Odd Fellows
- Eastern Star
- Rainbow for Girls
- DeMolay
- Shriners
- Job's Daughters
- Daughters of the Nile
- Elks
- Christian Science
- Church of Jesus Christ of Latter-day Saints (Mormons)
- Jehovah's Witnesses
- gurus
- Scientology
- Islam
- religious communes
- spiritism
- Buddhism
- Hinduism
- Tibetan Buddhism
- Unity
- Rosicrucianism
- Baha'i
- theosophy
- Pokémon cards and characters
- Harry Potter
- fortune tellers
- tarot cards
- Ouija boards
- séances
- mediums
- palmistry
- astrology
- color therapy
- levitation
- astral travel
- horoscope
- lucky charms
- black magic
- demon worship
- spirit guides
- clairvoyance

- crystals
- New Age
- Native (Indian) curiosity
- Eastern religions
- witchcraft
- voodoo
- satanism
- hypnotism

Although this is not a list of every possible doorway, it should give you an idea of what gives permission for demons to enter the soul and flesh of believers.

DELIVERANCE IS THE CHILDREN'S BREAD

The good news is that deliverance is the children's bread. To qualify for deliverance and to minister deliverance, you must simply be one of God's children!

In Matthew 15:22–28 (NKJV), we read an extraordinary account of Jesus delivering a child from demonic possession. But the circumstances surrounding this deliverance is what makes it stand out.

> And behold, a woman of Canaan came from that region and cried out to Him, saying, "Have mercy on me, O Lord, Son of David! My daughter is severely demon-possessed." But He answered her not a word. And His disciples came and urged Him, saying, "Send her away, for she cries out after us." But He answered and said, "I was not sent except to the lost sheep of the house of Israel." Then she came and worshiped Him, saying, "Lord, help me!" But He answered and said, "It is not good to take the children's bread and throw it to the little dogs." And she said, "Yes, Lord, yet even the little dogs eat the crumbs which fall from their masters' table." Then Jesus answered and said to her, "O woman, great is your faith! Let it be to you as you desire." And her daughter was healed from that very hour.

Let's set the scene here. Jesus was with His disciples at the Sea of Galilee and suddenly told His disciples they were going to Tyre and Sidon. Each of them must have wondered why. Those cities were on the Mediterranean coast, and the people who lived there were not Jews—that was Baal country. It was not only a Gentile region, it was about thirty-five miles away.

We don't know how long Jesus stayed in the region, but His next stop was Decapolis, which was on the east side of the Sea of Galilee. That means Jesus walked as many as one hundred miles during His trip from the Sea of Galilee out to Tyre and Sidon and back to Decapolis.

Until Jesus reached Decapolis, the only thing recorded about what Jesus did was bringing deliverance to a grievously vexed daughter and salvation to the terribly troubled mother, but there is great teaching here. Deliverance and healing are the *children's bread*! My now-deceased friend Frank Hammond named his ministry Children's Bread.

Knowing Jesus, He made that long journey just to minister to the Gentile mother and her daughter, who was in need of deliverance. We will never know for sure. Personally, I believe He had already heard this woman's prayer.

An interesting thing about this story is that the woman was a Canaanite, a Gentile. Respectable Jewish men in Jesus' day would never speak openly and publicly with a Gentile woman. But we know that Jesus turned tradition on its head on more than one occasion.

Jesus initially ignored the woman long enough for His disciples to become irritated. They asked Him to send her away, likely thinking He was never going to respond to her because she was a Gentile. But Jesus did answer her, saying, "I am not sent but unto the lost sheep of the house of Israel" (Matt. 15:24). Jesus was essentially saying that she didn't qualify for help because she wasn't under the covenant God made with the children of Israel.

Knowing that Jesus was the Son of God, the woman then knelt

at His feet, worshipping Him and begging for help. Jesus said, "It is not right to take the children's bread and toss it to the dogs" (Matt. 15:26, NIV).

The desperate mother did not give up, pointing out that even dogs get to eat the crumbs that fall from their masters' tables. She knew that because of Jesus' power and authority, even crumbs would be enough to heal her daughter. She had great faith! Jesus praised her for her faith and healed her daughter.

Do you know that by faith we are the children of Abraham and heirs according to the promise (Gal. 3:7–9)? As believers we are covenant qualified.

If you are Christ's, then you are Abraham's offspring and heirs according to the promise. We don't have to settle for the crumbs, because we are children of God. Healing and deliverance are for the children!

CHAPTER 3

SETTING THE TORMENTED FREE

THERE ARE AT least twenty-seven mentions of Jesus and His disciples casting out evil spirits in the New Testament. (See the appendix for a list of scriptures that address deliverance.) It is clear that casting out demons was part of Jesus' ministry. One such instance is mentioned in Mark 5:1–17:

> And they came over unto the other side of the sea, into the country of the Gadarenes. And when he was come out of the ship, immediately there met him out of the tombs a man with an unclean spirit, who had his dwelling among the tombs; and no man could bind him, no, not with chains: because that he had been often bound with fetters and chains, and the chains had been plucked asunder by him, and the fetters broken in pieces: neither could any man tame him. And always, night and day, he was in the mountains, and in the tombs, crying, and cutting himself with stones.
>
> But when he saw Jesus afar off, he ran and worshiped him, and cried with a loud voice, and said, What have I to do with thee, Jesus, thou Son of the most high God? I adjure thee by God, that thou torment me not. For he said unto him, Come out of the man, thou unclean spirit.
>
> And he asked him, What is thy name? [All demons have names.] And he answered, saying, My name is Legion: for we are many. And he besought him much that he would not send them away out of the country. Now there was there nigh unto the mountains a great herd of swine feeding. And all the

devils besought him, saying, Send us into the swine, that we may enter into them.

And forthwith Jesus gave them leave. And the unclean spirits went out, and entered into the swine: and the herd ran violently down a steep place into the sea, (they were about two thousand;) and were choked in the sea. And they that fed the swine fled, and told it in the city, and in the country. And they went out to see what it was that was done. And they come to Jesus, and see him that was possessed with the devil, and had the legion, sitting, and clothed, and in his right mind: and they were afraid.

And they that saw it told them how it befell to him that was possessed with the devil, and also concerning the swine. And they began to pray him to depart out of their coasts.

Quite a story! There is a lot of deliverance truth here. It reminds me of some of the requests we get for deliverance: "I'm tormented. No one can help me. I've tried everything."

This demon named Legion certainly knew who Jesus was; he had already been cast from heaven, and the demons knew Jesus was coming to free the man. All demons know Jesus and tremble at His name. Jesus said, "I saw Satan fall from heaven" (Luke 10:18, NLT). He saw him fall from heaven because He was the One who cast him out: "The great dragon was hurled down—that ancient serpent called the devil, or Satan, who leads the whole world astray" (Rev. 12:9, NIV). He was hurled to the earth, so he knows well the authority of Jesus' name.

Reading of this tormented man takes me back to when I was beginning seminary. I worked for the local electric company as a meter reader. When you read meters, eventually you wind up in everyone's backyard. You learn to watch out for dogs. I even encountered a protective goose one time. He would not allow me in the yard and was very aggressive. I didn't know if geese would bite, but I respected this one. (I later read that geese can be very territorial and "have a reputation for attacking or chasing anyone that crosses their path....They will even attack gorillas."[1])

I'll never forget this particular day. There was a house in south Fort Worth, a corner lot with no fence and a detached garage that was near the alley and could be entered from the side street.

As I was leaving the yard, I noticed a chain that led into the open garage. As a meter reader you learn to respect what might be on the other end of a chain. As I eased by the garage, I looked to see what was on the other end of the chain. I expected a large dog. But it wasn't. My heart beats heavy even as I write this. It was a man! He was crouched on the ground like an animal. I did not investigate any further. Actually it startled me. I quickly moved to the next house but could not get it off my mind and heart.

I asked fellow workers about it later. Several had seen him in the months before and had reported it. I recall one of the workers said, "Oh, you mean the crazy guy on Davis Avenue." It seemed that the man's parents didn't have the means to hospitalize him or maybe even were ignorant of how to care for him. When they were gone, he was chained in the garage with food and water, and some shade and shelter. Horrible!

The memory still troubles me to this day. Even after all these years, I could take you right to that house. I could even tell you where the electric meter was on the back.

We see this kind of bondage in people who come for deliverance. Not often, but we do see people in deep shame and bondage, not always by their choosing—perhaps, again, like Mary of Magdala.

I recall another similar situation during my days as a meter reader. This house was also on a corner lot. There were bushes surrounding the yard, and you had to separate them to gain entrance. When I walked into the yard, I saw a woman, haggardly dressed with her back to me. So as not to startle her, I gently announced my presence. I said, "Electric company meter reader."

She turned immediately. She looked like a witch from the movies. She shook her finger in my direction and said, "J. Frank Norris, James J. Segress, and y-o-u—God's preachers!" She said it in an evil tone, followed by a cackling laugh.

I can't explain what I felt. My legs got very heavy, and I could barely move. She was cackling the whole time. I finally made it out of the yard and sat on the curb. I had heard of J. Frank Norris, though I did not know him. He was a renowned preacher in the fundamental Baptist movement. But I didn't know the other man.

As I sat on the curb, I tried to digest what had just happened. As I moved on down the street, I asked people about this woman. I got all kinds of answers. "Oh, she's crazy. People just leave her alone. Kids are afraid of her."

Still, I wondered, "How did she know I was a preacher?" She didn't, but the demons in her did.

While in seminary, I had a very humble and great professor named Peter Connally. He was a very well-known evangelist in Scotland and told one day of being in a revival crusade. The host pastor asked him to witness to a woman who claimed to be a witch. He agreed and went to this woman's house. Before he knocked at her door, he heard, "Come in, Peter Connally. I've been expecting you," and she cackled with laughter. He said, "I went inside but could not speak. My legs got heavy, and I could hardly walk. I knew I was in the presence of a demon, but sadly at the time I didn't know what to do. I made my way to the door with heavy heart and left."

He added, "I'm telling you this because demons are real, and you need to prepare yourself."

I now know that as blood-washed children of God, we don't have to be afraid of demons. We have authority over evil spirits and the power to command them to go. Mark 16:17 tells us, "And these signs shall follow them that believe; in my name shall they cast out devils." Jesus has given us the authority of His name over all the power of the enemy!

THE MOST DIFFICULT CASES

We don't know much about what happened to the man with demons in Gadara in Mark 5, except that he was completely freed. Where he had been naked, out of his mind, and a problem to others, he was now clothed, in his right mind, and wanting to follow Jesus.

Without doubt the most difficult individuals we deal with are those who have been diagnosed with mental disorders. If it were like some of the spiritual warfare movements teach, then we could just circle the mental institutions and bind the entire kingdom of mind-tormenting spirits.

The question is really not that paranoia and other mental disorders are caused by demon powers; rather it is *how* the demons cause them. Without doubt many people in this condition need medical help. Often the individual needs both spiritual and physiological help. Sometimes the person needs some medical attention so that they can be delivered.

When a lie has been believed, it is very difficult to deal with demons until the lie has been renounced. The problem is the deception is so powerful that the individual does not perceive it to be a lie. He becomes so fully blinded by the lie that he is unable to see the truth. Perhaps he became so comfortable in the lie that he is unwilling to believe the truth. He is convinced that the government is persecuting him or that secret agents are assigned to spy and gather information against him. He is so convinced that it is very difficult for him to confess it as a lie. He often becomes suspicious of you because you don't believe the story. There is no doubt that what they perceive is very real to them. So the dilemma is how to bring freedom to those suffering from disorders of the mind.

I assure you it is more than simply commanding demons to go in the name of Jesus. If it were that simple, I would be at the mental hospitals right now. I have been there; I have prayed for institutionalized people. I have spent many hours in the psychiatric wings of the prisons; I have heard the demons react when I would walk down the halls or come by their cells. I have heard the screams down the corridors as the sounds from the chapel services spilled into the prison. It is more than just speaking the name of Jesus over a mentally ill person. It is complex, and until the legal rights of those demon powers have been removed (by the individual or parents), freedom does not come.

The name of Jesus will stir them regardless. Demons hate and fear that name. Some people with mental disorders cannot even read the Bible for the torment that comes. Some read it and are only able to see condemnation and judgment. The thing I know is that there is always a root, sometimes many roots. The problem is finding it and removing permissions that demons have gained. Often the demons have already done their damage, and even when they leave, God's supernatural healing is needed. It is truth that enables us to be free. Believing lies empowers the demon.

A TRUTH ENCOUNTER

Deliverance is not a power encounter; it is a truth encounter. The Holy Spirit so wonderfully brings truth to us and forces the demons to react in obedience to commands in the authority of the Lord Jesus Christ.

Deliverance is like being in a courtroom where Jehovah God is seated at the judge's bench. He is the judge of all truth and righteousness. It is His legal system. The law is what He has spoken! Whatever God speaks becomes law. You can't see His face, just His glory. Holy angels encircle the bench and proclaim His holiness. He is the righteous judge.

> Henceforth there is laid up for me a crown of righteousness, which the Lord, *the righteous judge*, shall give me at that day: and not to me only, but unto all them also that love his appearing.
> —2 TIMOTHY 4:8, EMPHASIS ADDED

God's courtroom is no ordinary courtroom; only truth will be recognized here. You see, deliverance is not about power, and it is not just about authority, though we certainly have it in Jesus Christ's name. Deliverance is about the truth.

One particular scripture about deliverance resounds in my spirit: "Behold, I give unto you power to tread on serpents and scorpions, and over all the power of the enemy: and nothing shall by any means hurt you" (Luke 10:19). Who gave us power and authority over the kingdom of darkness? *Jesus!* We have been given power of attorney, legal authority, to act in Jesus' name! The authority was and is His name, and He commissioned you and me to act in the authority of His name. As blood-washed children of God, we can take authority over evil spirits and command them to go. With great power and authority in the name of Jesus, we are to speak freedom!

CHAPTER 4

A DIVINE ENCOUNTER FOR DELIVERANCE

I WANT TO SHARE a special moment that happened in Corpus Christi a few years ago. I was scheduled to preach in several area prisons and decided Corpus was the most convenient to the prisons in Beeville, Three Rivers, and San Diego, Texas. I love to fish but didn't think I would have time because of the many services I had planned. I took my rod and reel just in case.

I got there and called Chaplain David Villareal at the Garza East unit where I was to be that evening. "I'm so glad you called. I tried to reach you, but you had already left home. Brother Don, we got a new warden on the unit today and he canceled all weeknight activities. I'm so sorry, but we can't have church tonight."

Well, I know those things happen; it's just part of prison ministry. So I said to myself, I'll just go fishing. I have fished many times in Corpus Christi.

Today would be different. Generally, I fish from the marina area where there are "T" heads and "L" heads that allow you to drive out and fish from the parklike area. I bought my bait from one of the shrimp boats in the area and headed for my fishing spot, but I absent-mindedly drove right past it. When I realized what I had done, I was already a few blocks past and decided to continue along the bayside drive for a while because I had spotted a pier in the distance. I thought I would try the pier first. When I arrived at the little public park, I could see one person on the pier. I gathered up my fishing gear and headed to the end of the pier. As I got closer to the end, I could see that it was a woman, and she had no fishing gear; she was just gazing into the water.

I wondered why a woman would be out there alone and with no fishing equipment, but I didn't want to know. I just wanted to fish. I went to the opposite side of the pier about one hundred feet from where she was. As I began to fish and was reeling in one small fish after the other, I could see her making her way little by little over to where I was. I just wanted to fish so I sort of ignored her. After a moment, she started a conversation: "You sure are catching a lot of fish. Do you always put them back?"

I confess I was not overly friendly. I told her I always put the fish back. I didn't know at this time that this was an anointed, appointed, ordained moment from God. I just kept fishing.

She continued to talk, and as she did, I began to listen with more interest. She told me she was a doctor. I just listened, but in my mind, I was saying, "Yeah, you're a doctor."

She told me she couldn't practice because she had been admitted to an institution for psychosis about a year ago. She told me she had attempted suicide a couple of times. I listened more intently. I asked her why she was on the pier. She said, "I seem just drawn to the water; there's something final about the water. You can cut your wrist and survive. You can overdose and survive, but there's something final about the water."

I looked at the choppy bay waters and glanced back at the shoreline. It was a pretty long swim. She explained how despondent and terribly depressed she was because of her situation. She was there to commit suicide!

I began to put away my fishing gear because now I knew why the service had been canceled. Now I knew why I had "absent-mindedly" driven past my fishing spot. I knew this was an ordained moment! Just as I was ready to witness to her, other people began to show up, and it spoiled the private moment. I understood that too.

I said, "Ma'am, I don't want you to misunderstand, but would you mind walking back to my car with me and sit for a few minutes in the front seat of the car? I want to talk with you and pray for you." She did not hesitate, stating that she knew she needed prayer.

As we walked toward the car, I found out that she was saved and was confident of her relationship to Christ. Even though she did not attend an evangelistic church, she remembered the day she asked Christ to be her Savior. I asked her if she believed in angels. "Oh, yes, I do. I believe they have intervened many times in my life."

I then asked her if she believed in demons. She hesitated a moment. "Yes, I suppose I do."

We arrived at the car and sat in the front seat. I said, "I don't think you are psychotic, though that may have been your diagnosis. I believe you are tormented with evil spirits of depression and suicide, and I further believe God has heard your cry for help. I believe that's why we are seated here at this moment."

I told her if she wanted to be free and if she had no unforgiveness or unconfessed sin in her life, in the name of Jesus Christ I could rebuke the demons.

She was ready! "Please do it!" she said.

First I had a word of prayer acknowledging and thanking God for His presence. I asked the Holy Spirit to give me direction and accomplish her freedom through biblical deliverance.

I explained to her that I was going to bind evil spirits in the name of Jesus Christ, and when I did so, she might experience some physical sensations, symptoms such as nausea, stomach tightness, tingling sensations, eyes fluttering, burning in parts of her body, and so on. She nodded that she understood. I took authority over the evil spirits and bound them in the name of Jesus Christ. I commanded that they could not split, divide, multiply, fragment, or clone; that they couldn't hide or use any form of trickery; and that they could not harm her or go to anyone else. I commanded them to attention and said that when commanded to go, they would go immediately and into the abyss.

After the evil spirits were bound, I asked if she experienced any unusual feelings or symptoms. "Oh, yes, my lips are burning, and my hands; both hands are tingling and burning."

They were there, and they were nervous about what was to follow. They manifested through the discomfort she described. I told her she might feel them come up and out of her mouth when I commanded them to go. I could see her body heaving from deep exhaling as the demons were expelled. I could see and hear the deep sigh of relief! I asked her what she was feeling.

"Oh, the fog is gone. [It wasn't foggy.] Oh, I can even see more clearly; things are sharp and distinct," she remarked. "I have never felt such peace in all of my life!"

I talked with her briefly about what had happened. I encouraged her to go to a Bible-teaching church and had prayer with her again. She was free in the name of Jesus Christ! It was an appointed, anointed, ordained time!

I sent her some materials to read and a letter of encouragement. A few weeks after that, she called our home while I was out of town and spoke to my wife, telling her what had happened to her life as a result of this moment ordained by God. She called again a few weeks after that to let me know she was doing fine.

I was recently back in Corpus Christi, and I called to check on her. It was now two years later. When her husband answered, I introduced myself and said, "I don't know if you know who I am..."

He interrupted me with, "Yes, yes, I know who you are." He told me his wife was not at home, but that she was a different person. "Thank God, her life is different now."

I think it was a little like Jesus meeting Mary of Magdala. One encounter with Jesus changed this woman's life, and God wants to use all of us to minister deliverance in His name. I've said it before, but it bears repeating: God is looking for an army, not an audience!

TRAFFICKED AS A CHILD

That story reminds me of a request for deliverance I received from a woman in New England. This was on her application in the field asking for background information: "On my mother's side there was much abuse. My grandmother and her sisters were all sexually abused by their father. He also beat his wife. My mother was raped by her cousin, and when she told my grandmother, my grandmother denied it. My mother, my aunt, and both my sisters..."

"Uh oh," I thought, "an ancestral curse."

We don't have background info from Mary Magdalene, but I know she didn't choose to have seven demons. No little girl says, "When I grow up, I want to be sexually immoral."

So the woman from New England did come. She did receive deliverance, and we have her video testimony. If you want to see it, go to our website. What I'm about to tell you really happened! While I have permission to use her real name, I won't. I'll just refer to her as Lisa.

Lisa was born in a typical New England family: mom, dad, sister, and cat. She said her dad was a workaholic and was gone most of the time. Her mom took her to church, and she walked the aisle to receive Christ at age five. This was also when her horror story began. She had a five-year-old neighbor friend, and at times they would spend the night with each other. However, her friend's father was a pedophile and sex trafficker!

I won't go into the grim details, but her friend's father started touching Lisa inappropriately when she would sleep over. Then he began to molest her in his basement. She thought if she told her mom, he would hurt her. Lisa didn't know it at the time, but she was being trained to be sex trafficked.[1] Could anything like this have happened to Mary Magdalene?

One day Lisa's friend called and said she and her dad were going to the mall and asked if she would like to go. "I never got to do anything like that, so I went with them."[2]

At the mall, her friend's dad handed Lisa off to another man, who took her into a restroom, abused her in a stall, and then choked her until she passed out. When she came to, he walked her through the mall to another restroom and repeated the abuse.

He then showed me a gun and put the pistol in my mouth. He knew my cat's name and my sister's name. He said he would kill them if I ever told my mother, and she wouldn't believe me anyway and would not love me anymore. Then he told me I was a good girl and handed me back to my friend's dad.

We were in the food court, and my friend's dad said we will get pizza soon. But he took me to an Old Navy department store to the men's shopping area and put me in the clothes changing room. He told me three or four men would come in with pants to try on and each pair would have money in the pockets. You know what to do!

He came back after a while and took the money. There were three or four men that came in. "You did a good job," he said. "Let's go get some pizza." We had pizza, and he took me home. I was five years old and being sex trafficked.[3]

They always rubbed a liquid in her mouth that she later discovered was a tranquilizing drug that causes people to feel separated or detached from their body or physical environment. Dissociative drugs are similar to psychedelics in that they can cause hallucinations and other changes in thoughts, emotions, and consciousness. Lisa eventually became addicted to it, and her friend's dad continued to use her.

At five, six, and seven years old, Lisa was tied up in bathrooms of motels and abused repeatedly. When she was eight years old, her friend invited her to an amusement park in another city. Instead of actually visiting the park, her friend's dad handed Lisa to another man, who held her at gunpoint and allowed her to be abused repeatedly for several days. Lisa became depressed and started entertaining thoughts of suicide. "My mom asked me, 'What happened to you?' and I just couldn't tell her because I was afraid," Lisa said.

The abuse ended around the age of ten when Lisa stopped spending time with that friend, but as a teenager she became addicted to drugs and alcohol. Then in college she was sexually assaulted.

I hated myself and went into a deep depression. My mom eventually checked me into a mental hospital. I really just didn't care about anything. I felt worthless and actually wanted to die.

I wanted someone who loved me for who I was, someone I could trust and lean on. I had learned to hate authority, these people who were giving me advice and had no idea what really goes on in the world. They couldn't even know how ugly the world was, and they are giving me advice. I hated it.[4]

Lisa wanted to be loved and have a normal life. She met a guy and got married. They had three children but struggled to make the marriage work and ultimately divorced. But after recommitting her life to Christ, Lisa began to see her life change. She eventually met a man who could love her unconditionally. I'll call him Eli. Also divorced with children, Eli was an upright man who loved the Lord. They dated and fell in love, and today they have a beautiful blended family and happily serve the Lord at their church.

When she came to our office for deliverance, she wanted to be free of the trauma from the abuse she suffered. During the deliverance session, I commanded a demon to leave that had been in her ancestry for more than five hundred years. I asked what gave him permission, and he said incest. Lisa didn't give him that permission; she had been subject to the curses of her ancestry. But God set her completely free!

You may think this is a pretty unusual story. You are wrong. I see it all the time. Five years old is also a common age for the abuse to start. It may be an uncle, cousin, stepbrother, stepfather— there are any number of scenarios, virtually always from ancestral curse.

Stories like Lisa's make me wonder if this is what happened to Mary Magdalene in the little fishing village of Magdala. We know Jesus rescued her from the grip of seven demons. Jesus didn't condemn her but freed her. He freed Lisa too. The promised Messiah came for people just like Mary Magdalene—and Lisa.

> For unto us a child is born, unto us a son is given: and the government shall be upon his shoulder: and his name shall be called Wonderful, Counselor, The mighty God, The everlasting Father, The Prince of Peace.
>
> —ISAIAH 9:6

In our office we see hundreds of people, including women who have been abused and misused all their lives. At times I actually get angry with demons and their works of destruction. When people who should be doing deliverance are critical of it, I want to say like Jesus when Herod tried to stop Him, *"Go tell that fox I will be doing deliverance today and tomorrow."*

> And he said unto them, Go ye, and tell that fox, Behold, I cast out devils, and I do cures today and tomorrow, and the third day I shall be perfected. Nevertheless I must walk to day, and tomorrow, and the day following: for it cannot be that a prophet perish out of Jerusalem. O Jerusalem, Jerusalem, which killest the prophets, and stone them that are sent unto thee; how often would I have gathered thy children together, as a hen doth gather her brood under her wings, and ye would not!
>
> —LUKE 13:32–34

Jesus set people free every day, wherever He went, and regardless of the opposition!

Foxes are unclean. They are a nuisance. They can carry deadly disease. Jesus said, "Go tell that unclean, disease-carrying nuisance that I'll be casting out demons and healing the sick both today and tomorrow. And when I rise from the dead on the third day, I'll be making it possible for all believers to do the same. You will see 'little Jesuses' all over the world doing this work in My name!"

It is our responsibility as believers not only to walk in freedom but to help others find deliverance. Let me tell you what we do when someone comes to our ministry seeking deliverance.

CHAPTER 5

THE DELIVERANCE SESSION

SEVERAL YEARS AGO, before a need for knee-replacement surgery ended my golf outings, I was playing golf with a couple of friends at Bear Creek Golf Course near the Dallas-Fort Worth airport. You may be wondering if I was a good golfer. I will tell you that I almost never lost. That's not a boast—because I only played with people I could beat!

This was an unusual day because while I was playing golf, God was sending a man who would greatly impact my life. The man was Stephen Strang. As my two friends and I were leaving the course, bags hanging on our shoulders, three men were coming onto the course, golf bags draped over their shoulders.

I knew two of the men very well. One was the late Marcus Lamb, founder and president of Daystar Television Network. (Marcus would also later endorse the book that came out of that meeting.) The other man was my pastor, Dr. Frank Harber, who taught for ten years at Southwestern Theological Seminary, the world's largest seminary. Dr. Harber now has a law degree and pursues cases involving religious rights all the way to the Supreme Court.

Steve was in town to be a guest on Daystar. Marcus Lamb and my pastor were best friends. They were also very good golfers, and if you were a guest on the network, you likely would be invited to play golf.

As we met, my pastor said, "Steve, I want you to meet a man who has the most unusual ministry, Don Dickerman." I had heard of Stephen Strang and knew a little about *Charisma*, the Christian

magazine he founded. It seemed like the backward way to intro-
duce us.

Steve asked, "What is this unusual ministry?"

My pastor said, "Don casts out demons and sees people healed."
Now talking directly to me, Steve said, "I know a thousand pastors
who need this!"

I said, "I do too, but I don't know any who want it."

Steve asked if I had anything I had written. I told him I had
a couple of self-published books, *Serpents in the Sanctuary* and
Turmoil in the Temple. He asked if I would send them to him,
saying he might be interested in publishing my writings. I did send
him the material, and he sent me a nice letter and a publishing contract. That is how *When Pigs Move In* was born.

My now-deceased friend Frank Hammond was excited for me.
A great man and great friend, Frank wrote *Pigs in the Parlor*. My
book would have a similar theme. Pigs, being unclean, still get into
the lives of people. I want to give you some things that God has
shown me, how I cast out demons.

THE FOUR PRINCIPLES

I had a request from a man in California. Oh boy, what a story. He
was a man who also wrote to my friend David Berkowitz, known
as the Son of Sam. I'll call the man in California, Gary. He was
struggling like so many. He would share his problems with David,
and David told him he needed deliverance. He told him about me.
I communicated with Gary, and he begged me to come to him. I
explained to him all of the reasons I could not do that. His job was
telephone bill collection.

I shared his story with a friend of mine. He said, "I'll go with
you and pay for most of it." Gary's story was so unusual, almost
intriguing. After much prayer and consternation, I decided to go.
I began to analyze his demon problem, and God showed me some
simple but powerful principles of deliverance.

I ran them by my friend Frank Hammond. He was elated and said, "That's it." He corrected some of my English (Frank was a Baylor graduate), but he said, "That's it!" I will now share those principles with you.

These four principles never change, and there is no shortcut or better way to approach deliverance. People are always saying stuff like, "Jesus just cast them out with a simple command." I am not Jesus, and neither are you. This is scriptural, practical, and proven.

1. You either have demons or you don't.

Not everything is a demon. There are only four principles, and they never change, anywhere in the world with anyone. The first principle is you either do or you don't! I find many times people who thought their problem was surely demons were dealing with the flesh. Most often it is people who think they could not possibly be dealing with demons who have demons. The first principle is *you do or you don't.*

2. If you do have demons, there had to be a permission.

As we have discussed, for demons to enter, there must be a legal entryway, an open door. The possibilities are virtually unlimited, and having demons does not make someone a bad person. The obvious permissions include ancestral curses (most people have no idea what may have happened in their ancestry to give demons a right to their lives); sins (like murder, rape, incest, fraternal oaths, and vows) that have not been confessed; soul ties; spoken curses; witchcraft; and false religion. There are many possibilities. The second principle is *explore the possibilities—what are the permissions?*

3. There is no permission that cannot be removed in Jesus' name.

When it is confessed, denounced, and renounced, any permission can be canceled. I call this the prosecution. Think about some

Bible heroes. Moses was a murderer; he killed a man. King David took a man's wife and then his life. The great apostle Paul killed people. If Moses, King David, or the apostle Paul came for deliverance, they all would be confessing murder. What is the key to successful deliverance? Honest desire to be free. *Cancel by confession and renunciation.*

At this point, you are commanding demons, and they are responding to you through the candidate. With every response received from the demon, I command, "Will that stand as truth before Jehovah God?" We have found that they will not lie to Jehovah God—there's no God like Jehovah! Remember, you are a prosecutor, and God is the righteous Judge. You are representing the candidate, but you are prosecuting the demons. Anything can be confessed, renounced, or denounced—anything. *Make sure you get the boss.* You will likely run into Apollyon. (See the information on Apollyon in chapter 6.)

4. The name of Jesus is always sufficient.

Demons are just spirits. We always win.

Now you are casting out demons. See if any of the demons have done any damage to the individual. Most likely they have, so command them to put everything back in order just as Jehovah God intends for it to be. Command; don't request! That doesn't mean raise your voice; it means don't let it go. Stay after it until it's done and you are satisfied it is done. *Cast the demons out in Jesus' name.*

I tell the candidate how easy it is to stay free. I do this every night. No one is there but me. I raise my hand in the darkness and quote aloud 1 John 1:9: "If we confess our sins, he is faithful and just to forgive us our sins, and to cleanse us from all unrighteousness." Then I confess and claim to be free from all unrighteousness. It is a promise. Then I command any spirit that got access to my life to leave immediately and not leave anything behind. You'd be surprised how many times I have released a deep sigh. I thank God and begin my prayers.

I have found that speaking in tongues is counterproductive in deliverance sessions. Demons often curse me in tongues, and we do not allow tongues in deliverance sessions. While tongues is obviously a legitimate gift, in my many years of deliverance, I have found that the name of Jesus is all sufficient!

"Tongues" are practiced by many non-Christian groups, including in paganism and Shamanism. One religious group in Japan believes glossolalia could cause their followers to remember past lives. Other religious groups have been observed practicing some form of ecstatic, unintelligible speech. If you listened to their worship frenzy you would think it sounds strangely familiar.

Again, biblical tongues is a legitimate gift, but you need nothing more than the name of Jesus! There is no place for tongues in deliverance.

SOME POSSIBLE MANIFESTATIONS DURING DELIVERANCE

Pastor Greg Locke has created a list of manifestations that are common in deliverances.[1] I have yet to see a head spin as in *The Exorcist*, but I have seen the following.

- Screaming
- Sweating
- Burping
- Coughing
- Sneezing
- Yawning
- Sudden urge to urinate
- Passing gas
- Falling
- Trembling
- Spitting
- Cursing
- Sobbing
- Runny/bloody nose
- Watery/itchy eyes
- Lightheadedness
- Tingling
- Heat/burning sensation

- Bitter taste
- Ringing ears
- Muscle spasms
- Body pains/ headaches
- Stiff hands
- Itching
- Nervousness
- Twitching
- Vomiting

- Dizziness
- Violent outbursts
- Chest tightness
- Choking sensation
- Demonic visions
- Tension release/peace
- Heavy breathing
- Drooling/foaming at the mouth
- Roaring

VARIOUS WAYS DEMONS MANIFEST

Demons usually manifest as creatures or characters of some kind, so it is important to share in advance that it is very likely the person receiving deliverance will have some visual image. Demons take many forms, but here are several we have encountered:

- Albatross
- Alligator
- Amoeba
- Anaconda
- Angel (fallen)
- Ant
- Anteater/aardvark
- Antelope
- Armadillo
- Armor

- Asp
- Auger (a boring drill bit)
- Baboon
- Basilisk
- Bat
- Bear
- Beast
- Beaver
- Beetle

- Behemoth
- Bird (robin)
- Black panther
- Blob
- Blowfish
- Blue jay
- Boa
- Boar
- Boll weevil
- Buffalo
- Bug
- Bulldog
- Bullfrog
- Bumblebees
- Butterfly
- Buzzard
- Camel
- Canary
- Capricorn (a goat)
- Cardinal
- Cat: alley, black
- Catalog: holder of curses
- Caterpillar

- Catfish
- Centaur (half man/ half horse)
- Centipede
- Chameleon
- Chicken (rooster)
- Clam
- Cloud (storm)
- Clown
- Cobra, King
- Cockroach (hard shell)
- Court jester
- Cow (calf)
- Coyote
- Crab
- Crane
- Cricket
- Crow
- Dam
- Deer
- Dinosaur (white)
- Dog: German shepherd, mongrel
- Donkey

- Dragon
- Duck
- Eagle
- Eel
- Elephant
- Excrement
- Ferret
- Fish (goldfish, sucker)
- Flea
- Fly
- Fox
- Frog (flying)
- Gargoyle (half man/ half gargoyle)
- Gazelle
- Germ
- Ghost
- Gnat
- Goat
- Goose
- Gopher
- Gorilla
- Grasshopper
- Grass burr

- Grebe
- Grey herring
- Griffin
- Hammer
- Hand
- Hawk
- Hippo
- Hookworm
- Horse (with horns)
- Iguana
- Indian chief
- Jackal
- Jellyfish
- Jester (joker)
- Juggernaut
- Leech
- Lemur
- Leopard
- Leper
- Leviathan
- Lion
- Lizard
- Lobster
- Lynx

- Macaw
- Maggot (on a carcass)
- Man (in cape, with hood, with no face, and so on)
- Mastadon
- Maze
- Mealworm
- Mermaid
- Millipede
- Minotaur (half man/ half bull)
- Mole
- Monkey
- Moose
- Mortae (like a skull cap with many snakes hanging from it)
- Mosquito
- Moth
- Mountain (snow capped)
- Mountain lion
- Mouse
- Munchkin
- Muskrat

- Ocean
- Ocelot
- Octopus
- Octopus/spider
- Opossum
- Ostrich
- Owl
- Parrot
- Peacock
- Pegasus (winged horse)
- Pelican
- Pharaoh
- Phoenix
- Plant (that strangles)
- Pollen
- Porcupine
- Potato bug
- Pterodactyl
- Puff adder
- Python
- Rabbit
- Raccoon
- Rag doll (blue/white)

- Rat
- Raven
- Razor
- Rhinoceros
- Ring of fire
- Roach
- Roadrunner
- Robin
- Rock
- Rooster
- Saddle blanket
- Salamander
- Salmon
- Scarecrow
- Scorpion
- Scum
- Seagull
- Seahorse
- Serpent (constric-tors, with venom, or feathered)
- Shark
- Shrimp
- Skeleton
- Skunk
- Slug
- Snail
- Snakes (nest of snakes)
- Soldier (in armor)
- Songbird
- Sparrow
- Spider
- Spider woman
- Squid
- Squirrel
- Star (black, red)
- Stick
- Stingray
- Sun
- Swan
- Sword
- Swordfish
- Tarantula
- Tasmanian devil
- Teddy bear
- Termite
- Tick
- Tiger

- Toad
- Tower
- Tree
- Tree frog
- Turkey
- Turtle
- Tyrannosaurus rex
- Unicorn
- Water bug
- Weed
- Vulture

- Walrus
- Warrior
- Wasp (yellow jacket)
- Weasel
- Wildebeest
- Witch
- Wizard
- Wolf
- Woodpecker
- Woolly mammoth

While the type of manifestation is not always important, there are times it may help us recognize the connecting story or the open door from generational standpoints. Always remember that Satan himself can manifest as an angel of light. The first and favorite work of a demon is deception.

IF YOU CAME TO OUR OFFICE FOR DELIVERANCE...

If you felt you were being tormented by demons and came to our office for deliverance, you would be asked to complete a questionnaire with symptoms of demonic attack. Simply checking a yes or no tells our team a little bit about how to prepare for the deliverance session. The list of symptoms includes:

- A compulsive desire to blaspheme God

- A revulsion against the Bible, including a desire to tear it up or destroy it

- Compulsive thoughts of suicide or murder

- Deep feelings of bitterness and hatred toward others without reason: Jews, other races, the church, strong Christian leaders

- Any compulsive temptations that push you toward thoughts or behavior you truly do not want to think or engage in

- Compulsive desires to tear other people down, even if it means lying to do so

- Terrifying feelings of guilt even after honest confession is made to the Lord

- Certain physical symptoms that may appear suddenly or leave quickly and for which there are no physical or physiological reasons

- Choking sensations

- Pains that seem to move around and for which there is no medical cause

- Feelings of tightness about the head or eyes

- Dizziness, blackouts, or fainting seizures

- Deep depression and despondency (frequently and at significant times)

- Sudden surges of violent rage, uncontrollable anger, or seething feelings of hostility

- Terrifying doubt of one's salvation even though they once knew the joy of salvation

- Seizures of panic or other fear that is terrifying

- Dreams or nightmares that are of a horrific nature and often recurring

- Clairvoyant dreams that may even come true as these are most often demonic

- Abnormal or perverted sexual desires

- Questions and challenges to God's Word

- Sleep or eating disorders without a physical cause

- Most compulsions and obsessions

- Rebellion and hatred for authority

- Bizarre terrifying thoughts that seem to come from nowhere and that the person cannot control

- Fascination with the occult

- Involvement in criminal activity

- Extremely low self-image (feeling unworthy, like a failure, no good, and other emotions that constantly undermine the self-identity)

- Constant confusion in one's thinking (sometimes having great difficulty remembering things)

- Inability to believe (even when the person wants to)

- Mocking and blasphemous thoughts against preaching/teaching of the Word of God

- Perceptual distortions—perceiving anger or hostility in others when it doesn't really exist

- Seeing only judgment in the Scriptures

- Horrible nightmares causing fear (as they often have demonic images)

- Violent thoughts (suicidal, homicidal, self-abuse, and so on)

- Hatred and bitterness toward others for no justifiable reason

- Tremendous hostility or fear when encountering someone involved in deliverance work

- Feelings of being watched or sensing an evil presence

- Irrational fears, panic attacks, phobias

- Irrational anger, rage

- Irrational guilt, self-condemnation to the extreme

- Desire to do what is right but the inability to carry it out

- Sudden personality and attitude changes that are severe contrasts (causing the person to appear schizophrenic)

- Bipolar disorder

- A strong aversion to Scripture reading and prayer (especially one-on-one)

- A dark countenance (a steely or hollow look in the eyes, contraction of the pupils, facial features that contort or change, often an inability to look at a person directly)

- Lying, exaggerating, or stealing compulsively (often wondering why)

- Drug abuse (especially when there are demonic hallucinations)

- Eating obsessions, including bulimia and anorexia nervosa

- Compulsive sexual sins (especially perversions)

- Irrational laughter or crying

- Sudden speaking of a language not previously known (often an ethnic language of ancestors)

- Negative reactions to the name and blood of Jesus Christ (verbally or through body language)

- Extreme restlessness (especially in a spiritual environment)

- Uncontrollable cutting and mocking tongue

- Vulgar language and actions

- Loss of time (from minutes to hours; ending up someplace, not knowing how you got there; regularly doing things of which there is no memory)

- Extreme sleepiness around spiritual things

- Demonstration of extraordinary abilities (either ESP or telekinesis)

- Voices heard in the mind that mock, intimidate, accuse, threaten, or bargain

- Voice that refers to the individual in the third person

- Supernatural experiences, such as hauntings, movement or disappearance of objects, and other strange manifestations

- Seizures that last too long and/or are too regular

- Blackouts

- Sudden temporary interference with bodily functions, such as buzzing in the ears, an inability to speak or hear, severe headache, hypersensitivity in hearing or touch, chills or overwhelming heat in body, numbness in the arms or legs, or temporary paralysis

Having a couple of symptoms may not indicate anything, but these are common symptoms of things that demons do. When I have an idea of what the person is dealing with, I can identify possible entry points.

PREPARING FOR DELIVERANCE

If you are in need of deliverance, there are some things you can do to help bring about your freedom. If you came to us for deliverance, here are a few things we would share before we made an appointment.

- You must first be born again (you must be one of the children). The human spirit must surrender in order for demon spirits to be dealt with. The human spirit must desire to be free from the influence and misdirection of the demon spirit. When the human spirit becomes too comfortable with a situation to yield it to God, the demon spirit is strengthened. We have learned that it is fruitless to try to cast out demons against someone's will. The human spirit is you, and it is me. That's why deliverance and healing are called "the children's bread" (Matt. 15:26). That's what Jesus called it. It is for believers.

- You must renounce curses and soul ties. All curses—whether they are generational, physical, mental, trauma-related, sin-related, spoken, and so on—must be renounced as they are entryways for demon powers. Here is a sample prayer:

Father, I repent of anger, bitterness, hatred, rebellion, resentment and revenge, envy, jealousy and strife, lust, witchcraft, idolatry, and all the works of the flesh. I put it all under the blood of Jesus, and by doing so I break Satan's power and legal rights to my life. I break the power of generational curses and deny permission of any demon spirit to my life. I repent of and denounce any contract I made with Satan; since he is a liar, no contract is binding. By the blood of Jesus I free myself from any pact with the devil. I renounce all unholy oaths, vows, pledges, and ceremonies. Jesus is my Savior and Lord. He is my deliverer and my healer, and He broke the power of the curse! I choose to be free, and I will be free by the resurrection power of Jesus

Christ according to His holy Word and in the authority of His name. Amen.

Sexual relationships outside of marriage are called soul ties, and each one could be an entry point for demon spirits. The ties must be broken by confessing them as sin and then choosing to be free from them. When you pray, it would be best if you denounce each one by name; do the best you can with that. The deliverance process involves canceling permission of evil spirits to be in our lives. This renunciation will cancel consent that was granted through soul ties. The prayer can be something like this:

Father, I confess the sin of sexual relations outside of marriage. I renounce that sinful activity in Jesus' name. I call back that part of me that was given to another, and I refuse that part of another that may have come to me. I denounce all soul ties and choose to be free in Jesus Christ's name. Amen.

- You must believe what God's Word says despite your preconceived ideas about deliverance. You must come into agreement with the Word of God. If you want genuine freedom, you must be in spiritual alignment; that is, your spirit must agree with what God says in His Word; your soul must believe and speak what God's Word says; and your flesh must agree in obedience to the truth of God's Word. Coming into agreement with God's Word can cancel any legal consent that demons may have. Here is an example of how you can pray to come into agreement with the Word:

Heavenly Father, I come to You humbly, acknowledging my need for Your truth and freedom. I confess any thoughts, beliefs, or actions that have opposed or doubted Your Word, and I choose now to believe fully in what Your Word says. I declare that my spirit agrees with Your Word, and I claim the freedom You have promised. In Jesus' name, amen.

- There can be no unforgiveness. In order for deliverance to be successful, there can be no unforgiveness in your life. Unforgiveness is legal permission for demons to torment believers (Matt. 18:23–35). Do not neglect the area of forgiveness for yourself. You must forgive yourself in order to be free. A typical prayer might be as follows:

Father, because You have forgiven me, I choose to forgive others. I forgive everyone who has hurt me, lied to me, or disappointed me. I confess unforgiveness as sin and repent of it. I receive Your forgiveness and apply it to my life by forgiving myself. Thank You for Your grace and mercy. In Jesus' name, amen.

- If there was ever any involvement (however innocent) in satanic activities, witchcraft, cults, or occultic activities, it must be renounced. You can pray something along these lines:

Father, I denounce any bond or agreement I ever made with Satan and the kingdom of darkness. I know there can be no valid contract with a liar, and I renounce any words, oaths, or pledges made to Satan. I choose to be totally free from them. I choose to be cleansed from any ties with Satan, in Jesus' name. Amen.

For complete deliverance you must be willing to turn away from certain strongholds—maybe old friends, things you once did, or old habits and hangouts.

God will deliver you from your areas of weakness, but you must be willing to do your part, which may mean choosing new friends and new activities. You must learn to hate the things that cause you to fall! You must hate demons and count them as your enemies.

CANCELING PERMISSIONS PRAYER

During the deliverance session, I often have people repeat this prayer after me:

> *Father, I thank You for Jesus and for my salvation through Him. He is my Savior, and I am the sinner. I am so grateful to be washed in His blood. And because You have forgiven me, I choose to forgive others.*
>
> *I repent of anger, bitterness, and hatred, and of rebellion, resentment, and revenge. I repent of envy, jealousy and strife, fear, doubt and unbelief, witchcraft, idolatry, and all the works of the flesh. I denounce the sins of my ancestors. I separate and cut myself off from all generational curses. I renounce all unholy oaths and vows, pledges, and ceremonies, and I choose to be free from all of those curses. I denounce and confess as sin all unholy soul ties and choose to be free from them. I put everything under the blood of Jesus and by doing so, I break Satan's power in my life.*
>
> *Jesus Christ is my Savior and Lord. He's my Deliverer and my Healer, and He broke the power of curse. I choose to be free, and I will be free, in Jesus' name.*

GENERAL COMMAND FOR BINDING DEMONS

After all permissions are canceled, the following is a general prayer I use to bind demon spirits. (I find it's best for the deliverance candidate to keep their eyes closed and not pray but to keep their mind open to the demon's response.)

In the name of the Lord Jesus Christ, I now bind every spirit in any way associated with _____, whether in him, attached to him, or anyway connected with his life. I now call you under the authority of the living, resurrected Lord Jesus, the One who defeated your master. You are commanded that you will not harm him, that you will not split, divide, multiply, fragment, or clone, or use any form of demonic trickery or deception. If you have already done so, you are commanded to rejoin as one kingdom. There will be no passing on of duties nor calling on others to replace you. All traffic will be one way, and that will be out and into the abyss. I forbid the use of revolving doors and entry by other demon powers. You will not harm him nor will you leave him and go to anyone else. Whether hiding or sleeping, using shelves or dark corners, coming and going, or floating in free circulation, you are now under the authority of Jesus Christ and you will be obedient. All hiding places are destroyed.

I remove your crowns and robes and earned authority and privilege. You are commanded that you cannot communicate with other demons at this time in any way to scheme, plot, plan, or devise a way to retain this kingdom. The kingdom will be completely and totally demolished.

You are commanded that you will return everything that you have stolen, you will repair any damage you have caused, and every disorder you have created, you will put back in order just as Jehovah God intends for it to be. You will not receive any outside assistance or interference. To demons present, you are commanded to retrieve every seed or egg, and you are commanded to uproot everything planted. Nothing will be left behind, and every doorway will be closed and locked. This command is in the name of the Lord Jesus and must be obeyed. When commanded, you will go immediately and directly into the abyss and never return.

I now call the highest-ranking demon power to the front, inside or outside. You come forward right now and identify yourself by the name Jehovah God knows you by. Who are you?

You are now prosecuting the demons. If the highest-ranking demon is outside (meaning it is attached to the person rather than having entered his soulish area), and it most likely will be, determine its name, geographical territory, permission to access the person, function, how long it has been associated with the person, how many demons are present on the outside, who they are, and so on. When permissions are canceled or it is determined that no permission remains, command the demons to return to the heavenlies and to not send any other demons to replace them. Then proceed to the inside kingdom. Most of the outside spirits will have inside spirits by the same name. Get rid of the outside spirits first.

All kingdoms have leaders. You want the head guy. He may not be identified as a prince; he may have another title. Healing comes when the source has been identified and confessed and demons expelled!

GONE OUT VS. CAST OUT

Don't be surprised that demons know Scripture; not only do they know it, but they also know how to twist it! What I am about to say is not revolutionary revelation, but it certainly opened my eyes as a key truth to deliverance ministry and to walking in freedom. This is something you must know to effectively deal with the kingdom of darkness! It concerns the demons' favorite scripture, Matthew 12:43–45:

> When the unclean spirit is gone out of a man, he walketh through dry places, seeking rest, and findeth none. Then he saith, I will return into my house from whence I came out; and when he is come, he findeth it empty, swept, and garnished. Then goeth he, and taketh with himself seven other spirits more wicked than himself, and they enter in and dwell there: and the last state of that man is worse than the first. Even so shall it be also unto this wicked generation.

This scripture puzzled me, and for months I could not reconcile this with other Scripture verses. I had to stop working on the book *When Pigs Move In* because these verses made no sense to me. Why cast them out if they can come back stronger? I asked for weeks for the Holy Spirit to enlighten me and show me truth.

This information is perhaps the most important I can share with those interested in deliverance ministry. Get this phrase locked in your mind: "Gone out or cast out." It is a key to ministering in truth. All my life I had heard preachers making reference to this verse and teaching that the demons can come back unless the house is filled with the Holy Spirit, faithful Bible reading, worship, prayer, and giving: "You have to fill the house." That is not even implied in the Scripture passage.

In Matthew 12 Jesus reproved the Pharisees and the generation of Israel to which He came. He healed and cast out demons. He rebuked the people for their unbelief and likened the nation to one who has demons. He spoke of them as a generation that were resolved to continue in the possession and under the power of Satan, despite all God's attempts to rescue them and free them. Jesus used a parable to compare them to one out of whom the devil is gone but returns with double force. The devil is here called *the unclean spirit.*

The parable represents Satan and his demons possessing men's bodies. Matthew Henry wrote:

Christ having lately cast out a devil, and they having said *he had a devil*, gave occasion to show how much they were under the power of Satan. This is a further proof that Christ did not cast out devils by compact with the devil, for then he [the demon] would soon have returned again; but Christ's ejectment of him was final, and such as barred a re-entry: we find him charging the evil spirit to *go out, and enter no more*, Mk. 9:25.[2]

What a great statement! There was no deal with Satan as the Jews had accused Him. There are two key issues in clarifying this horribly misused scripture:

1. It was a parable.

2. The term is *gone out*, not *cast out*.

I will say that again: *gone out*, not *cast out*!
Another great insight from Matthew Henry reads:

The application of the parable makes it to represent the case of the body of the Jewish church and nation: *So shall it be with this wicked generation*, that now resist, and will finally reject, the gospel of Christ....And then he shall take a durable possession here, and the state of this people is likely to be more desperately damnable...than it was before Christ came among them, or would have been if Satan had never been cast out.[3]

Clearly Jesus made this statement in the parable in regard to what He called "a wicked generation."

I have been doing this for a few years! Virtually all believers who have a casual knowledge of Scripture misunderstand and misapply Matthew 12:43–45 here. This is what they say: "If you don't keep the house filled, then the cast-out demons will come back seven times stronger." That is *not* true! That is not what is being taught here. If, as most believe, demons can return in double force once they have been cast out, wouldn't it be unwise to cast them out? What would allow demons to do this, to be cast out and yet later return? That makes no sense.

Look carefully at the parable Jesus used. The demons here were not cast out; they were gone out—apparently they left to try to find a better home, knowing they could return because there was still an open door. When the demons decided to return, it was not because the house had not been filled (so often and erroneously taught). The house was in good shape; it was garnished, clean, and decorated. The demons knew they could go back because they knew they still had legal permission. Their legal rights to be there had never been canceled.

When demons are cast out in the name of Jesus, there is finality. Those particular demons cannot return! However, there are plenty of demons who can and possibly will enter if legal rights are granted. That an individual can continue a downward spiral is true. Whether a person goes through deliverance or not, if they grant other demons opportunity, those other demons can enter. It is so important to know this. Demons love to intimidate deliverance candidates with lies and threats.

DRY PLACES

Never do we command demons to go into "dry places," which seems to be where they congregate and make their plans and evil strategies. Demons have done a good job at using these scriptures to confuse people and prevent them from seeking deliverance. I have had many people ask me, "Now what do I do to keep them from coming back seven times stronger?" Most preachers even make misleading comments about this section of Scripture. You have heard words such as, "Be sure and keep the house filled so the demons don't come back stronger."

The demons love it. Keeping people in ignorance and fear is their specialty. Across many, many years of ministry I have never seen this happen—someone being worse off because they experienced deliverance. Never! However, someone who continues in a life-style that initially granted permission will once again be entangled because doors stay open. There is a big difference. Don't be intimidated by confusion and lies; the demons cannot come back stronger because those same demons cannot come back.

When I leave my office, I go out knowing I can come back and could even invite some friends to come back with me. I have a door; I have the keys. However, if the owner of the building evicts me, takes the keys back, and demands that I leave, I can't come back. Big difference—gone out and cast out. Leaving of your own volition is very different from being kicked out!

The commands we give when casting out demons is that they go into the abyss, the pit of hell, and never return. That does not mean the individual cannot continue to live a dysfunctional life-style by being disobedient to God. Some do make choices to disobey and grant legal rights to demons. Choices always remain, and bad choices generally open doors to other demons.

Don't give demons too much credit. Don't fear them, and don't let them gain an advantage by misuse of God's Holy Word!

CHAPTER 6

NAMES, WORKS, AND MANIFESTATIONS

ESSICA HAD A history of medical problems. Diagnosed with bipolar disorder, she had been on antidepressants and mood-altering medication for many years. She also had undergone several major surgeries. She suffered from constant back pain and chronic fatigue syndrome. She told me that although she had never been "diagnosed," she always felt that she had a learning disability and could not retain much of what she read, especially the Bible. "I often feel very confused, and I struggle with decisions," she said. I have heard this so many times prior to deliverances.

Well, there were obviously many opportunities for demons to gain access to her life. She still had some anger, bitterness, and resentment toward all those who abused her throughout her life. But she said she could release that and confess it as sin. She also had unforgiveness toward her first husband.

It was time to begin, and we prayed together affirming our salvation and then repenting of unforgiveness, anger, bitterness, hatred, resentment, and kindred sins. We also affirmed together that we received the full work of the cross, breaking the power of all curses and canceling the right of any demonic power to her life. Her husband prayed this along with us.

I explained that I would be binding evil spirits in the name of the Lord Jesus Christ and commanding them to be obedient in His name. I told her it might help if she closed her eyes so she would not be distracted. "Tell me what you feel, hear, or see when I am commanding the spirits," I said.

She was already feeling nausea and trembling, she said.

I discovered a very powerful demon who made Jessica incredibly fearful, and I suspected that this demon spirit came in through Jessica watching scary movies. Very rarely does a person become somnambulistic (in a trancelike state where the demon speaks through them) during deliverance, but it does occur. The person will actually be unaware of what is taking place, and the demons will speak through his or her voice. This was not the case here. Jessica was in full control of her faculties, and as I bound the evil spirits in Jesus Christ's name, she dropped her head and closed her eyes.

I asked her to tell me what thoughts came to her mind—words or names or what she saw or felt—as I commanded spirits to respond. She told me she was feeling very hot and had some tightness in her chest. She also mentioned tingling in her arms. I commanded, always in the name of the Lord Jesus Christ, that the "prince" demon—the boss, the demon power in charge—come forward and identify himself. Immediately she named the prince demon.

I recognized the name right away. I run into this spirit quite often; there must be a million that carry that identity. This spirit boasted that there were too many present for me to handle. The demon spoke through her, "You are too weary, and you will have to stop and rest. You will not be able to cast me out." This was a ploy to make Jessica believe she was being selfish by taking my time and energy, or that we would not be successful. I was tired, but I had no doubts about being successful because it has nothing to do with my strength!

The demon revealed his function and purposes in Jessica's life to be confusion, disorder, and death. One by one, we began to tear his kingdom down. This spirit was there by consent of the abuse she suffered as a child. Then a spirit who identified his function as confusion surfaced, and his work was to keep her unstable. There was also a spirit linked with this one with an assignment of instability and insecurity.

An interesting revelation for me was a spirit whose function was sexual abuse, not causing her to abuse others, but somehow inviting sexual abuse *from* others. I began to ponder the spirit. Was it seductive, deceptive, a coconspirator in murder? I had encountered this spirit before.

Another spirit identified itself whose function was denial. This spirit also came from humiliation as a child. A spirit identifying his function as dishonor came in through one of her cosmetic surgeries. This spirit often has a doorway of a "reprobate mind," according to Romans 1:24, choosing to "dishonour their own bodies." This falls in the same category as body piercings or tattoos. It is sometimes revealed as a demon spirit functioning in vanity.

Jessica said she wanted to move to the floor. So she left her chair and knelt on the floor, at times with her hands to the floor and her head down, other times with her body erect but head tilted down and eyes closed. She raised her head and said, "I am so negative in my thinking and speech. There surely must be something there." Her mother was very negative and doubtful. She was right; there was a spirit there by permission of a generational curse from her mother and grandmother whose function was negativity.

Deliverance is so amazing. The Holy Spirit wonderfully brings truth to us and forces the demons to react in obedience to commands in the authority of the Lord Jesus Christ. With each release, Jessica had deep sighs as the demons left and went to the pit of hell as commanded. Toward the end of this wonderful night, I commanded one of the remaining boastful demons to tell me where his master was. There was a weak response: "He's in the pit." That is exactly where he had been commanded to go earlier!

IDENTIFYING DEMON SPIRITS

Demons can be identified in four ways: by name, by function, by where they inhabit the candidate's body, and by how they manifest.

1. Demonic names

Demon names are often confused with demon functions or demon manifestations. A common misnomer is to call a demon by its function or how it manifests. For example, a fear spirit will simply be called Fear. A spirit that manifests as a python will be called Python. However, that is not the demon's name but what it does or how it manifests in a person's life. Every demon has a name. Every demon was an angel of the Lord at one time, and each has a name given to it by God. Their names are usually not common human names as we know them. The names the demons have will generally be like ancient biblical names or something possibly from Greek or Roman mythology, usually not Jim or Bob.

Obtaining the names of the demons is important to the success of the deliverance. When a demon is confronted and commanded to give its name, it will be reluctant to do so. Like any common criminal, as long as they are unidentified, they are able to continue their work with little chance of being brought to justice. Once identified, they will be easier to nail down and made to cease their work. In each kingdom, no matter their function, there will almost always be more than one of them to contend with. It is not as important to identify all the demons by name as it is to identify the names of the demonic princes themselves. After the princes are identified and their permissions are canceled, they can be commanded to take the remainder of their kingdoms and to go into the abyss.

2. Demon functions

These are just that. It is what a demon has permission to do in a believer's life. For example, fear is a function. Again, do not let the demons get away with using that as their name. It is simply what they do.

3. Body location

This can help greatly in identifying the demons and what they do. Virtually every demon will be in or on the body someplace. Scorpion spirits, for example, will generally inhabit the abdomen or torso. Spider spirits will generally be located in and around the head. Serpents can be found all over the body but will many times be in the abdomen or wrapped around the spine or torso.

4. Demonic manifestations

This is how a demon can appear in a person's life. Every demon will manifest as a creature of some type, usually as a creature of darkness. Common manifestations are snakes, scorpions, spiders, bats, or dragons. These are common but not a given. The demons can manifest as many other creatures. What is important to know is that the way the demon manifests can tell a lot about who they are and what they do. A common example is a scorpion spirit. These types of spirits will almost always operate in the fear and anxiety kingdoms but can also cause rejection, anger, hatred, or any of many other problems. Remember, nothing is a given.

Every demon has a name they were given by Jehovah God when they were created, and the name is significant as to their function. If they were created to minister to the mind, for instance, then you can be sure that as a demon they are "killing, stealing, and destroying" in the mind.

For decades I have been collecting demon names I've encountered in deliverance sessions. Here are just a few of them:

Aberjinan, Absalom, Acton, Adian, Aella, Aeoro, Alpha, Amonforth: Self, Amoz, Amyloc, Andor, Andrew, Anglin, Angus, Anikadin, Anspaad, Antesus, Armageddon, Artie, Assimov, Azorian, Baal, Bahni, Balof, Barclay, Barrabus, Basil, Belial, Bickery, Biltread, Bob, Bobam, Bobo, Bolla, Brockland, Butro, Byzentine, Cagen, Calipso, Cameron, Camille, Caracus, Carlie, Caus, Cee, Charlemagne, Charpé, Claudius, Clementine, Closko, Colecka, Corinthia, Credome, Crimeo, Curlion, Danby, Daniel, Darius, Death, Demetrius, Dimitri, Dizzy, Doubtking, Driddle, Dublu, Duvin, Elsinor, El Wormo, Epalace, Errmacuse, Estavan, Fairfield, Flitch, Flotran, Fortus, Gaius, Gale, Gangleesh, Gliddarde, Goober, Haley, Heidel, Helifa, Helwig, Heron, Hexel, Hiedin, Hilasheal, Horus, Hunck, Hyman, Ibod, Ibus, Igamous, Iccubus, Igron, Imus, Inglos, Ireland, Iris, Irksho, Ivan, Jabel, Jarie, Jarman, Jason, Jehogah, Jerichem, Jerwise, Jessie, Jezebel, Joel, Josiah,

Juno, Justus, Kaluses, Kanica, Killo, Kipschan, Kyuza, Laban, Labem, Labrich, Landau, Lakifi, Lani, Laron, Lason, Lawrence, Lemier, Leon, Leviasian, Leviathan, Liena, Longfellow, Lucas, Lucifer, Luko, Mace, Machio, Magon, MaHa Bone, Majirus, Malarkioni, Malchut, Marcus, Masterly, Meshach, Mezhobic, Michael, Milkik, Mishaba, Molar, Morron, Moses, Mris, Mystery, Mytog, Nahum, Nazabut, Nuron, Oda, Olaf, O'riely, Ophram, Orethro, Osmos, Othonal, Ottowa, Oxsaya, Pacifier, Panlail, Pathios, Paula, Perez, Pharoih, Piantus, Player, Pladius, Poindexter, Ponday, Pourah, Pribius, Pricero, Quandry, Quiznor, Rakle, Ramadama, Raul, Refuelic, Regatuda: Salvation, Rencor: Of Salvation, Renda, Rhelea, Ronniexum, Rufaldo, St. Jude, Salazar, Salvator, Sapphire, Saqua, Samhain, Samuel, Saur, Seli, Seth, Shaaktel, Shabada, Shamain, Shambach, Shamreal, Sharequa, Shaya, Sherez, Shona, Shotis, Shustamain, Shyrice: Salvation, Silencer, Siphor, Six, Spearnach, Star, Subar, Sweet, Syrian, Syrpt, Taldor, Tamar, Tekoline, Tododo, Tolay, Tolly, Towzer, Trojan, Tubal-Cain, Turkistry, Underminer, Van, Vasyylia, Victor, Visimo, Washton, Wayan, Wendra, Who Are You, Wilkins, Xavier, Xerbac, Yanada, Yata, Yu-Are-He, Zana, Zarbon, Zel, Zim, Zolack

All these demons have works related to doubt and confusion, so you may find this list helpful if you are dealing with someone who is bound in this area. As I said, this has been a journey of many years in an effort to gain insight and pass it on. All demons have names!

BLOOD, SWEAT, AND FEARS—HOW ONE DEMON CAN BE IN MULTIPLE PEOPLE

You should also know that one territorial demon can inhabit multitudes of people. Principalities and powers are just that. They are over principalities with a particular power. I did not learn this by attending seminary or receiving a doctoral degree. I learned by experience and focus—blood, sweat, and fears! I sensed the Lord tell me to find out everything I could about demons. I kept records and information from every deliverance.

I pushed and pressed into every deliverance and learned that the principalities split and place part of themselves into people. I remember dealing with a man from Ethiopia, and one of the demons said, "I am baby Beelzebub; he put me here." Beelzebub was also present on the outside of the body. We virtually always deal with splits of principalities.

The most common principality I have encountered is Apollyon, or Abaddon. His work is always fear-related. In my opinion and experience he may be the highest-ranking demon under Satan.

Some have described him as a two-headed dragon, which is absolutely wrong. This is one demon, always manifesting as a scorpion. He is named in Revelation 9:11 as Apollyon in the Greek, the language the New Testament was written in, and Abaddon in Hebrew. The scripture clearly says his sting is in his tail, and he is called the "angel of the bottomless pit," a pretty impressive title.

This demon claims to be on the first tier below Satan and says he has access to about 90 percent of the world. I don't know if that is true, but I've never done a deliverance anywhere or with anyone from around the world where Apollyon was not present. He is responsible for fear and things fear related, including rejection. He always organizes as a military, and the demons under him have a rank. It took me years in deliverance to find this out—blood, sweat, and years!

One day I was reading these words in Proverbs 30:27: "The locusts have no king, yet go they forth all of them by bands." I said, "That's what I am seeing." The scorpions are in rank like a military. Ten or fifteen Bible translations indicate that they march in order, like a military. Often when I would locate a fear-related spirit and demand his rank in the kingdom, I would get answers such as "I am a corporal," or "I am a general."

After months of seeing this pattern, I commanded one of the

spirits, who claimed to be a general, "I don't want to talk to you. I want to speak to the commander-in-chief. Who is it?"

It replied, "That would be Apollyon."

The demon power Apollyon came forth. I have since dealt with him thousands of times. He is likely the highest-ranking demon present, and if you have not dealt with him, you probably have some unfinished deliverances.

Usually, he will have another principality working with him. This is true in virtually all situations. The prince of doubt and confusion is Orion. This demon generally appears as the color purple and is always an octopus on the head, a skull-cap octopus with many tentacles going into the mind and head, twisting truth. There are many such demons in his kingdom that cause confusion, skepticism, doubt, disbelief, unbelief, and sometimes physical problems with vision, headaches, and tightness in the head and neck area. He is a blocking spirit!

I was visiting a Texas prison once, and the chaplain had a deliverance minister there to cast out demons from an inmate. I arrived toward the end of the deliverance. A couple of inmates I knew were there praying during that session. One of them pulled me aside and said, "Brother Don, I saw this huge octopus thing standing behind him, and he was attached with tentacles that looked like wires to different parts of his body. It was larger than [the deliverance candidate]. As commands were given, you could see this thing begin to tremble. I saw this, Brother Don! When the final command was given, that thing released backward and fell out of sight. I saw this, Brother Don!"

This is a pretty accurate description. Not all demons are inside. Some are attached to certain parts of the body. This is why part of our command in binding demons includes the phrase "whether inside, outside, attached, or floating in free circulation."

Here are some of the regulars found in Apollyon's scorpion army of fear and its fear-related military structure:

- **Feelings of guilt/shame:** Haberlowe, Vermo, Lock, Rendonhale, Ramadama, Ubersev

- **Depression/hopelessness:** Apollyus, Tallorous, Pradylis, Gaston, Ezra, Mesal, Undicer

- **Feelings of gloom:** Archibald, Azorian, Beldon, Karpesh, Coda, Hexatar, Jambres

- **Anger:** Risellen, Rahab, Rashayton, Ristoff, Shontex, Vertotall, Risnofin

- **Self-hatred:** Aster, Jira, Zenim, Pantera, Estantaffe, Jelzar, Masterath, Spinx, Randy

- **Rejection:** Akraba, Racka, Rabar, Nazaraba, Oxsaya, Felix, Randolph

- **Rape:** Lust, Baracus, Benquist, Horus, Netyn, Spartan, Traylor, Jew, Joshishe, Tartac

- **Insecurity:** Elenta, Errmacuse, Codimay, Raquilt, Visimo, Cynic, Paloncho

- **Hearing voices/seeing things:** El Dimo, Jeff, Randy, Cindy, Shockadula, Vetchkup

- **Inexplicable pain:** Orion, Woteige, Argon, Ash, Augnoton, Vicus

- **Inferiority:** Elenta, Errmacuse, Codimay, Raquilt, Visimo, Bisimo, Hagar

- **Incredible loneliness:** Felix, Oxsaya, Elenta, Errmacuse, Codimay, Bisimo, Orion

- **Doubt/unbelief:** Orion, Closko, Danby, Raul, Calipso, Juno

- **Obsessive-compulsive thoughts:** Steven, Krulon, Kaleno, Glabbring

- **Feeling a presence:** Chentagua, Marco, Apollyon, Blackwell, Letoe, Ezra

- **Nightmares and sleep disorders:** Masshallert, Sleeper Inkwell, Sartoohe, Shevelert, Tussarlaire

All the demons I just listed were cast out of one person. Of the 120,000 or so demon names I have encountered, I include the ones I've encountered most often in part 2.

LET ME TELL YOU ABOUT YEMAYA

I know this demon well. You may want to look up this demon on the internet. She came to my office, and we visited. (All demons are male, but they can manifest as female.)

Yemaya is Santeria's ocean goddess mermaid. Originally from the Yoruba religion, Yemaya was brought over to the Americas by enslaved Africans as early as the sixteenth century.

Well, I didn't know any of this when I first encountered the "Queen of the Sea." However, a woman from Puerto Rico had come for deliverance. She is now a friend and administrative assistant at a large church. She does Bible studies online with a friend in Florida. The friend had sent in an application for deliverance and said, "I want to be here when she comes. She is from the Dominican Republic and may speak to you in Spanish."

So the woman from the Dominican Republic—I will call her Carol—agreed. Her husband had come with her and was being seen by one of our other ministers. Carol had prepared for our session and was ready for deliverance. We talked and went through a typical prayer and canceled all permissions. But just before we started, Carol said, "I have been hearing some unusual names in my mind, and I think they may be names of demons. I wrote some down," and she handed me a piece of paper.

I said, "Well, we will just see." The first name on the list was Yemaya. I said, "Is there a demon power present named Yemaya? Carol leaned forward and threw her hair back over her head, looking like the Starbucks lady. Her face contorted a little. She threw her chest out very seductively and put her feet together like a mermaid!

She smiled at me and said, "Do you like me, Don?" I'd never had that happen before, so I said, "Well, do you like me?" She said, still smiling very seductively, "No, right now I'm a lesbian, but I can change my gender anytime I want to."

Her friend's eyes almost popped out of her head as she took it all in. I knew I had just encountered something new to me.

"You can change your gender? Do you have anything to do with the gender confusion going on in this country?"

"Yes, I do," she said coyly.

Now check this out. This is amazing. I commanded this demon to reveal how long it had been in the family. "I came into her family in 1595. The Yoruba tribes in Africa worshipped me as the goddess of life and blessings. I am the Queen of the Sea!"

"Yeah, well, you're gonna bow to our King today!" I said.

"We all bow to your King," the demon replied.

This evil spirit had mermen and mermaid demons with her, many minions of sea creatures. I said, "So how did you get to the Dominican Republic?" Her immediate response was, "On the boats. They dropped us off in Haiti and the Dominican Republic, and we merged with Santeria." The demon was getting weak and less seductive.

"So you are also a principality, and your territory is what?"

"Waters, gender, and sexual disorientation. The sailors pray to me."

"Well, your rights to [Carol's] life are forever removed, and you will leave her now and repair any damage you have caused. Confess in the name of Jesus that you will fully obey that command!"

"I confess," the spirit said, and with a deep sigh, Yemaya was gone.

Carol put her hair back in place and repositioned herself in the chair, and then we got the rest of them. When I arrived home, I went straight to my computer to check out this name. There it was, just as the demon had said through Carol.

Remember when the all-rookie deliverance team of believers came back with glowing reports: "Lord, even the demons are subject to us in your name!" (Luke 10:17, ESV)? Jesus joined in their joy.

Yemaya is actually a well-known spirit, but that was my first meeting. Remember, demons are not female but can manifest even as angels of light. They have all been defeated and tremble at the name of Jesus—all of them.

CHAPTER 7

STAYING FREE

COMMIT THIS TRUTH to memory: Staying free is your responsibility. You are the gatekeeper of what gets into your life. It's not a matter of what if you fall; it's a matter of *when* you fall, because our nature is sin. But God has said clearly in 1 John 1:9, "If we confess our sins, he is faithful and just to forgive us our sins, and to cleanse us from all unrighteousness." In other words, if you will confess your sin, He will forgive you and put you right back into fellowship with Him.

Maintaining freedom is easy. It involves not doing things that open doors to demonic powers. It is more about not doing than doing. We need to know our limitations and recognize our boundaries so we can remain free and not open doors to demon powers.

ADMIT IT AND QUIT IT

The apostle John described true fellowship with Jesus Christ as walking in the light. Believers walk in the light by, among other things, honestly admitting they sin: "If we say that we have no sin, we deceive ourselves, and the truth is not in us. If we confess our sins, he is faithful and just to forgive us our sins, and to cleanse us from all unrighteousness" (1 John 1:8–9).

Jesus is the light (1 John 1:5; John 1:4–9). He even described Himself as light (John 9:5; 12:35–36). He is the light of the world, with holiness that shines into the darkness of this fallen and sinful world. But if we want to have a genuine relationship and unbroken fellowship with God, we must live in His light by obeying His Word. And when we mess up, miss the mark, or cross the line, we need to openly confess. John explained, "If we say that we have not sinned, we make him a liar, and his word is not in us" (1 John 1:10). Admit it and quit it!

Confess your sin as soon as you recognize it. If you don't, guilt will consume you, as it did David: "When I kept silent, my bones grew old through my groaning all the day long. For day and night Your hand was heavy upon me; my vitality was turned into the drought of summer" (Ps. 32:3–4, NKJV). But David knew the solution: "Finally, I confessed all my sins to you and stopped trying to hide my guilt. I said to myself, 'I will confess my rebellion to the LORD.' And you forgave me! All my guilt is gone" (Ps. 32:5, NLT). Confess it and address it.

A key word all through Scripture is *confess*. That's how you got saved—confessing with your mouth and believing with your heart that God raised Jesus from the dead. The word *confess* refers to acknowledging or admitting a sin. When we confess our sins to God, we are acknowledging that we have gone against His Word and broken His law, and because of that we deserve punishment. When we confess, we are stating with humility that we have sinned against God.

Don't misunderstand. At the moment of our salvation, the moment we choose to accept Jesus as our Savior, all our sins are forgiven—every single one of them. Jesus paid the price for our sins on the cross, once and for all time, accepting the punishment that we deserved (Eph. 1:7; Rom. 5:6–11; Heb. 10:1–18). All our sins—the things we did in the past, the way we are messing up in the present, and how we will miss the mark in the future—are forgiven through the blood of Jesus Christ.

Yet Jesus taught us to ask for God's forgiveness daily: "And forgive us our debts, as we forgive our debtors" (Matt. 6:12). That is because even after salvation, believers frequently mess up (Phil. 3:12; Jas. 3:2, 8; 4:17). Just because you are a believer does not mean you are perfect. You are going to sin because you are human. That is why the Word says, "If we confess our sins, he is faithful and just to forgive us our sins, and to cleanse us from all unrighteousness" (1 John 1:9).

Becoming a believer does not make us sinless, but hopefully it will make us sin less. And when we do sin, if we confess those sins, they won't hinder our fellowship with the Lord.

The first step is to admit our sins to ourselves: "For I acknowledge my transgressions: and my sin is ever before me" (Ps. 51:3). Trying to hide or cover up sins is never a good plan: "He that covereth his sins shall not prosper: but whoso confesseth and forsaketh them shall have mercy" (Prov. 28:13). The next step is to confess our sins to God so we can receive His forgiveness, mercy, and grace. Sometimes we may also need to confess to someone else when we have sinned against them. The Word of God instructs us to confess our sins to other members of the body of Christ and to ask for forgiveness from those we have hurt:

> Confess your faults one to another, and pray one for another, that ye may be healed. The effectual fervent prayer of a righteous man availeth much.
>
> —JAMES 5:16

> Therefore if thou bring thy gift to the altar, and there rememberest that thy brother hath ought against thee; leave there thy gift before the altar, and go thy way; first be reconciled to thy brother, and then come and offer thy gift. Agree with thine adversary quickly, whiles thou art in the way with him; lest at any time the adversary deliver thee to the judge, and the judge deliver thee to the officer, and thou be cast into prison.
>
> —MATTHEW 5:23–25

> And be ye kind one to another, tenderhearted, forgiving one another, even as God for Christ's sake hath forgiven you.
>
> —EPHESIANS 4:32

> Forbearing one another, and forgiving one another, if any man have a quarrel against any: even as Christ forgave you, so also do ye.
>
> —COLOSSIANS 3:13

The Bible tells a story about a man who was sick for a long time:

> Now a certain man was there who had an infirmity thirty-eight years. When Jesus saw him lying there, and knew that he already had been in that condition a long time, He said to him, "Do you want to be made well?" The sick man answered Him, "Sir, I have no man to put me into the pool when the water is stirred up; but while I am coming, another steps down before me." Jesus said to him, "Rise, take up your bed and walk."...Afterward Jesus found him in the temple, and said to him, "See, you have been made well. Sin no more, lest a worse thing come upon you."
>
> —JOHN 5:5–8, 14, NKJV

This section of Scripture confirms that sickness is in the world because of sin—not necessarily our sin, but it is always directly or indirectly related to unconfessed sin. Jesus certainly indicated that when He said to the healed man, "Sin no more, lest a worse thing come upon you." Change your lifestyle. Don't do what you did before or the results next time could be even worse.

The Book of Psalms indicates the same. Look at Psalm 107:17: "Fools because of their transgression, and because of their iniquities, are afflicted." One version reads like this: "Some were fools through their sinful ways, and because of their iniquities suffered affliction" (ESV).

Now, that is not to say that if someone is sick it's because of unconfessed sin in their life. It is implied by Jesus, but the sickness could also be from ancestral sin that has not been dealt with. It could be that we live in a sinful world and have been exposed to sickness. We can't always know why. That is the case here in the account of the man who had been sick for thirty-eight years. None of the methods involving human participation were used; it was a sovereign act of God. It is not beyond speculation that a childhood sin may have caused his sickness, but to me it's clear that ancestral sin likely brought about his disease. It is also clear that this man was a believer; moments after he was healed, he was in the temple, where Jesus saw him and gave the admonishment. Perhaps he was there to give thanks for his healing.

I have seen people receive deliverance and healing and then return to a lifestyle that brought on the conditions initially. This is unacceptable to God. Opening a door for demons is what this is all about—they are the tormentors; they bring about sickness and disease. Jesus basically said to this man who had been sovereignly healed, "Whatever allowed this into your life before, don't do it again."

Remember, He initially asked this man, "Would you like to be healed?" He gave him the opportunity to confess his need. Confession always precedes receiving from God. Confess it and address it. Stop it and drop it. Cast it out and last it out. The five-word summary of this story is *admit it and quit it.*

PROTECTIVE BOUNDARIES FOR THE FREED

Have you ever heard anyone say, "God, let me out of the box"?

In an effort to experience more of God, some people get out from under sound doctrine and allow their itching ears to be scratched by preachers and teachers of unsound doctrine. The apostle Paul warned Timothy about this:

> For the time will come when they will not endure sound doctrine; but after their own lusts shall they heap to themselves teachers, having itching ears; and they shall turn away their ears from the truth, and shall be turned unto fables.
> —2 TIMOTHY 4:3–4

I am not referring to the host of people who left good, solid but incomplete doctrine and traditional teaching that was denominational and restrictive for new churches that teach doctrine that does not limit the working of the Holy Spirit. I am talking about others who have ventured out, perhaps venturing too far out.

Some of these people have entertained their own lusts to be recognized by others as being spiritual. Just as Paul wrote to

Timothy, the time will come, and I believe it now is, when people will not endure sound doctrine but will, after their own lust, heap to themselves teachers, having itching ears. If the box we want to get out of is the Bible and sound doctrine—then we need to get back in. The things we believe and speak must line up with sound Bible doctrine. The apostle Paul addressed this issue and advised believers "that we should no longer be children, tossed to and fro and carried about with every wind of doctrine" (Eph. 4:14, NKJV). If we allow ourselves to step out of the box of sound doctrine, we will become empty and without satisfaction in our Christian experience—and we will open wide the doorway for demonic intrusion.

Remember that when Peter got out of the boat, it was at the invitation of Jesus (Matt. 14:22–33). He experienced a great moment—a miracle—but then he got back in the boat. He was "out" because Jesus was there, but he got back in when Jesus did. The miracles you seek will happen because Jesus is there, not because you got out of the boat or the box.

I believe most people have gotten out of the box because they sincerely desire more of God and more from God. Most have realized that it is not happening, and not likely to happen, where they are presently worshipping. Sound doctrine will stand the test. Let your box be God's Word. There is security and safety in the box because God stands behind His Word.

> God is not a man, that he should lie; neither the son of man, that he should repent: hath he said, and shall he not do it? or hath he spoken, and shall he not make it good?
> —NUMBERS 23:19

> So shall my word be that goeth forth out of my mouth: it shall not return unto me void, but it shall accomplish that which I please, and it shall prosper in the thing whereto I sent it.
> —ISAIAH 55:11

All Scripture is given by inspiration of God, and is profitable for doctrine, for reproof, for correction, for instruction in righteousness, that the man of God may be complete, thoroughly equipped for every good work.

—2 Timothy 3:16–17, nkjv

But as for you, speak the things which are proper for sound doctrine.

—Titus 2:1, nkjv

We do harm to ourselves when we go against God's law and His spiritual principles. As some have said, we don't really break God's commandments; we break ourselves against His commandments. We don't break the commandments; the commandments break us. When we try to change what God has put into place, we find ourselves fighting against God.

GOD'S PROTECTION

God protects what is His. Remember how God protected the patriarchs in their unsettled condition. When they came as strangers to Canaan and were sojourners in the land, they were but few and could have easily been defeated and swallowed up. There were many who wanted them destroyed, yet no man was allowed to do them wrong. God held back the hand of the Canaanites, Philistines, and Egyptians.

Kings were reproved and plagued for their sakes. Mighty Pharaoh was unable to resist God. God had called leaders for His people. They were the anointed of the Lord. They were sanctified by His grace and glory. They had received the unction of His Spirit. They were His prophets and preachers, instructed in the things of God by God. They were commissioned to instruct others. They were called and separated out by God. Therefore, if any touched them, they touched the apple of God's eye; if any harmed them, it was at their own peril.

I have experienced this godly protection without even being aware there was an attempt to harm this ministry. Many years ago, not long after I had started going into prisons, I received a check from the Texas Department of Corrections Inmate Trust Fund for more than six hundred dollars. The check was an offering from more than five hundred inmates at a particular prison in Texas. They had collectively drawn a dollar or so from their accounts to send me as a love offering for being faithful in coming to their prison. The chaplain called me to explain what an act of love it was from the inmate congregation. That just overwhelmed me. It still does when I think about it.

At the time, I didn't even know the inmate trust fund existed, let alone how it worked. Basically, it's like a bank account for inmates. If a loved one sends them money, it goes into this fund. Through paper transactions, an inmate could draw from his account at the commissary or even ask that a check be sent to someone on the outside. Most inmates have little or nothing in their accounts. During a prison church service, the congregation had decided they wanted to help support our ministry for being faithful in coming there. I didn't know anything about it.

Naturally, five hundred inmates sending individual withdrawal slips designated to go to me caused some attention in the prison system. A few weeks after I had received the check, the chaplain called again, almost crying, and his voice was broken. He told me the warden of the prison had banned me from coming there, convinced that I must be bringing in drugs or something illegal, which was why the inmates were sending me money. The chaplain apologized and told me the men would be praying. I really didn't know what to do, so I did nothing.

About three weeks after this took place, the chaplain called again and told me the warden had experienced a bad heart attack and died. He informed me that I was once again welcome on the unit.

I received a similar phone call from the prison director in New York State. This was many years later. In a very kind conversation, he told me that a particular prison ministry in New York had made a complaint about me. The complaint was that I only came to New York prisons to find out which inmates had money. The director said, "We don't believe that, and we have great appreciation for what you do. However, we have to investigate this woman's complaint, and until we have completed our investigation, you will no longer be able to minister in New York State prisons."

I did not know this lady, nor did I have any idea why such a charge would be made. It's very expensive to make a trip from Texas to New York. I don't know that I had ever received any money from a New York inmate. Knowing that someone had lied about me and our ministry caused me great pain. I didn't know what to do, so once again I did nothing. I still don't know who this woman was.

A couple of months passed, and I received another phone call from the director. He was very apologetic and professional. "Don, there is no problem with you or your ministry, and you are welcome to come here anytime." He further said, "By the way, the woman who made this complaint has since lost her family and her ministry."

I consider myself the apple of God's eye. (See Deuteronomy 32:10; Psalm 17:8; and Zechariah 2:8.) I know that I am called by His name, and I know I am anointed. That's not boastful to say that; I didn't have anything to do with it. My job is to be faithful.

KEEP THE DOORS CLOSED

A curse without a cause—don't the demons wish they could torment believers without legal rights? Don't they wish they had more than the power of a lie? We'd all be sick or dead if it worked that way. If demons could do whatever damage they chose, whenever they chose, we would be in big trouble. However, they are limited by the truth of God's Word and the principles set forth by God Himself. Look at the scriptural truth tucked away in Proverbs 26:2: "Like a flitting sparrow, like a flying swallow, so a curse without cause shall not alight" (NKJV).

There will be no causeless curse. That is, curses can't just happen because demons want them to; there must be a legitimate cause—no consent, no curse.

Of more importance than recognizing the curse is discovering the cause. I believe if you can receive this truth, it will help you greatly in your spiritual walk. Demons must have legal rights, rights that are recognized by Jehovah God, to gain access to believers. Here are some obvious causes that can bring a curse, opening the door to demonic strongholds in your life.

Ancestry

> I the LORD thy God am a jealous God, visiting the iniquity of the fathers upon the children unto the third and fourth generation of them that hate me.
> —EXODUS 20:5

As we have seen, iniquity of the ancestors may be a cause for a curse. It is our job to denounce it—to separate ourselves from generational sins that may have brought demons into the family.

Lying

If you tell a lie, you might get a demon. If you live a lie, you have a demon. What you attempt to cover, God will expose. What you expose and confess to God, He will cover. Believing a lie is the power of the demon. Victory as a believer hinges upon truth. Lies—telling them, living them, believing them—are cause for curse.

Unforgiveness

> ...delivered him to the torturers until he should pay all that was due to him. So My heavenly Father also will do to you if each of you, from his heart, does not forgive his brother his trespasses.
> —MATTHEW 18:34–35, NKJV

Unforgiveness. It would be helpful to research everything the New Testament has to say about this sin. Sometimes it is more involved than merely confessing it. Often the demons that came through unforgiveness have built themselves a kingdom, and they must be cast out. Refusing to forgive is cause for curse.

Of course, this includes forgiving yourself. Many times I have had deliverance candidates insist they had no unforgiveness toward anyone—anyone else, that is. But they held great resentment and unforgiveness toward themselves.

Anger, bitterness, hatred, and related sins

> Be angry, and do not sin: do not let the sun go down on your wrath....And do not grieve the Holy Spirit of God, by whom you were sealed for the day of redemption. Let all bitterness, wrath, anger, clamor, and evil speaking be put away from you, with all malice.
>
> —EPHESIANS 4:26, 30–31, NKJV

Virtually all the sins in this category are easy to justify. Because we make excuses for harboring these sins, it seems OK to continue in them. "Well, you'd be hurt too if you had experienced what I have," we reason. These are all causes for curses.

Rejection, perception, dejection

These are very tough root causes for curses. Rejection is horrible. Whether it is real or perceived, it is still one of life's most intense feelings.

> He is despised and rejected by men, a Man of sorrows and acquainted with grief. And we hid, as it were, our faces from Him; He was despised, and we did not esteem Him.
>
> —ISAIAH 53:3, NKJV

Jesus certainly understands rejection. He relates to all our feelings. He was tempted in all points like as we are yet without sin (Heb. 4:15). I believe issues of rejection are responsible for many of today's disorders. To be acquainted with grief; to be despised and to know and feel it; to have feelings of no self-worth, no esteem; to feel unaccepted; to have strong feelings that you simply cannot measure up in the eyes of others—these can be the vilest of painful emotions. These are not only unspeakably painful feelings, but when they are based upon a perception, they are cause for curse. In many of these cases, the cause becomes the curse. All these lies must be resisted with truth.

I am not listing all the causes for curses, but just a few of the most common ones I encounter. Cause is a legal right that demons have to torment believers. Any and all causes can be removed through repentance, confession, and renunciation and denunciation. Receiving and applying the work of the cross and coming into agreement with what God says in His Word bring freedom.

Here are additional commonly encountered causes.

Trauma

Everyone has experienced some trauma in their life. The way we manage the trauma generally determines whether demons get access or not. Disappointment is a big door opener for demons. Remember, the Word tells us to stand, not to fight:

> Put on the whole armour of God, that ye may be able to *stand* against the wiles of the devil. For we wrestle not against flesh and blood, but against principalities, against powers, against the rulers of the darkness of this world, against spiritual wickedness in high places. Wherefore take unto you the whole armour of God, that ye may be able to withstand in the evil day, and having done all, to *stand. Stand* therefore...
> —EPHESIANS 6:11–14, EMPHASIS ADDED

Often the best thing we can do is the only thing we can do. We can always stand on truth; we can always choose our thoughts.

Irrational fears

Irrational fears are obvious doorways to fear demons. Sometimes they are evidence that demons are already there. It is so easy to magnify the wrong thing; to focus on the what-ifs in certain situations is needless exasperation of a virtual nonissue. I see that people who fear air travel have an extreme issue with focus. The more they focus on the what-ifs and the more they think and talk about it, the more real the fear becomes to them.

What you can always know about fear is that it is a spirit, and God didn't give it to you: "For God hath not given us the spirit of fear; but of power, and of love, and of a sound mind" (2 Tim. 1:7). So irrational fear is indication of a demon that is already there. To prevent giving strength to a demon already present or possibly opening a door to a new one, resist lies with truth and stand on that truth. Simply put, the truth is that airline travel is safe.

OTHER DOOR OPENERS

So many things we experience could be door openers for demons. Generally, this is based upon how we respond to the experience. Dejection and disappointment are neighbors to depression. Betrayal can be there too, with all the questions of "Why me?" and "How could this happen?" Again, Jesus understands these feelings. Emotional wounds as well as physical wounds were included in the price He paid.

Abandonment is definitely a possible doorway for demons. These traumas have to be covered with the blood of Jesus, and that most often involves forgiving. Childhood abuse—abuser or abused—is a cause for curse.

Sexual impurity—there is really no need to comment on this issue. You know if it applies, and you know what needs to be done. Admit it and quit it. Sexual addiction is a demon. Sexual impurity opens the door. Often this is rooted in the ancestry or perhaps some abuse in the early childhood. Receiving or causing sexual abuse, perversions, sexual relations outside of marriage, pornography, and births out of wedlock are all causes for curses.

Dishonoring your body—alcohol, drugs, nicotine, body piercings, tattoos, vanity enhancements—any and all could be cause for curse.

Occult/secret organizations—pledges, oaths, vows, and ceremonies—any organization that offers a way to God without salvation through Jesus Christ is a cause for curse.

Doubt is a choice. Unbelief is something people decide to do. It not only opens doors for demons, but it also empowers demons who are already present. Pride generally is the prop that holds up doubt and unbelief. Not only have I found this to be scripturally true, but I have also seen that often the same type of demon power runs these kingdoms. He is generally a leviathan in his creative nature. What do I mean by that?

Demons all have a creative identity, such as a serpent or a scorpion, as Jesus indicated in Luke 10:18–19. Leviathan is not the name of a demon but rather a type. You can read about him in Job and the psalms. Similarly, I hear people say, "Oh, they have the python spirit." Python is not the name of a spirit. It is a type of spirit, a serpent spirit. Doubt, unbelief, skepticism, and pride are all cause for curse.

Cause for curse is simply legal permission that demons have gained through either the decisions made by our ancestors or the experiences of our own life. Remember, there are no curses without cause. While our lives may be affected indirectly by demons that torment other individuals, we maintain the security of what comes and goes directly into our lives. We stay in control by confessing open doorways and casting out demon spirits. There is no cause that cannot be canceled through Christ.

REMOVING THE CAUSE

I have briefly discussed causeless curses. God's Word says there are none. So if one does have demon spirits, the key is removing the cause. Here's a simple step-by-step procedure that is always true. It is a simple way to examine and proceed.

- Cause—What event(s) gave legal permission for demons to torment?

- Curse—What is the result from that root cause? All demons kill, steal, and destroy. What is being stolen from you? What is damaged? What is dying?

- Consequence—This is tied to the curse; the curse is tied to the cause. You can't remove the curse until you have dealt with the cause.

- Choice—God always honors our choices. Choosing to hold on to a legitimate cause for curse extends the consequences. I have seldom seen a demon leave without being cast out.

- Confess—Until there is confession of sin and agreement and alignment with truth, demons do not have to leave. Confession cancels permission.

- Confront/cast out—Demons must be cast out; they cannot be counseled or medicated out. Jesus said, "Cast out demons."

- Cure—Once the demon spirits have been removed, often physical healing takes place and emotional wounds begin to mend. That is God's process, and it always works.

Sometimes it sounds too simple. But I tell you, it is no more complicated than this.

THE WORD

It seems everyone wants to hear from God; everybody wants a word. If you want to hear from God, you must hear His Word. God has already spoken through His Word, and His Word "is a discerner of the thoughts and intents of the heart" (Heb. 4:12). Simply put, your thoughts—your thoughts from God—must line up with the already spoken Word of God. We must come into agreement with the Word of God.

It is interesting that Hebrews 4:12 tells us the Word of God is able to invade our entire being—spirit, soul, and body. An absolute key for genuine freedom is spiritual alignment; that is, our spirit agreeing with what God says in His Word, our soul (mind, will, emotions, and personality) believing and speaking what God's Word says, and our flesh agreeing in obedience to the truth of God's Word.

There is an interesting verse the apostle James wrote to believers:

> Do ye think that the scripture saith in vain, The spirit that dwelleth in us lusteth to envy?
>
> —JAMES 4:5

What? The spirit that dwells in us? "But if I'm a believer, only the Holy Spirit can dwell in me." Is that what you're thinking? What spirit do you suppose James is referring to here? Our human spirit most likely, but maybe evil spirits that dwell in our souls and bodies. Evil spirits must be cast out; our human spirits must be cast down. There must be agreement in our being for healing and fullness of God's presence.

You see, the Word gets into even the joints and marrow, and the Word brings healing. Coming into agreement with truth that God has already spoken allows us to receive and apply the promises of the Word.

Whenever God speaks, whatever He says automatically becomes law. In His legal system, alignment with truth brings freedom. The opposite is true as well. Rebellion, refusal to receive His Word as truth, means to believe a lie, and the lie empowers demons. Empowered demons bring destruction, death, disease, and further deception to the believer. The job of every demon is to steal, kill, and destroy. The problem is that believers don't believe. More accurately, our belief is often tempered with conditions. The Word of God is alive! It is alive and powerful. How can that be?

> In the beginning was the Word, and the Word was with God, and the Word was God....And the Word became flesh, and dwelt among us, (and we beheld his glory, the glory as of the only begotten of the Father,) full of grace and truth.
> —JOHN 1:1, 14

The Word of God is alive because Jesus is the Word. It is powerful because Jesus is the Word. What an incredible truth. When you speak the Word, you actually speak His presence right into your life and your situation. "Your word is truth" (John 17:17, NKJV). Discerning disciples must weigh their words against God's Word. It is truth that liberates, and His Word is truth.

When Mary was holding the baby Jesus in her arms, I wonder, did she know she was holding the One who was holding all creation in His grip? Maybe she knew, but I doubt that she could possibly comprehend that He was in the beginning with God and that He was and is God. Could she have known that while she was holding Him, He was actually holding her? Could she have known that He spoke everything into being and that when He speaks, all creation obeys?

I think we too are not able to receive the magnitude of power and authority that is ours in His name. I believe it is a little more than simply speaking His name; it is *believing* that His name is above every name. It is living daily, moment by moment, in that amazing truth. His Word is truth. We are empowered by the truth of His Word, the presence of His Holy Spirit, and exercising His name in our lives.

CHAPTER 8

PRINCIPALITIES AND POWERS

WHEN A PERSON comes to me for deliverance, often territorial spirits come with them. They come to defend the kingdom they have established and cause doubt, confusion, or fear to try to block or hinder the deliverance. Often I can sense their presence; there is usually an attack on my mind or on the person's mind. I can tell when leading a person in prayer if the demon doesn't want a particular part of the prayer prayed.

Early in my ministry I didn't understand this and could not successfully deal with it. One day the Holy Spirit showed me how to distinguish between spirits on the inside and demon powers who are present on the outside, generally territorial spirits.

Virtually every demon power within a person has a territorial spirit in the heavenly realm, or in the atmosphere. The demons on the inside are like a cell, or a seed, from the territorial demon. So now I first address the outside territorial spirits and determine if they have any legal rights to be there. They communicate with me through the individual. They are being confronted in the name of Jesus, and I command from them their names, the names recognized by Jehovah God. Once I get their names, I command that they reveal their creative purpose. For instance, I may ask, "When God created you as a holy angel, what did He create you to do?"

An example of the answer that comes would be, "To bring peace." So immediately I know that as a demon he now does the opposite. Remember, they oppose God! I also command the demon to reveal his assigned geographical territory on the earth—I know he has one, and I insist that he reveal it. Generally, it will be the same area where the person was born, or perhaps where they presently live.

Then I command the spirits to answer, before Jehovah God, this one question: "Do you have legal permission to be here?" When the answer is no, and it usually is, I command them to return to their place in the heavenlies, to not come back, and to not send others to replace them. They leave. I have documented these events over the years, as I always take notes. I have thousands of names of territorial spirits and their territories, some of which are included in part 2 of this book.

These demons are principalities and powers. I used to try to cast these demons into the abyss. "Not possible," they would respond. "You can send me back to the heavenlies, but you cannot send me to the abyss." Hmm…I learned this to be true. I could, however, clean out the kingdom of demons on the inside or attached to the person and send them to the abyss, and I do.

There are two levels of this battle, and until we recognize this, we will not be successful.

In one deliverance session, one of the territorial spirits boasted of his high rank. I commanded him to reveal where he would be in level of authority beneath Satan. He responded with, "I am three tiers beneath him."

I said, "Will you call him here? I want to ask him something."

Immediately the response was, "He won't come."

"You don't even know where he is, do you?" I asked.

"No, I don't, but he won't come here."

Interesting. With eight billion people in the world, why would Satan come here? He has a lofty position in the heavenly realm; he is not omnipresent. He is not in all places, nor can he be in more than one place at a time. His underlings carry out his plans and desires.

WHAT ARE PRINCIPALITIES AND POWERS?

The phrase *principalities and powers* occurs six times in the Bible, always in the King James Version and its derivatives. Some versions translate it variously as "rulers and authorities," "forces and authorities," and "rulers and powers." The principalities and powers of Satan are in a similar structure of power and authority as the holy angels who did not rebel and oppose God. These demonic creatures wield power in the unseen realms to oppose anything and anyone that is of God.

The first mention of principalities and powers is in Romans 8:37–39:

> Nay, in all these things we are more than conquerors through him that loved us. For I am persuaded, that neither death, nor life, nor angels, nor principalities, nor powers, nor things present, nor things to come, nor height, nor depth, nor any other creature, shall be able to separate us from the love of God, which is in Christ Jesus our Lord.

These verses are about the victory we have in Christ. We are "more than conquerors" because no force—not life, not death, not angels, not demons, indeed nothing—can separate us from the love of God, which is in Christ Jesus. It seems that the "powers" referred to here are those with miraculous powers, whether false teachers and prophets or the very demonic entities that empower them. It is clear that no power, whatever it may be, can separate us from the love of God. "In Christ Jesus" is important wording here, for it is in Christ that our victory is assured. It is in His name that we can obtain and maintain victory.

The second mention of principalities and powers is found in Ephesians 1:20–21:

> Which he wrought in Christ, when he raised him from the dead, and set him at his own right hand in the heavenly

110

places, far above all principality, and power, and might, and dominion, and every name that is named, not only in this world, but also in that which is to come.

I like that it says Christ is "far above" all principality—not just above but far above! Not just principalities and powers and might and dominion, but *all* principalities and power and might and dominion—*all* of them. This is an overwhelming signal that every power is beneath the name of Jesus!

Ephesians 3:10–11 presents the third picture of principalities and powers in the heavenly realms:

> To the intent that now unto the principalities and powers in heavenly places might be known by the church the manifold wisdom of God, according to the eternal purpose which he purposed in Christ Jesus our Lord.

Here, it seems the revelation is to the angelic hosts showing the wisdom and purpose of God. Angels, both holy and unholy, observe the glory of God and the preeminence of Christ above all creatures in the church. Verse 10 in the NIV reads, "Now, through the church..." and seems to indicate that God is showing that His redemptive plan includes both Jews and Gentiles. Perhaps the angels, who desire to look into man's salvation, may not have had full knowledge of God's plan, and it is being revealed through the church. These angelic beings, referred to as *principalities and powers*, are divided into two factions—those who remained true to God and those who joined in Satan's rebellion against God.

The fourth reference is in Ephesians 6:12, which declares the battle we are engaged in:

> For we wrestle not against flesh and blood, but against principalities, against powers, against the rulers of the darkness of this world, against spiritual wickedness in high places.

The Amplified Classic Edition (AMPC) records it this way: "For we are not wrestling with flesh and blood [contending only with physical opponents], but against the despotisms, against the powers, against [the master spirits who are] the world rulers of this present darkness, against the spirit forces of wickedness in the heavenly (supernatural) sphere."

Despotism is an interesting word used to describe these powers and is defined by Oxford Languages as "the exercise of absolute power, especially in a cruel and oppressive way." There is a sophisticated hierarchy of evil in the heavenly realm; these spirits direct legions of demons toward us. They are always looking for open doors through which to attack.

It is as though we are facing an army of dark powers that have been disarmed from real power. Wouldn't they just kill us all if they could? They attack us through lies, threats, deceptions, sickness, and various diseases—always as a result of disobedience in our lives, or many times in the lives of our ancestors.

One of the clearest examples is the generational results that can be visibly observed as a result of incest and inbreeding. What took place before and during one's birth can be manifested in abnormalities that are readily recognized. Sin in the world! Our actions and reactions to the lies and temptations of demons most often determine the outcome. Propaganda in the evil realm is satanic misinformation and is distributed by and through the principalities and powers. Colossians 1:16 reads:

> For by him were all things created, that are in heaven, and that are in earth, visible and invisible, whether they be thrones, or dominions, or principalities, or powers: all things were created by him, and for him.

This is the fifth mention of principalities and powers. Here is the clear statement that God is the Creator and ruler over all authorities! Whatever power the evil spirits possess, they are always subject to the rule of our sovereign God, who, according to Daniel 4:35 and Isaiah 46:10–11, uses even the wicked for bringing about His perfect plan and purpose.

In Colossians 2:15 we see again that Jesus is the ultimate power over all other powers: "Having disarmed principalities and powers, He made a public spectacle of them, triumphing over them in it" (NKJV). As ancient armies would return to announce their victory, sometimes they returned with the enemies' body armor tied to the horses and the body of the enemy leader strapped to the chariot wheels, making a triumphal entry back into the city. This was a display of public humiliation of the enemy. So Jesus Christ has made a public spectacle of demon powers through His death, burial, and resurrection!

There is no power that is not subject to His control and beneath His name. Principalities and powers, rulers of darkness, and spiritual wickedness in high places have all been disarmed by the cross. The Savior, by His death and resurrection, took dominion from them. I have never encountered a demonic power that does not recognize this as truth. It is in His name that we have victory.

There is reference to principalities and powers in Titus 3:1: "Put them in mind to be subject to principalities and powers, to obey magistrates, to be ready to every good work." Here they refer to those governmental authorities under whom we dwell. They are duly constituted authorities.

By using the phrase *principalities and powers*, God's Word is telling us there is a hierarchical structure to the kingdom of darkness—a sophisticated government where fallen angels, evil spirits, and demons are ranked one above the other according to their power and authority. These evil spirits exercise influence over people, geographical areas, cities, and nations. This evil, Satan-ruled hierarchy is a *copycat* form of government similar to God's.

CONTENDING WITH THE DEVIL

I think Christians make a mistake when they believe they have been given authority to challenge these powers in the heavenly realm. I will simply ask, "If we have that authority, why then does it not work? And why limit it to a particular location?" If through a human being's declaration to principalities and powers we can change their actions, why not extend it to the whole earth? I have never seen a positive result from Christians engaging in spiritual warfare with heavenly realm powers.

I have seen the opposite happen with churches dissolving, ministries crumbling, and individuals suffering sickness and multitudes of difficulties. Our God-given authority has to do with *individuals*, to pray for nations, not against principalities and powers. Jesus sent His disciples to the people, not against heavenly realm powers. He did not bind the evil prince of Jerusalem; instead, He admonished us to pray for the peace of Jerusalem. He did not pray against heavenly realm powers; He prayed for people. He sent believers commissioned to preach the good news to nations, not to pray against the demonic powers.

Principalities are the chief rulers of the kingdom of darkness; they are first in rank or power and constitute a high order of evil spirits. Every place you see the word *principality* in the King James Version New Testament, it is the Greek noun *arche,* defined as that which is first in time, order, or place.[1] This word is used at least seven times in the Scriptures to denote angelic or demonic rulers. The word *powers* is from the Greek noun *exousia* and means one who possesses authority or influence.[2] It is the word used in Ephesians 6:12 to represent the angelic or demonic authorities that operate in the spirit realm.

DON'T PICK A FIGHT WITH A PRINCIPALITY

I was recently in Canada for some deliverance seminars and nights of ministry. One of the ladies I met in Kingston, where there are many prisons, said, "Sometimes my husband and I drive by the

Kingston pen and just bind up all the spirits there." What? I wonder what she was thinking! Did she really believe her "binding up" of all the demons there changed anything? It is a troubling doctrine being preached and taught today that we have some kind of authority in the heavenlies. If this is so, we should get to the hospitals and psychiatric centers—but it doesn't work, and it is very dangerous and foolish to attempt it. Pick a fight with a principality? Please.

While I was in this same city in Canada, a man who is involved in deliverance ministry told me of a group there that did "prayer marching and pulling down strongholds" in the city. He said they have tried to get him involved, but he feels that what they are doing is not scriptural. He told me there were twenty-five or thirty people who did this. I asked him what kind of success they had experienced after a couple of years. "I don't know of any," he said. "They're all sick or their families are falling apart. I think they have disbanded."

Ephesians 6:12 also speaks about the "rulers of the darkness of this age" (NKJV). To my knowledge, this term is only found in this verse. "Rulers" is translated from the Greek noun *kosmokrator*, which is defined as lord of the world, the prince of this age.[3] The god of this world, Satan, is indicated here.

The last group mentioned in Ephesians 6:12 is "spiritual hosts of wickedness in the heavenly places" (NKJV), or wicked spirits that operate in high places. Here, the Greek word *epouranios* refers to the dwelling place of God as well as the abode of angels and evil spirits. This also translates to "heavenly places," a sphere of activity or existence that is above that of the earth.[4]

There is an interesting statement in *Vine's Expository Dictionary of New Testament Words*:

> The context ("not against flesh and blood") shows that no earthly potentates are indicated, but spirit powers, who, under the permissive will of God, and in consequence of human sin, exercise satanic and therefore antagonistic authority over the

world in its present condition of spiritual darkness and alienation from God.[5]

How true, "in consequence of human sin"—as given permission by our unconfessed sin! Our ignorant disobedience comes into play here as well. The god of this world is Satan, according to the Bible. He has in place a governmental hierarchy doubtlessly patterned after God's, with numerous levels of authority and power. I don't know how many levels of demonic bureaucracy are between Satan and the demons we deal with on our plain, but it is vast.

THE DEMONIC REALM

The Word of God teaches that Satan is the prince or ruler of this present world order, which includes the systems and governments of mankind and the present condition of human affairs. He is the commander and chief, exercising authority over the rulers of the darkness of this world, which includes principalities, powers, authorities, and every wicked spirit.

Paul also declared that Satan exercises authority as the god of this world in 2 Corinthians 4:4: "in whom the god of this world hath blinded the minds of them which believe not, lest the light of the glorious gospel of Christ, who is the image of God, should shine unto them." Scripture reveals that Jesus Christ and the apostle Paul clearly taught that Satan is the god and ruler of this present world. This is why the world is in such a mess. But God had a plan that included exalting Christ above all principalities and authority.

This is very difficult to grasp since we are talking about an invisible kingdom.

Think with me. If you were the devil, how would you organize your countless numbers of fallen angels? Since he is not able to be everywhere present at all times, he must be in a place of rule where he delegates his authority and his wishes to be carried out. Imagine yourself in this dark but lofty position of evil. You are "god of the earth," and you are aware that there are eight billion human beings on the earth. Do you think you would form a cabinet of the most brilliant and most powerful of the demons? How many levels of government would you need? Remember, you are "warring against the saints"; you are opposing the work of God.

I'm thinking I might start with at least one demon for each of the seven continents. These would have to be the best. I would see to it that those seven chose demons under them to rule various areas of these continents; they would be principalities. After the regions are established, I would also make lesser principalities for specific regions in these territories. For instance, in the United States it would be very similar to the governmental structure we have in place. One powerful demon ruling with many advisers and cabinet members, and then those that rule divisional or regional areas of the country, one over particular states, one over certain counties, one over county seat cities and local towns. Each of these rulers would have a large government of their own to manage the affairs of darkness—one over communities and neighborhoods, blocks of the streets, certain houses. There would be multitudes of workers in the vast kingdom of darkness.

There would be so many in this governmental structure of evil that special appointees would be given territories over waters, mountains, deserts, trees, barren remote areas—covering all the earth. By the way, I have encountered demon powers who describe their territories and responsibilities in such terms. For instance, I know the prince of Texas and many of his subordinates. I have encountered many principalities of certain counties and cities and many of their underlings. I know the princes of many states and regions in the world. They show up, and under oath before Jehovah God they reveal their territories.

I have encountered hundreds of territorial spirits; I have recorded their names and geographical areas. I don't fight with them; they come to protect their kingdoms on the inside of the individual. I do not have authority to cast them down or else I would do so for the entire world. I do, however, command them to return to the heavenly realm and not interfere with the individual's deliverance. They always obey.

How many demons are working in this vast network of evil against God and His people? Billions? Thousands of thousands? Remembering that they are spirits, I don't suppose there is any value in speculating. Demon powers that are in or attached to people are minions of higher-ranking spirits. These we can and do cast into the abyss. I have found that they can split, divide, multiply, fragment, clone, and use various other ways of deceiving and evading the deliverance process. I always forbid them from doing this in my commands to demon powers. I also have found that these spirit beings have the ability to make decisions. Many of them seem to have, for lack of a better description, brat personalities. They communicate with other demons and actually call for help to those in higher rank.

There is obviously a demonic hierarchy, and we deal with some of the lowest-ranking soldiers. You can imagine a line of reporting that goes through many demonic powers before it reaches Satan himself. Demons we deal with likely report to regional or territorial spirits—spirits over communities, cities, counties, states, regions, countries, nations, hemispheres, and the world system. They are likely more complex than we can comprehend.

Without doubt there is a system of rank and power in place. The powers we deal with are on assignment from higher-ranking evil spirits, like principalities. But let it suffice here to say that Satan is not who most people think he is. He is a defeated foe, right now, at this moment. He is defeated. It is important that we remember Satan only has power over us that we give to him, that we yield. He was disarmed at Calvary, publicly humiliated.

> And having spoiled principalities and powers, he made a shew of them openly, triumphing over them in it.
> —COLOSSIANS 2:15

"He made a shew of them openly." This is what the Romans would do when they returned victorious from a battle. They would display the enemy in humiliation. They gloried in their triumph by showing the enemy soundly defeated. They made a show of the defeated enemy. So did Jesus with His shed blood and glorious resurrection! Jesus, in defeating Satan, made him and all his principalities and powers like Barney Fife, the feisty deputy of *The Andy Griffith Show*. He had lots of boasting power, but he had no bullets for his gun. He was a threat and no more. Fear, lies, and deceit have become the power of Satan and his demon spirits concerning believers. The power they have over believers is the lies we believe and the biblical ignorance we tolerate.

However, Christians are beginning to understand the principle of binding and loosing. The words that Jesus spoke are coming alive to them. "Behold, I give unto you power...over all the power of the enemy" (Luke 10:19).

It is a bad day for the devil when that truth comes alive in believers today. Speak to those demons in the name of Jesus. Tell the demons that you face, "You are defeated. I have victory in Christ Jesus. I am in Him, and He is in me. And He that is within me is greater than he that is in the world. *You* back off; you are the one going to hell, not me. You are the one with a problem, not me. I have eternal life living in me. You have a bad future ahead of you, and you and your principalities and powers are all under the feet of Jesus. You back off! Go, in the name of Jesus Christ. I overcome you by the blood and the power of His name. I resist you, I rebuke you, and you must be obedient!"

You have been given power of attorney; use it. Do it. Give Satan and all his principalities and powers a bad day.

CHAPTER 9

DEALING WITH STRONGHOLDS

IN THIS CHAPTER we are going to take a closer look at how to recognize and avoid the demonic strongholds that will quickly take hold in the life of a person who has not successfully locked and bolted the doors shut by confessing all known sin, walking in obedience to the Word of God, and focusing only on those things over which God has given His children authority through His righteousness and salvation.

There are some boundaries we should not cross. There are some places we should not go. We will look at how to recognize and avoid demonic strongholds that could be sources of demonic oppression and intrusion. Whether you have already been delivered from demonic interference and are now seeking to understand how to "keep the pigs out" or need teaching to help you understand and recognize where you may have opened a doorway allowing demons to rush in, you will discover some of the strongholds that need to be eradicated from your life, and you will learn to stay within the Father's protective boundaries in the future.

DEPRESSED, DETACHED, AND DISTANT

Bill Morgan will likely be the head of my ministry when I retire. He was trained by some of the materials I have shared in this book. Bill told me about a deliverance encounter a year or so ago, when a middle-aged man I will call Sam came in for deliverance.

> He was the most depressed, detached, and distant person I had seen come through the office in a while. His life was

falling apart. Apparently, he was recently divorced. I think his business had gone under or was about to do so. His kids wanted nothing to do with him, and he didn't really have any friends.

In preparing for deliverance, I will typically brief the candidate on three areas:

- The four-step deliverance process itself
- A biblical discussion on demons
- A review of the paperwork that was submitted in advance

As Sam got comfortable with the conversations and began to really understand the concept of a "clean temple" within us, he pointed out something that wasn't listed in his paperwork. He confessed to me that once his temple was cleaned, he intended to kill himself right after the session. He essentially said "I'm done" and that he felt he would soon be ready to cross over to the next life.

Something hit my spirit like a ton of bricks. All of the sudden, there was intense "fire in my belly." The Holy Spirit kicked in high gear and Sam was bathed in prayer and "re-educated" on who we are in Christ. We have resources for people that are struggling with insecurity. In this session, they were used for suicidal ideations.

All of our resources are biblically based. Hopefully, we can agree that the Scriptures are either all true or none of them are true, but we cannot pick and choose the truth. Did you know that there are about 100 scriptures that declare who we are in Christ?

We call these "Biblical Truths to Practice Believing," and I shared these with Sam.

As a sort of "spiritual stretching" exercise, Sam was asked to read the scriptures. If he chose in his free will to agree with them and apply them to his life, then he would simply repeat them out loud in order to give them back to the Lord. Sam did this.

Some of these include:

I am God's...
possession (Genesis 17:8; 1 Corinthians 6:20)
child (John 1:12)
chosen (Ephesians 1:4)

I have been...
redeemed by the blood (Revelation 5:9)
set free from sin / condemnation (Romans 8:12)
given a sound mind (2 Timothy 1:7)
given the Holy Spirit (2 Corinthians 1:22)

I am...
sanctified (1 Corinthians 6:11)
loved eternally (1 Peter 1:5)
one with the Lord (1 Corinthians 6:17)

I have...
all things in Christ (2 Corinthians 5:17)
power to witness (Acts 1:8)
the mind of Christ (1 Corinthians 2:16)

I can...
do all things through Christ (Philippians 4:13)
quench all the fiery darts (Ephesians 6:16)
defeat (overcome) the enemy (Revelation 12:11)

I cannot...
be separated from God's love (Romans 8:35–39)
be taken out of my Father's hand (John 10:29)
be condemned (1 Corinthians 11:32)

As Sam went through the entire list, his faith began to strengthen. His spirit agreed with the Holy Spirit as he pressed further into Jesus. His soul (psyche) was transforming as he submitted to Jesus and surrendered his will to the will of Jesus. Sam was now ready to begin our deliverance session.

It wasn't long before the usual suspects showed up and admitted they were the spirits behind influencing him to take his life along with a whole bunch of other negative and dark stuff that has been weighing Sam down all his life.

Because Sam was willing to trust Jesus, the Holy Spirit eradicated the demons, and he became a new man. When he finished the session, Sam was radiating with joy and a sense of great victory. He felt love, loved by the Father, and loved by Jesus, and he loved the feeling of freedom! His soul and spirit were clean and free. Sam now has a testimony from being put to the test and walking back from the edge of death by simply walking in faith that Jesus can and did set him free that day. Sam is an overcomer!

Freedom from demonic oppression is a choice. If we want to be free, we can be free, no matter the circumstances, but we must surrender fully to Jesus.

TERRIBLE TURN DUE TO ADDICTIONS

Recently, a man in his forties came through a deliverance session really wanting to be free from demonic oppression that had been haunting him for decades. Let's call him Chris. I'll let Bill tell the rest of the story.

> We have a healthy backlog of candidates in line for limited deliverance ministry sessions each day. Chris had promptly completed his paperwork online and patiently waited his turn for over a month before coming to the office.
>
> Chris said he grew up in the church. He led worship and taught the Scriptures. He was well liked by his friends and companions but took a terrible turn due to addictions. I noticed that the paperwork was a bit light on background detail. Thus, coming into the appointment, my expectation was that this

session could be a nothing burger, where Chris might simply need encouragement.

Our paperwork is similar to a medical questionnaire. We have a comprehensive form with many questions in order to identify and isolate possible strongholds. Once strongholds are identified, we know the usual suspects of demons that run those kingdoms and may be involved with the candidate. This technique really helps to compress time identifying the prince demon(s)—those in charge.

By many accounts, Chris was going to be an in-and-out kind of session, as there was not much going on according to the paperwork. We reviewed the deliverance process itself. We reviewed biblical scriptures regarding demons. Scriptures establish that demons have both a ranking system and territories, usually organized by strongholds similar to unions. Electricians may impact the nervous system. Plumbers may impact the digestive system, and so on. We got to discussing Chris' paperwork, and I commented that there really wasn't much going on that I could see based on what he reported.

It was at this point that Chris came clean. "Actually," he said, "there is one more thing." I think he felt compelled by the Holy Spirit to deal with this head-on, because he flat-out said, "Look, I did twenty years in prison for my crime. I'm out now and reformed. I make beautiful, expensive custom furniture by hand as an artisan. I love the Lord. I've forgiven everyone that I can think of including myself, but there is a sin that continues to be a burden. You see, I was a crack addict. One time, during a purchasing transaction, I was high on crack and murdered a prostitute."

Obviously, murder and prostitution qualify as doorways for demons. We launched into one of the most thorough ministry sessions I've ever witnessed. Chris nailed his strongholds to the cross and let the Holy Spirit cleanse him in such a profound way that until then I had not seen that level of joy and glory overcome someone during a ministry session.

You may have heard Don talk about Orion, Apollyon,

MaHa Bone, Baphomet, and many other high-ranking demons. Chris had them all, and they admitted to influencing his choices to engage in criminal behavior. But Chris strived, sought the Lord with all his heart, and knocked on Christ's door—and Chris got delivered. He received the freedom that he sought and became a new man, glowing with the peace and presence of the Lord.

This was one of the best deliverance sessions I have ever witnessed where the Lord displayed His majesty and set the captive free. People often wonder if they can receive that kind of freedom themselves. Indeed, we all can—if we choose to do so.

Jesus gave us His "first commandment" in Mark 12:30: "And thou shalt love the Lord thy God with all thy heart, and with all thy soul [psyche], and with all thy mind, and with all thy strength: this is the first commandment." Most of the time, even 99 percent of the time, is not all; it's some. When we choose of our free will to go all-in for Jesus with our heart, soul, mind, and strength, we will find Jesus waiting to receive and beautifully restore us.

Chris traded his shame that day for the glory of our King. Jesus sealed that transaction with His blood.

FREED FROM NIGHT TERRORS

Our office administrator, Cherie Flowers, is also one of our ministers. She had a deliverance session with a woman from San Angelo, Texas, which is several hours' drive to our office in Bedford. I guess you could say it was a pretty typical deliverance. However, during the deliverance the woman mentioned that her four-year-old son had night terrors and would wake up screaming every night. Boy, we hear that a lot.

As Cherie continued with the deliverance, the woman said, "I'm seeing a bat manifesting." It is very common for the candidate to see a manifestation like this.

Among the commands Cherie gave this demon was, "Do you have anything to do with the night terrors?"

The demon responded, "Yes, I do."

Cherie said, "Leave that child right now and never torment him again!"

Distance never mattered to Jesus.

So the woman went home and told her husband, who said, "Let's go see if he has seen a bat in the room."

They went and asked the little boy, and he said, "No, Batman doesn't come in my room." He didn't know what a bat was. They found a picture of a bat and showed him. "Oh, that's the monster that comes in the corner at night, but Mommy killed him today!"

The demons' permission to the child was ancestral. The mother broke that curse and removed its permission to access her child. No more night terrors!

THE MOST COMMON STRONGHOLDS

The most common legal stronghold I have encountered is unforgiveness. We see this all the time. The lie demons use here is causing a person to feel justified in their anger and bitterness toward someone else or toward themselves, and sometimes even anger toward God.

> And whenever you stand praying, if you have anything against anyone, forgive him, that your Father in heaven may also forgive you your trespasses. But if you do not forgive, neither will your Father in heaven forgive your trespasses.
> —MARK 11:25–26, NKJV

Forgiveness is not option; it is a must. The closing words in the powerful parable about unforgiveness are "delivered him to the torturers....So My heavenly father also will do to you if each of you, from his heart, does not forgive his brother his trespasses" (Matt. 18:34–35, NKJV).

When Peter questioned Jesus about how many times a man had to forgive, he argued that seven times seemed enough, but Jesus said, "I do not say to you, up to seven times, but up to seventy times seven" (Matt. 18:22, MEV). After speaking these astounding words to Peter, Jesus completed the emphasis with a parable about the consequences of not forgiving.

He told of a man who had a great debt but could not pay it. His debt was insurmountable, and he was about to lose his wife and children. He owed the equivalent of millions of dollars, and foreclosure was imminent. (See Matthew 18:23–35.) The man went to his master and begged for patience and forgiveness. "Then the master of that servant was moved with compassion, released him, and forgave him the debt" (v. 27, NKJV). He had a debt he could not pay, and he was forgiven. That debtor is a picture of us.

But then this man who had received great grace and forgiveness went to one of his peers to collect a debt of about forty dollars. The man who had received great forgiveness pursued a small debt with vengeance. He put his hands on the man's throat and threatened him with prison. Even though his debtor pleaded for patience and made a promise to pay, he had the man cast into prison.

This is a vivid picture of how heaven sees our acts of unforgiveness. We have received grace beyond measure, unconditional love, and forgiveness for a debt we could not pay. Yet so often we refuse to forgive someone on our same level.

The master who had forgiven the great debt had these words for this man: "'You wicked servant! I forgave you all that debt because you begged me. Should you not also have had compassion on your fellow servant, just as I had pity on you?' And his master was angry, and delivered him to the torturers until he should pay all that was due to him" (Matt. 18:32–34, NKJV).

The picture is clear; forgiveness is not optional if you want to be free. Look at the strong words of Jesus after He spoke the parable.

> So My heavenly father also will do to you if each of you, from
> his heart, does not forgive his brother his trespasses.
> —MATTHEW 18:35, NKJV

Unforgiveness is like the ultimate insult to God, and it carries a severe penalty for believers. God turns the unforgiving believer over to the torturers, to evil spirits. No, not in the sense of losing one's salvation, but many believers today live in torment because they refuse to forgive. Unforgiveness grieves the Holy Spirit of God.

> And do not grieve the Holy Spirit of God, by whom you were
> sealed for the day of redemption. Let all bitterness, wrath,
> anger, clamor, and evil speaking be put away from you, with
> all malice. And be kind to one another, tenderhearted, for-
> giving one another, even as God in Christ forgave you.
> —EPHESIANS 4:30–32, NKJV

Unforgiveness is sin. Sin can only be removed by confession and repentance. I will tell you without blinking that if you have unforgiveness in your life, you have demons in your life.

Forgiveness is not an act of the will, nor is it an agreement that it is the right thing to do. Unforgiveness must be repented of before God. It is a sweet-smelling fragrance to God, and He always receives our forgiveness of others. Healing comes through forgiveness.

Unforgiveness is torment. God turns those who refuse to forgive over to the tormentors. Those who forgive He looses from bondage. Forgiveness is what we received at salvation. Forgiveness is honored by God. We are being Christlike—like God's Son—when we forgive. Once the unforgiveness is gone, the demons that came by that permission must be cast out. They don't necessarily leave just because you repented. Cast them out.

One of the things we see healed on a regular basis when this is done is fibromyalgia. We also see levels of arthritis healed. Here is a simple thought: If pleasant words and a cheerful heart are health to the bones, what are anger and bitterness to the bones? If repentance and departing from evil is health and marrow to the bones, what is holding on to unforgiveness?

> Pleasant words are like a honeycomb, sweetness to the soul and health to the bones.
>
> —PROVERBS 16:24, NKJV

> A merry heart does good, like medicine, but a broken spirit dries the bones.
>
> —PROVERBS 17:22, NKJV

> Do not be wise in your own eyes; fear the LORD and depart from evil. It will be health to your flesh, and strength to your bones.
>
> —PROVERBS 3:7–8, NKJV

WHAT FORGIVENESS IS NOT

Some people don't forgive because they misunderstand what it is. It is not saying that what happened is OK. It will always be painful; the deeds that hurt and offended you will always be wrong and always be painful when you remember them. When Jesus forgave me, He did not say sin was OK. Sin is ugly; it took Him to the cross. What He said was, "I love you anyway, in spite of the sin and the ugly, painful deeds."

You can do that. You can look at the person who has offended you and say, "I wish no harm for you. I want God to love you as He loves me. If vengeance is in order, I turn that over to God. I did not deserve forgiveness when God forgave me." The person who offended you may not deserve your forgiveness either, but because it is God's way and God's instruction to do so, you do it.

I'll never forget a meeting I attended. Neither will our team members who were there with me. At the altar call I gave, a lady stepped from her seat and came forward. Many others had also come, and our ministry associates were praying with various individuals. However, when this lady came, others came with her. I didn't know it at the time, but it was her family—grown children and spouses. The woman was so large she could hardly stand. She also had become very rigid as I talked to her. I invited her to sit in the first chair next to the aisle.

As I bent to talk with her, she told me she knew she had demons because she could not forgive. I said, "Sure, you can forgive. You just choose to do it." She insisted that she could not. She also said that many times she had pledged that she would never forgive. She had a few tears in her eyes. "It's my mom," she told me. "I'll never forgive her. Even though she is dead, I will not forgive her."

I talked with her some more and told her that she could not be free from her torment until she forgave.

"I can't say it; I can't even say the words."

"Yes, you can; just say these words after me." I kept insisting that she look at me, and I encouraged her, "Just speak the words, 'I forgive my mother.'"

"I can't do it," she said. "If I forgive her, then she wins." Her family circled her seat and held hands.

"No," I said, "if you forgive her, you win, and your family wins."

She struggled and mumbled but just couldn't get the words out. Finally, she did, with words that seemed to bolt from her mouth: "I forgive my mother!" When she spoke those words, her family fell to the ground in unison, and she burst into tears. Her family lay silently on the floor as I very simply and softly, in the name of Jesus, commanded the demons to go. They did; their right to her and her family was broken in that moment.

James 3:14–17 (NKJV) gives some warnings about possible gateways similar to unforgiveness.

> But if you have bitter envy and self-seeking in your hearts, do not boast and lie against the truth. This wisdom does not descend from above, but is earthly, sensual, demonic. For where envy and self-seeking exist, confusion and every evil thing are there. But the wisdom that is from above is first

pure, then peaceable, gentle, willing to yield, full of mercy and good fruits, without partiality and without hypocrisy.

If you have recognized the presence of unforgiveness or any of these related strongholds in your life, and you want to be free of the demons who inhabit these strongholds, pray this prayer:

Heavenly Father, I ask You to forgive me for not forgiving. I acknowledge that unforgiveness is sin, and I repent before You and ask You to give me peace. I forgive all those who have hurt me, and I thank You for forgiving me for harboring bitterness and anger toward them. I choose to forgive myself, and I receive and apply Your forgiveness to my life. I want the peace that You give. I thank You for Jesus and the forgiveness provided at the cross. In Jesus' name, amen.

UNJUSTIFIED SUSPICIONS—THE TOUGHEST CHALLENGE

...casting down imaginations and every high thing that exalts itself against the knowledge of God, and bringing into captivity every thought to the obedience of Christ.
—2 Corinthians 10:5, nkjv

Without doubt, the most difficult individuals we deal with are those who have been diagnosed with mental disorders. If it were like what the spiritual warfare movements teach, then we could just circle the mental institutions and bind all the mind-tormenting spirits.

This is a tough one for several reasons. I am somewhat acquainted with it. My mother was diagnosed as paranoid schizophrenic. She attempted suicide nine times in a six-week period. She was tormented in her mind. This was before I knew about deliverance as I do now. Since her death I have many times tried to discover what may have happened in her life that could have allowed this. I don't know. Her two sisters committed suicide. If they were abused as children, I don't know about it; none of my relatives know about it. While I suspect that may have been the problem, I don't know.

I can't find anything in her ancestry that helps me to answer the mystery, but there was a source. It was the work of demons. My friend Frank Hammond was convinced that rejection is at the root of paranoia and schizophrenia. I have had many experiences to confirm that; however, there may be multiple things that come together to bring this about. Delusion is maximum deception. Paranoia is defined as "a mental condition characterized by delusions of persecution, unwarranted jealousy, or exaggerated self-importance; unjustified suspicion and mistrust of others."[1] Unjustified suspicion—I see this a lot in the ministry. Unfortunately, it is also often among those who claim to be God-called ministers.

The paranoia is so strong that to the individual it is real. They see something. They hear something. Something is going on.

As I mentioned before, when a lie has been believed, it is very difficult to deal with demons until the lie is renounced. The deception is so powerful the individual does not perceive it to be a lie. They become so fully blinded by the lie that they are unable to see the truth. They are so convinced that it is very difficult for them to confess it as a lie.

It is always the same and never the same. It is the neighbors plotting against them, coworkers telling false stories about them, hearing people outside their house or in their house, or witches and warlocks putting curses on them. The torment they are in is real. There is no doubt that what they perceive is likely very real to them. So the dilemma is how to bring freedom to those suffering from disorders of the mind.

There is more to it than simply commanding demons to go in the name of Jesus. It is complex, and deliverance and freedom do not come until the legal rights of those demon powers have been removed. There is always a root, and sometimes there are many roots. The problem is finding the roots and removing permissions that demons have gained.

One of the things we've experienced in this area is a common need for attention. Sometimes it's the only way a person knows to gain sympathy and importance. This is often the case with those who claim to have been victims of satanic ritual abuse (SRA). We have also learned that in most cases the supposed abuse never happened. The individual may believe it happened, but generally it is a lie. Unfortunately, some who claim to be victims only identified themselves as victims after a "counselor" convinced them.

Now, I also think there are some instances where these things really happen, but not nearly to the numbers of people claiming it happened. We used to see a lot of these folks. We found limited success and also discovered that there was seldom any evidence to confirm the stories. This became all too common. There were no names, no addresses, no crime reports, and no way to verify any of it.

A friend and local pastor of a large Southern Baptist church called me one night. "Maybe you can help me. We are at our wits' end in knowing how to deal with a young lady. We have taken her in our home to try to help her. We have tried casting out demons, and it just seems to go on and on. We don't know what to do."

He began to tell me her story, and as he did, I knew I had heard it many times. It was the familiar SRA story, although I don't want to minimize what may be a very real problem for some. As he told me her story, I said, "The reason you can't help her is because it didn't happen."

There was silence on the other end of the phone. After a moment, he said, "You mean she's lying?"

Part of her sad story was that when she stayed at a motel the church was paying for, her father busted open the door and brutally raped her. I said, "Take her to the police. I'm betting she won't go."

Again, there was silence. "You're right," he said. "We tried to take her there, but once we arrived, she wouldn't go in." Of course, there were demons involved, but the demons had permission because she was believing and perpetuating the lie.

I always seem to end these stories with the same thing. It is truth

133

that enables us to be free. Lies empower the demons. Unjustified suspicions and drawing wrong conclusions not only can give demon spirits access to your mind but also cause you to hurt others based upon your wrong conclusion. Unjustified suspicions can lead to believing a lie! In a nutshell, believing a lie gives power to demons. It is the truth that will set people free.

THE TOUGHEST SPIRIT

The following passage clearly teaches that deliverance is part of Jesus' job description.

> The Spirit of the LORD is upon Me, because He has anointed Me to preach the gospel to the poor; He has sent Me to heal the brokenhearted, to proclaim liberty to the captives and recovery of sight to the blind, to set at liberty those who are oppressed; to proclaim the acceptable year of the LORD.
> —LUKE 4:18–19, NKJV

Jesus was sent to be:

- the breaker of the bondage
- the bearer of the burden
- the blesser of the bruised
- the binder of the brokenhearted
- the beacon to the blind

All of that is included in His anointed duties, for He came for the purpose of destroying the works of the devil.

Satan stripped Job. He shamed Peter. He slammed Paul. He buffeted Paul with "a thorn in the flesh" (2 Cor. 12:7). But Jesus is the grace giver. He is the righteous restorer. The bottom line in all deliverance is Jesus.

Why does the subject of demons create so much controversy?

Have you ever given much thought to why no one is comfortable when the subject of demons comes up? What's the problem? Can you talk about it with your friends? How about with your pastor or church leaders? Since Jesus spent approximately one-third of His ministry dealing with demons and healing, why do we only talk about the other two-thirds? Do you suppose He was only speaking on the level of understanding the poor, unintelligent people of His time? What a prideful assumption and insult to Jesus!

Would the Creator of all things deceive us into believing that demons existed only in an unenlightened generation? Is it realistic to think that now that man has become so smart, we know that demons really don't exist? Can we truly classify all our problems into categories other than spiritual causes? Did demon spirits just go away? Did they ever really exist? What do you do with the scriptural accounts of them and Jesus' direct dealing with them? How do you account for this? Most people choose to ignore it. What about you?

What I know is that if you don't recognize this as biblical truth, you can't deal with evil spirits as the source of many problems.

I have personally seen about thirty thousand Christians freed of demonization—believers healed of demonic oppression. The atoning work of Jesus included "to heal the brokenhearted, to preach deliverance to the captives, and recovering of sight to the blind, to set at liberty them that are bruised" (Luke 4:18). I have experienced this happening; there are thousands of testimonies.

The Holy Spirit has shown me that it is not my job to convince or persuade people about the reality of demonic spirits that oppress believers. Rather I am just to present truth. So I am comfortable in presenting truth and leaving the results to Him.

Often I have been asked if there was a particular spirit that proved more difficult than others. The strength of the spirit depends upon the amount of permission it is given. However, there is one spirit I have encountered that is tougher than all the others.

The unteachable person is perhaps the most frustrating. I don't know if there is an unteachable spirit involved, but the person who will not accept teaching is a very difficult person to bring to deliverance. These people will not submit to truth, and it is often because they think they already know the truth. They have believed a lie for so long that it is virtually impossible to show them truth.

This person reverts to the lie. Some people have erroneous teachings about deliverance in their minds, and that in itself becomes bondage. That is why we spend so much effort in getting an individual prepared for deliverance. The unteachable spirit is virtually impossible to minister to because of the choice to remain in darkness.

Homosexual spirits are often difficult because there are also, generally, some genetic problems along with learned habits. Other demon powers of fear, rejection, anger, and pride give strength to this spirit. But homosexual spirits are not the toughest.

As I mentioned, mental disorders often present a whole set of problems. Disorder spirits with all the confusion, fear, and doubt are difficult. However, the most trying spirit of all is the human spirit. You see, the human spirit is not subject to the name of Jesus. It can resist Jesus or it can yield, whichever it chooses. It has free will. It is when the demon spirit becomes so ingrained with the human spirit that it becomes extremely hard.

Remember, the human spirit must surrender for demon spirits to be dealt with. The human spirit must desire to be free from the influence and misdirection of the demon spirit. When the human spirit becomes too comfortable with a situation to yield it to God, the demon spirit is strengthened. It is pointless to try to cast out demons against someone's will. Deliverance is not for those who choose to live in darkness. The choice to remain in sin disqualifies one for freedom. Refusal to denounce and confess sin is a choice to obey the human spirit in rebellion against God.

To clarify, the most difficult spirit is not the prince of Persia, not the king of the bottomless pit, and not some high-ranking, ruling spirit in the heavenlies. It is your human spirit. This is the only spirit I have encountered that does not tremble at the name of Jesus. Until the human will is surrendered and by grace through faith is born again, it is a very difficult spirit to deal with.

People who are born again, Spirit-filled, and zealous for God still have a human will and spirit. They can still disobey; they can and often do yield to the desires of the flesh. Disobedience is a doorway. Pride is an entry point—just go down the list of sins; they are gateways for demon spirits into the lives of believers. The toughest spirit you will deal with is your human spirit.

CHAPTER 10

WHY ARE PULPITS SO SILENT?

THE CHURCH TODAY is weak, anemic, sick, and in bondage. God's people are hurting. We are just like the unsaved when it comes to sickness, divorce, and other areas of bondage. The reason for this, I believe, is simple: The message of freedom from demonic powers is not being preached.

Pastor, what will you do when your members come to you and ask for help in this area? If it has not already happened, it will. The numbers will increase, and I assure you that you will not be able to escape it. Sure, you can send them to a counselor. You can recommend a Christian psychologist. But Jesus did not say, "Counsel them out," or, "Medicate them out." Neither can you get them out by being more religious. You can't wish them out or will them out. Jesus said to cast them out, and that is the role of the church!

We have been given authority over "all the power of the enemy" (Luke 10:19). So why won't the church step up and deal with this? Every church should have an active deliverance ministry, and every pastor should be able to lead someone through deliverance! I also believe that every pastor should go through deliverance as well.

If Jesus came to heal "all that were oppressed of the devil" (Acts 10:38), should we not let that Jesus come alive in us? Should we not be advancing against the kingdom of darkness with the authority Jesus has given us? There is plenty of truth in the Scriptures about the demonic but very little taught in our churches. Have we not been silent long enough?

EXPECTATION

The pages of the New Testament are filled with Jesus' miracles of healing and casting out of evil spirits. Why do our churches remain so silent about it? Why don't we experience these things? These passages give us some insight as to why.

> Great multitudes came together to hear, and to be healed by Him of their infirmities.
>
> —LUKE 5:15

> a great multitude of people out of all Judea and Jerusalem, and from the sea coast of Tyre and Sidon, which came to hear him, and to be healed of their diseases.
>
> —LUKE 6:17

Our responsibility is in the area of expectation. The people came not only to hear Him but also to be healed by Him. It seems today we only go to hear Him. I believe the responsibility for expectation is missing in the church. It is the fault not only of the preachers but also of congregants who don't want their pastors to preach and practice healing and deliverance. Demon powers are doing a good job of keeping this out of church. Think about it; this is what Jesus did and what He told us to do.

During a recent night of ministry, a woman came at the altar call and handed me a note. She could not hear, and she could not speak clearly. But she came expecting. That's what we do at our ministry nights—we pray for the sick and cast out demons. As I prayed for her, she gently fell to the ground and lay on the floor throughout the entire altar call time. When she was helped to her feet, she looked around in amazement and said, "I can hear you! I can hear you!" That's really exciting! We had many people healed that night; we always do.

One man told me he was healed as he came into the parking lot. "I have had this condition in my right cheekbone for years, but the pain left when I pulled into the parking lot." That's pretty incredible.

As I looked over the people in attendance at the meeting, I noticed something common in their eyes—expectation and need. I believe that in most congregations, need is common, but expectation is not. Someone needs to pump up the expectation level among believers. God is a faith God—God honors faith.

BEWARE OF SEEKING AFTER SIGNS

And Peter answered Him and said, "Lord, if it is You, command me to come to You on the water." So He said, "Come."
—MATTHEW 14:28–29, NKJV

"What is the call of God?" Don't we hear that phrase a lot? "God called me to do this or that," or, "I don't feel called of God." Be careful what you chase because you might catch it—or it might catch you! While we need more pastors willing to embrace the ministry of deliverance, we must beware of seeking after signs. Those pursuing a dream are not necessarily called of God. I know some people who are simply fulfilling a fleshly desire to feel important, to be recognized as spiritually significant, but their doctrine and lifestyle are contrary to Scripture. Their voice and vision are drowned out by their actions and attitudes.

"Many are called, but few are chosen" (Matt. 22:14). Many are called, but many are not. Some people are chasing after supernatural experiences. May I say that many people have caught a supernatural experience only to find that it is not of God. Not everything "supernatural" is the Spirit of God. Many are saying they hear what the Spirit of God is saying; there are some who say they see what the Spirit is showing—and they will tell you. May I say to you as gently as I know how, as kindly as I can: Much of it is phony baloney. I'm sorry; I know that seems harsh. But I have seen too much of it to dismiss it lightly.

It is a serious thing to claim to be the voice and eyes of God. Being spiritually accurate is confirmed by scriptural accountability.

If you have a more sure word of prophecy than we already have, you might be a prophet. If you don't, you might be a fortune teller.

Do you really know what you are looking for? What do you expect to receive in your next worship service? In the seminar, workshop, or weekend retreat, what are you looking for? I find in many of our sessions that people have been seeking "something," but they are not sure what it is. Don't we all want peace? Fulfillment? Purpose? I mean, isn't that really the longing of our hearts? Genuineness is our goal!

I find some things to be pretty much applicable in all situations. People do the best they can. I believe that. I also believe that our perspective of things often determines how we react in situations. If we see the task as overwhelming, it probably will be. If we see victory, if we see defeat—well, you see where I am going. When David was asked by his father to take food to his brothers who were fighting against the Philistine army, his older brother accused him of coming only to "see the battle" (1 Sam. 17:28).

David's response after hearing the Philistine insults to God and God's people was pretty much, "I didn't come to see the battle; I came to *be* the battle!" (See 1 Samuel 17:20–51.) Quite a difference. Seeing something and being something are two different things. Personally, I like *being* rather than just *seeing*. What you see is what you get. You can see an enemy too big to conquer or an enemy too big to miss. You can assess a situation by fear or by faith. You can base your decision on what others see or what God says.

Permission to proceed is the call of God. God's call is often simple and subtle. Look at God's call extended to Peter. In the storm, from the boat of normalcy, Peter requested permission to go to where Jesus was. The call, or permission to proceed, was simply, "Come" (Matt. 14:29). That's all, just "Come." If your desire is to be where Jesus is, you have permission to proceed. Notice that when Jesus got in the boat, so did Peter. It is better to be in the boat with Jesus than to be on the water without Jesus.

If Jesus calls you to be where He is, He will also make it possible for you to stay on top of things that would normally drown you. The call of God is an invitation to invest. Many times Jesus cautioned us to count the cost. His invitation requires an investment from us.

Don't venture outside God's calling for your life. I get "prophetic words" in my email inbox almost daily. The only problem is they are not prophetic at all. It's not that they are only seldom correct; they are never correct. I wonder why people are so attracted to this. Why do we seek after more signs from God when we don't even honor the sign that has already been given and will be the only sign given!

These people have special titles to enhance their deception. They call themselves "Prophet," "Apostle," or some other lofty title and claim to hear directly from God. The church has got to do better! Where are the genuine preachers who will proclaim the blood of Jesus and the power of His resurrection?

Some of you reading this fall into this category. Generally, when this happens, it is because the message has gone from focus on Jesus to focus only on the Holy Spirit. I believe this so grieves the Holy Spirit that permission is gained by demons to deceive and even to give false gifts and lead people into thinking they're following the Holy Spirit. Jesus must be the focus. A genuine infilling of the Holy Spirit will cause you to lift up Jesus. The Holy Spirit is honored when Jesus is magnified.

While every gift of God's Spirit is legitimate and valid, virtually all of them have been mimicked, mocked, and adulterated. Do you see why Jesus called sign seekers an "adulterous" people (Matt. 16:4)? They have polluted the simple, powerful message of the resurrection. Don't chase signs! I know folks who go to every seminar and meeting held. They've attended all the conferences and have all the books, CDs, and teaching materials, yet they can't seem to find peace. They constantly seek, I guess thinking that someday, somehow, through some speaker they will hear the "magic" words. There are no such words. God's Word has already been spoken, and the sign has already been given. The resurrection of Jesus was and is the sign.

If you want to damage your church, maybe destroy it, try going beyond what God's Word teaches. I know of churches that have been virtually destroyed by venturing out of their realm of authority.

We have not been given authority in the heavenlies. You cannot take back what never was yours. Principalities and powers have authority because it has been given to them by the sin and disobedience of people. Get the people saved; leave the principalities alone. They have rights by the people, and until the people submit, we have no rights to banish these spiritual kingdoms or take back cities or communities. We tread on very dangerous ground when we do this.

Listen, that's not a casual observation; it is the voice of many years of experience with this! Don't chase signs. Don't engage in territorial warfare. It's not wise, and it's not scriptural. It's not wise *because* it's not scriptural. Why not seek Jesus? If you want to be pure in your seeking and chasing, seek Him. Chase Him.

For those who seek signs and wonders, I wonder about the wonders they seek. What sign has importance other than the death, burial, and resurrection of God's Son? May I just say in love, don't be seduced. Don't compromise the simple truth of God's Word. Evil and adulterous people seek after signs. These are the words of Jesus, and they are for our admonition and spiritual safety.

EXUBERANT JOY IN THE HOLY SPIRIT

I want to turn your attention to a well-known passage in Luke's Gospel:

> At that, Jesus rejoiced, exuberant in the Holy Spirit. "I thank you, Father, Master of heaven and earth, that you hid these things from the know-it-alls and showed them to these innocent newcomers. Yes, Father, it pleased you to do it this way. I've been given it all by my Father! Only the Father knows who the Son is and only the Son knows who the Father is. The Son can introduce the Father to anyone he wants to."

He then turned in a private aside to his disciples. *"Fortunate the eyes that see what you're seeing! There are plenty of prophets and kings who would have given their right arm to see what you are seeing but never got so much as a glimpse, to hear what you are hearing but never got so much as a whisper."*
—Luke 10:21–24, msg, emphasis added

What had just happened that would cause such rejoicing by Jesus? I really like the way *The Message* breaks this down. The seventy disciples had just returned with joy. And Jesus rejoiced with them. Why? What had they done that produced such joy—joy in them and joy in Jesus?

Jesus chose seventy men and sent them with authority to heal the sick and cast out demons. These were not polished theologians but rather new believers, new followers. Jesus appointed them and anointed them with His authority. He gave simple instructions and sent them out as thirty-five two-man teams.

Astounded, they returned proclaiming, "Even the devils are subject unto us through thy name" (Luke 10:17). Even the devils! I can see the victorious smiles on their faces—a grin from ear to ear, the grin that comes from knowing victory through obedience. It comes when we have been instrumental in winning a soul to Christ. There is no such comparable joy. It was in their eyes and on their faces! This brought joy to Jesus.

I have experienced this feeling of joy. It also causes the angels to rejoice. Look how *The Message* relates this: "You hid these things from the know-it-alls and showed them to these innocent newcomers. Yes, Father, it pleased you to do it this way" (Luke 10:21).

I get to see this on a regular basis—folks being healed, demons obeying commands through the authority of Jesus' name. What deep joy.

As we look on this with reverential wonder, and as we perceive what it was that produced this ecstasy, we will also find rising in our hearts a measure of rejoicing in our spirit, as well as exaltation.

Rejoiced doesn't even seem to be a strong enough word. The Greek word translated "rejoiced" in Luke 10:21 is *agalliaō*. It means to jump for joy, to rejoice greatly, with exceeding joy, to exult.[1] The word *exult* means to "show or feel triumphant elation."[2] When Jesus rejoiced, it was a visible manifestation of His intense emotions, and His words conveyed both to His disciples and those of us reading the account the sheer depth of His emotions. We get an inside look at the heart of the Savior, the Redeemer, the Deliverer, the One who came to set us free.

I think I see an unbridled smile and an expression of victory that could be the equivalent of a fist pump or high five by Jesus. To exult, remember, is to show or feel triumphant elation. The thirty-five two-man rookie teams had obeyed His Word, and the demons had obeyed their commands. Jesus was not just pleased; He exulted. He was exuberant. He was overjoyed. He felt the triumph, and He showed it.

I like the picture I see here. Jesus exulted, and the Father was exalted. It is my desire to bring exultation to Jesus and exaltation to the Father. One produces the other. Jesus said that it seemed good to the Father. If it makes Jesus rejoice and seems good to the Father, why are we not doing it in the church today?

Jesus made sure the seventy men did not rejoice in the wrong thing. He basically said, "You have power over demons because I gave it to you, so don't lose sight of why you have such authority." We are in Christ, and Christ is in us. We are healed by the authority of His name.

I am ever aware that the things I see and experience in this ministry have simply been revealed to me, that I qualify not as wise and prudent but as a babe in His sight. I wouldn't want it any other way. I believe today that Jesus rejoices when we act in His name and believe His Word.

I believe there is way too much attention given to the Holy Spirit, and I believe that grieves Him. The focus should always be Jesus! God sent us His Holy Spirit to lift up Jesus, not to lift up the Holy

Spirit. Talk about Jesus, dwell on Jesus, and focus on Jesus. The authority we have been given is in *His* name.

Jesus' joy made Him break out into prayer. He praised God the Father for His wisdom, for His plan, and for His own unique relationship with God the Father. "I thank You, Father!" How many times I have said the same words. "Thank You, thank You, thank You because of the joy of seeing people delivered and healed!"

Rejoicing in our victories leads to "Thank You, Father" as it did with Jesus in Luke 10:21. Jesus then said, "All things are delivered to me of my Father...and he to whom the Son will reveal him" (v. 22). God the Father gave it to Jesus, and Jesus gave it to us, to me, a babe in Christ.

Does it confound the wise? You be the judge. Authority as a believer is not received or understood through education and accomplishment. Really, it is not even discovered; it is revealed. It is not hidden; it just cannot be seen through carnal eyes.

The parallel account in Matthew 10:1 says, "He gave them power against unclean spirits, to cast them out, and to heal all manner of sickness and all manner of disease." He gave authority to His twelve disciples and then to seventy rookies—babes, if you will—to cast out demons and to heal all kinds of sickness and disease.

I vividly recall how I expressed this the first time I experienced it, in Kingston, Ontario, Canada. I could take you right to the spot on the top step of the Kingston Prison for Women. I had just ministered my first deliverance. I commanded demons in the name of Jesus, and they obeyed. A tormented woman was set free.

I walked out of that prison, paused on the top step at the prison entrance, thrust the Bible in my right hand high above my head, and said, "Yes! In the name of Jesus, yes!" I left with joy, so I'm pretty sure I know what these men felt. I hope you do too.

EXPERIENCE AND THE TRUTH

What someone is taught must always be subject to what they have experienced. You can teach me that the gift of healing is no longer available to the church, but you can no longer convince me! I know by experience that Jehovah-Rapha is still in business! God is still the Lord God who heals (Exod. 15:26). The stripes on the back of Jesus Christ were purposeful. The blood from those stripes paid for our healing. You cannot talk me out of this.

You can tell me that believers cannot have demon powers in them, but you will never convince me. I have seen about thirty thousand people set free! I now know! Knowing is better than believing. You can believe it doesn't happen, but I know that it does! I used to believe that Jesus "went about doing good, and healing all that were oppressed of the devil" (Acts 10:38). Now I know it.

Experience is the best teacher. Man's theological ideas must take a back seat to life experience that is based upon scriptural truth. I implore you to read what I have shared with you here with an open and honest heart. I have no agenda in writing this book except to lift up Jesus Christ and expose Satan and his kingdom of darkness.

I believe pastors must get ready. There will be an onslaught of believers asking for deliverance. I can tell you personally that day is rapidly approaching, and I am touching the tip of it. All believers can experience the freedom that is available in Christ and not be limited to what a denomination imposes. Find the truth by experiencing it, and do not be ashamed to seek full freedom in Christ. If you are sincere in seeking, you will find the Holy Spirit; God will not give you a serpent. That is a scriptural promise from the lips of Jesus.

> If you then, being evil, know how to give good gifts to your children, how much more will your heavenly Father give the Holy Spirit to those who ask Him?
>
> —LUKE 11:13, NKJV

WHY IS IT SO HARD TO BELIEVE?

Believe Me that I am in the Father and the Father in Me, or else believe Me for the sake of the works themselves. Most assuredly, I say to you, he who believes in Me, the works that I do he will do also; and greater works than these he will do, because I go to My Father.

—JOHN 14:11–12, NKJV

Jesus was talking to His disciples about believing, using strong, emphatic words to encourage them (and us) to believe—simply believe.

I want to give you three of many reasons to believe.

1. Believe Him for His world's sake.

2. Believe Him for His Word's sake.

3. Believe Him for His works' sake.

Believe Him. Can you honestly look at the world and the miracles of creation and not be stirred in your belief? Can you read the miracles throughout God's Word and remain in unbelief? He told His disciples, "Believe Me then for the works' sake, but believe Me."

Unbelief is an insult to all three—the creation, the infallible holy Word of God, and the miraculous works of Jesus. To live in doubt is to live in opposition to God.

We cannot receive what God has for us apart from belief. It's not complicated. God is a faith God. He always has been. Abraham, through faith, became the "father of all them that believe" (Rom. 4:11). His faith was counted for righteousness (v. 3). Abraham "did not waver at the promise of God through unbelief, but was strengthened in faith, giving glory to God, and being fully convinced that what He had promised He was also able to perform" (vv. 20–21, NKJV). Unbelief robs you of God's blessings and of God receiving glory. Our access to God is through faith (Rom. 5:2).

Jesus rebuked the disciples for having no faith and little faith. He praised two Gentiles for having great faith—the woman of Canaan in Matthew 15 and the Roman centurion in Luke 7.

Jesus cried, "O Jerusalem, Jerusalem, the one who kills the prophets and stones those who are sent to her! How often I wanted to gather your children together, as a hen gathers her chicks under her wings, but you were not willing!" (Matt. 23:37, NKJV). I believe it was unbelief that caused Jesus to weep over the city. Our unbelief doubtless grieves the heart of God, and it limits the blessings of God. Unbelief binds the hands that bless. It grieves the giving, compassionate heart of God.

I believe it was unbelief that caused Jesus to weep as He went to the tomb of Lazarus. Instead of believing Jesus could and would raise Lazarus from the dead, Mary and Martha blamed Jesus for not being there.

Jesus chided Thomas for not believing: "Do not be unbelieving, but believing....Thomas, because you have seen Me, you have believed. Blessed are those who have not seen and yet have believed" (John 20:27, 29, NKJV).

Does believing make you vulnerable? Is it the what-if involved that causes you to hold back? Is it pride? I believe it's both.

His world. His Word. His works. Jesus gave us three reasons to believe. Isn't creation itself reason enough to believe? Look around; God so loved the world. Look at His holy Word that is tried and true; isn't that sufficient? Jesus said, "If you can believe Me for no other reason, believe Me for the works' sake." It seems as if frustration might have accented His words—*believe Me.*

> Verily, verily, I say unto you, He that believeth on me, the works that I do shall he do also; and greater works than these shall he do; because I go unto my Father.
>
> —JOHN 14:12

"Because I go unto my Father"? What does that mean? It means that the same authority God had given to Him, He was going to give to the church. Later He said, "As my Father hath sent me, even so send I you" (John 20:21).

This is hard for some to believe. Hence, not many mighty works are seen. The Word also says that Jesus could not do many mighty works in Nazareth because of their unbelief. Unbelief will prevent us from receiving all that God has for us, for "without faith it is impossible to please God" (Heb. 11:6, NIV).

Does it require a lot of faith? It involves taking a step, making a move. It requires getting out of the boat. Peter walked on water with a "little faith," but had he stayed in the boat with others who doubted, he could not have exercised even "little faith" (Matt. 14:31). Peter got out of the boat. Abraham started walking. What step do you need to take to express your faith in God and His Word? I think it also involves getting back in the boat when Jesus is in the boat.

Recently I had an unsuspecting medical need arise. I discovered I had three herniated disks in my neck. I'm not sure how the injury occurred. I saw four different doctors plus my son, who is a neurosurgeon. (One of his partners did the surgery.)

I believed God for my healing and received it through the hand of God and four very skilled doctors. May I say to you that believing God has nothing to do with not trusting Him to use people? God uses people to bring about His miraculous works. His healing and delivering power can be seen throughout His Word—and ordinary people are involved.

We don't need a Moses, a David, an Elijah—we need some vessel God can use to bless His people.

PART II

DEMONIC ENTITIES AND THEIR FUNCTIONS

CHAPTER 11

A CATALOG OF COMMON DEMON NAMES

ALL THE NAMES in this list have been encountered by our ministry teams. Some of the names have also been verified by other deliverance ministries. This is not a complete list but comes from hundreds of hours of diligent one-on-one ministry. The entries include what we know about these spirits. Sometimes we know their origin, function, or how they gain access to a person's life. Other times we only know the works related to that demon.

Demons are notoriously deceptive, but when I put them in a courtroom-type setting before Jehovah God and ask if what they are telling me will stand before Him as truth, they will not lie. I ask for their name and even how to spell it, and I believe what I have collected is reliable. That is partly because I and others in deliverance ministry have encountered the same spirits that use the same names again and again. I don't pretend to understand how those names are chosen, but collecting them has proven useful to me and others in deliverance ministry. I hope you will find the list informative as well.

Refer to chapter 5 for direction on how to cancel demons' permission and command them to leave. As I've said before, deliverance is not a power encounter; it's a truth encounter. Demons can't stand the truth, and they can't withstand the truth. You may think these demons are out of your league, but Jesus put them in your league. Our authority is in the name and blood of Jesus.

We are not to be intimidated by demons, but we are also not to be unwise. We cannot take them on in the flesh. This list is not intended for you to find demons associated with a person's problem and call them out in a deliverance session. It is mainly for confirmation. If you cast out a demon and discover its name, look here, and you just may find it.

A

Aaron—Its functions include fear, anxiety, and condemnation; also causes rheumatoid arthritis, obesity, acid reflux, choking, gluttony, and comfort eating; has manifested as an eagle and as a donkey; another name is Aranoid.

Abaddon—the scorpion of the bottomless pit "whose name in the Hebrew tongue is Abaddon, but in the Greek tongue hath his name Apollyon" (Rev. 9:11). See Apollyon.

Abid—Its functions include insecurity, need for attention, performing for attention/love, lust, flirtation, and confusion; has manifested as a serpent with venom in the central nervous system; attracts lust spirits in others.

abnormal menstrual cycle (dysmenorrhea)—See Ammon, Belial, and Molech/Moloch.

abortion—Spirits associated with this function include Alien, Alusha, Ammon, Andalava, Apollyon, Arbal, Baal, Babylon, Bagglee, Baphomet, Berder, Bon, Buddah, Cali/Kali, Cilad, Condor, Corsea, Darius, Debol, Dolthan, Dulcie, Ecala, Elion, Evan, Formanaux, Garrett, Halibus, Herod, Hipite (who said, "I kill children"), Illiers, Jasper, John, Lacia, Lamdech, Lola (who said, "I abort everything"), Midra, Moab, Molech/Moloch, Molecha, Naddius, Nakata, Nandrathal, Noek, Paul, Punta, Rahla, Relena, Saan, Sar, Seha, Sheba, Svenra, Taluth, Tamuz, Tork, Tubal-Cain, Undella, and Xylan. See Baal and Molech/Moloch.

Absalom—Its functions include anxiety, bitterness, vengeance, hatred, fragile X syndrome, betrayal, control, doubt, unbelief, vanity, pride, self-righteousness, frustration, alcohol and drug addiction, pornography/seduction, confusion, and rejection (2 Sam. 13:28–29);

has manifested as a dragon and a tick; permission gained from rebellion.

Abuki—damages ovaries and causes female problems.

abuse, sexual—this function is associated with Archer (claimed, "She's my target"; manifested as a pterodactyl and a pig), Herod, Henbal (causes people to attract abuse), Kabala, and Loloch (an incubus; part of Moloch's kingdom).

Achan—A territorial spirit over Eagle Mountain Lake in Texas and a ruling prince in Asia; its functions include rejection and eating disorders including anorexia; has manifested as a serpent with venom in mind.

achy legs—a work of several demons including Beelzebub, Budges, Kolar, Neva, Penchar, Pomed, Remberkuhl, Sano, Speer, and Toblar.

acne—a function of Bultepcah (called the little pimple maker), Endo, Diimus, Rivershone, Rohon, and Zertus.

ADD—frequently a work of Backeraba, Baphomet, Beelzebub, Blanche, and Delores. See Backeraba and Baphomet.

addiction—Though we may cast them out of people dealing with certain types of addictions, the following spirits are involved in all addictions: Alala, Boa, Dark (probably not its name but rather its description; a prince of all addiction who specializes in nicotine and sexual addiction; an incubus whose works also include feelings of worthlessness), Debarico (can cause and can be diseases of the heart, liver, and colon; also linked to stomach cancer), Delona (its works also include rejection and stress), Demok (a demonic prince under Chofarra whose works also include sexual perversion), Durham (manifested as a boar in the emotional heart and pressure in the head), Euphrates, Fiazl (its works also include rejection, fatigue, and rebellion), Jensa, Kinx (a ruler of addiction), Mercur, Quantum, Shelton, and Somar. See also nicotine.

alcohol addiction—When ministering to someone with alcohol addiction, we often cast out spirits that call themselves: Abaccus,

Abikor, Absalom, Adobe, Adolphus (also involved in food addiction), Alazar, Albacor, Albiton, Alchemy, Altoim, Alvaizeiton (a ruler of alcohol addiction), Amelia, Ames, Anaton, Angel, Artesia, Ashera, Avatar, Azbeltion, Azom, Babuk, Bacchus, Baldasado, Ballerdell, Balthazar (also involved in drug addiction), Barach, Barsh, Beast, Bethada, Blarney, Borcon, Buth, Calisima, Cameron, Caroline, Clabence, Conar, Dagon, Debarico, Demok, Donato, Doomdoc (a demon in the Freemasonry kingdom), Euphrates, Flo, Folca, Frederick, Gangleon, Grainohal, Gunther, Herbocius, Herden, Herod, Heryal, Hex, Hoard, Hooker, Horrik, Horus, Huble, Igneous, Inger, Jabar, Jarmon, Judas, Jugan, Justa, Kabala, Kanorkia, Katherine, Kaylah, Khan (manifests with confusion), Kilmion, Kinx, Kyme, Labayn, Lago, Lamen, Lancelot, Laramie, Leonardo, Letoe, Lider, Limen (its works include alcohol addiction with lust), Liver (its works include alcohol addiction with suffering), Lloyd, Lona, Lucid, Luciferl, Lurkin, Luther, Luwigi, Madera (also involved in nicotine addiction), Malo, Nigwid, Nikon, Noumeen, Paine, Pergas, Perlion, Petron, Pillar, Pisan, Raudel, Reezer, Regal, Reich, Rembold, Robart, Ronel, Roy, Rumaultin, Saldar, Satar, Satio, Satuway, Schumsud, Semik, Shabar, Shacami, Shoopla, Smagnol, Slater, Tacanowane, Tablough (pronounced Tab-loo), Tabogalesh, Taborg, Trin, Von, Waldorf, Walton, Wateranonca, Weiypa, Willoughby, Wenan, Wesley, Wilcox, Willie, Winston, The Worm, and Zor.

drug addiction—Spirits we often cast out of people dealing with drug addiction include: Alon, Bar, Beetle, Belach, Belkins, Boa, Butter (specifically cocaine addiction), Candor, Caraba, Carib, Ceronis, Chow, Clemeshter, Coldo, Conner, Crowl, Danfoy (specifically cocaine addiction; its name at creation was Mariah, which means joy, and it now does the opposite, bringing misery), Dark (again, probably not its name but rather its description), Darnus (manifested as a leviathan at the core of the person's emotions; in addition to addiction, its works include shame and self-mutilation, or cutting), Darvon (its works also include depression), Deckamon (its works also include child abuse and kidney damage), Doker (manifested as a dragon), Dominique (a destroyer of relationships with a cutting tongue; its works include nightmares, suicide, desperation, and hopelessness), Elium, Elkie (manifested as a maggot in the mind), Feeler, Fellkum, Figero, George, Grunder, Halius, Hammon, Hauben, Heathen, Hedra, Hygman, James, Leviticus (linked specifically to addiction to amphetamines), Lickidus (linked to addiction to marijuana and prescription drugs), Merlot (linked to both alcohol and food addiction), Meshura, Methdon, Mithly, Mizer, Molen, Narco, Neff, Nomad, Non, Peochious, Petratop, Prometheon, Pulperster, Quantum, Ramadama (linked to addiction to medication), Rightran (causes death through addiction), Selbek (linked to marijuana addiction), Septor, Seraph, Seven, Shormasha, Solomn, Somar, Sontag, Spence, Syrus, Talistan, Veronus, Zarthros, Zefna, Zeptarl, and Zippulus.

food addiction—Demons linked to addiction to food include: Ezik (causes chaos in addition to food addiction/comfort eating; also linked to nicotine addiction; has manifested as a beetle in the heart and a worm in the stomach), Fellkum, George, Ibon, Idrin, Joel, Merlot (linked to both alcohol and food addiction), Nathum, Nayrabeeano, Nelmecizer, Nemroah, Obadiah, Oblesq, Obsidius, Orapa, Oriell/O'Reily, Pig, Seherama, Starbright, Symie, and Zelt (manifested as a pig). See eating disorders and gluttony.

gambling addiction—Demons linked to this addiction include: Boleta, Carnivious, Finik, Gollack, and Nelmecizer.

nicotine addiction—Demons associated with nicotine use and addiction include Abathar, Achal, Addibus, Anadon, Aruba, Atcha, Ati, Azmos, Babuk, Bachnold, Bahah, Becola, Bescha, Black Lung, Brock (linked to emphysema from smoking), Bueleez, Caan, Caesar, Cancera, Carlos, Carmica, Catara, Cimmar, Coldo, Conar, Culardia, Cuse, Damion, Debo, Delneuth, Derbine, Dumas, Edelf, Elcon, Elwok, Emphesshea, Ezik, Exberiur, Euphrates, Felix, Fiazl, Flock, Fumelles, Geru (associated with snuff use), Grunder, Hammon,

Hauben, Hedra, Huble, Hygman, Idrin, Igneous (in sinuses), Ibon, Jabar, Jazze, Jefeer, Jemon, Jensa, Jeston, Joa, Jugan, Kajar, Klamor, Kreniel, Lazmon, Lona, Lionel (a leviathan in the chest), Madera, Maggi, Malo (pronounced May-lo), Marki, Matlar, Meloch, Mig, Mopar (associated with black lung), Moriah, Moroni, Muran, Namaan, Niad (linked to snuff use), Nicolaus, Niridel, Nochodeus (linked to desire for nicotine), Omas, Oshua, Palamor, Panelus, Pathecas, Pirus, Prilo, Rabaacah, Ragosorrit, Reich, Rico, Riley, Rock, Roho, Sar, Sargeeo, Sensa, Seraph, Shaschar, Sheleh, Shelton, Simba, Siptar, Solomn, Somar, Spence, Syrus, Taquwa, Tazar, Thist, Toner, Tooll, Torrel, Tulof, Vanchester, Viceroy, Yengawah, Tar, Tobrian, Tombo, and Zeptar.

sex addiction—Spirits we have cast out related to sex addiction include: Anthwerp, Belzeck, Blushedon, David (a watchman for the demonic kingdom whose works also include pornography, confusion, and self-condemnation; it manifested as a spider during deliverance and said, "I'm a cobra that strikes with words of self-condemnation, guilt, and shame"; another time it said, "I'm a pit bull"), Eefsullam (its works also include rebellion, anger, and a racing heart; it gained permission through drug use), Egore (a relationship robber that has manifested as a constrictor in the emotional heart; its functions include insecurity and sexual perversion along with addiction), Flow, Goltha, George, Gaddori, Legion, Lemnich, Maltie, Tidisala, and Welifore.

video game addiction—Demons we have cast out in relation to video game addiction include Adandoff, Arreanna, Bodosom, Bojour, Fohun, and Satio.

Addorkusila—a high-ranking spirit behind mental disorders.

Adelphi—causes confusion; manifested as a spider in the brain; permission was Scottish Rite (of Freemasonry).

agoraphobia—a function of Parani and Shamain.

AIDS—a destroyer of the immune system linked to Besetiosomo, Kalmar, Piner, and Xanthian.

Alexander—an incubus; its works include sexual attack, rebellion, rejection, insecurity, slothfulness, and stubbornness; works with Anthony and Beelzebub; manifested as a praying mantis in the chest; entered through unnecessary enemas during childhood. See Beelzebub.

allergies—often a work of the demons Agra, Alegra, Algra, Allum, Anisted, Asmodes, Belcher, Belgar, Boegal, and Boli.

Alvaizeiton—a devouring wolf whose functions include alcohol addiction; manifested as a serpent of addiction in the central nervous system; also causes addiction to the Holy Ghost, where a person focuses on the Holy Spirit instead of Jesus and the Father; under Wadridrianunco, a controller whose works include addiction to drugs, rock music, and alcohol. Another name for Alvaizeiton may be Algor.

Alzheimer's disease—Demons commonly associated with this illness include Adboa, Albert, Alkeen, Altathius (gained access from anger), Astoroth (causes memory loss and personality change), Blather, Dementia, Earl, Eltik, George, Gustov, Ham, Hilabel, Jackalyn, Juanita, Kareenda, Ladushka (linked to fear of Alzheimer's disease), Lani, Motor, Noah, Oncor, Outlaw, Paul, Rachman, Saradec, and Tinker. This is a tough one. We rarely see healing.

Amalek—Its works include paranoia, hatred, guilt, shame, anger, frigidity, fear of intimacy, and bitterness; manifested as a monster.

Ammon—territorial spirit that destroys marriages and relationships; its functions include incest, child abuse, anger, dysmenorrhea, hypertension, shingles, migraine headaches, sexual impurity, self-doubt, rejection, abortion, and the need for hysterectomies; works with Jezebel.

aneurism—A spirit called Ottowa is linked to aneurisms; it said, "I am a time bomb."

anger—a work associated with Belial, Blackwell, Dagon, Omar, and many other demons. I have collected pages and pages of names associated with anger, but these are the ones we most frequently encounter. See Belial and Dagon.

ankylosing spondylitis—inflammation in the spine and rib cage that over time can cause some of the bones in the spine to fuse. Demons linked to this condition include Dicer, Finlo, Mengering, Timov, Vomit, and Xato.

anorexia—Demons associated with this condition include Achan, Anthony, Apocalypse, Apollyus, Colash, Condo, Danar (its works include self-hatred and self-torture through not eating), Fuller, George, Jewel, Jewellette, Leachry, Loresha, Shamon El, Spartacus (linked to both anorexia and bulimia; manifested as a rat in the bowels), Tormencia, and Zacron. See Achan, Colash, and Shamon El.

Anthwerp—a serpent spirit whose venom is lust; it is linked to sex addiction, sexual perversion, and sleep disorders; has manifested as a weevil in the mind; entered through pneumonia, occult involvement, and incest; a scorpion; brought an imaginary lover; under Pashurmo.

Antichrist—All demons oppose Christ. Some key demons associated with this spirit are Abdullah, Ali, Allah, Anter, Baphomet, Benjamin, Cancer, El Lobo, Flaming, Flegger, Havastard (a murder spirit), Husain, Jabel, Lucifer, Mascar, Matalia, Molik, Terorarc, and Uostern.

Apollyon—called Abaddon in Hebrew (Rev. 9:11); it is the king of all fear, and anything that is fear-related will be in his kingdom: suicide, shame, hopelessness, rejection, intimidation, and the like. He is a scorpion spirit who claims to be directly under Satan. Because the demonic kingdom is organized like a military, Apollyon may have many types of demons with him, but he is the king of the bottomless pit and commander in chief of the demon soldiers. Orion will generally assist him. Apollyon's works also include pride, bipolar disorder, anger, hatred, violence, and destruction. It is a destiny thief, time thief, and sleep robber whose functions include wrong priorities, pain in heels/ankles, torture with thoughts of self-hatred/rejection, fear of abandonment, adultery, confusion, prostate problems, illnesses in the colon, IBS, diverticulitis, cerebral palsy, unforgiveness, and sexual perversion; has manifested as a serpent with the venom of self-promotion, a dog in the bowels, a lizard, a parasite in the blood causing candida infection, and of course, a scorpion. One of its permissions for gaining access was incest. Also known as Rashid; its God-given name at its creation was Logarith, meaning "God's reason."

Aranoid—Its functions include gluttony, comfort eating, obesity, fear, anxiety, and fear of water; has manifested as a donkey.

Argon—an intimacy thief and relationship robber whose works include anger, rejection, self-condemnation, poor circulation, frigidity, back and joint pain, worthlessness, and alcohol addiction; manifested as a jackal, a doll that is stiff/rigid, and a snake with venom in the mind; gained permission through Freemasonry in ancestry.

Artemis—the goddess Diana of the Ephesians (Acts 19:24–28); its works include diabetes, misery, homosexuality, and condemnation. Associated with Accishia, Asmodaus (whose functions include suicide, murder, violence, fear, and hopelessness), Juron, Nimo, and Suron.

Ashdar—associated with Aschtart, Astarte (a Phoenician goddess), Ashtoreth, and Simeramus. See Ishtar, Kali/Cali, and Queen of Heaven.

Ashtoreth—linked to all addiction, worthlessness, criticism, pride, deception, confusion, envy, strife, division, pornography, rebellion, stomach/bowel pain, hypertension, bitterness, and arthritis; a nasty spirit that is a relationship robber, joy thief, and peace robber; manifested as a scorpion of fear; entered through childhood sexual abuse.

Asmodes—a vision thief whose works include eye problems, retina disorders, osteoporosis, and allergies. See eye disorders.

Asmodeus—territorial spirit over Newark, Texas; makes women suffer.

Asmodeus—a lust spirit linked to bone and blood cancer, corruption of the mind, self-hatred, heart disease, suicide, self-destruction, problems with eyesight, depression, hopelessness, rejection, guilt, shame, and control; has manifested as a badger, a constrictor in the colon and nerves, and a vulture in the mind; gained permission through blasphemy.

autism—a mental condition characterized by great difficulty communicating with others and in using language and abstract concepts. This is a function of several demons, including Zorca the Great (says he is king), Absalom (a mind blocker), Delilah (linked to deceit in the mind), Holcomb (a deaf and dumb spirit), Legion (said, "We control him"), Demoniac (linked to intellectual disability with restlessness, driving, and pacing), P. Verde (a succubus that twists the mind with violence), Acorn (kills and destroys the mind), Ichabod (a serpent spirit that disconnects a person from God), Cornucopus (an autism prince who said, "Plenty of us here"), Kayaka (linked to mind control), Zodiac (said, "I twist the will of God into my will"), Dorkas (involved in OCD and control), Hordamarr the Great (causes speech development delay), King Etobie, Veritable (an autism prince), Horca (of the highest rank and order; is involved in mutilation and self-mutilation), Thomas (causes intellectual disabilities), Froggy (covers the mind with darkness; said, "I cover like a blanket with darkness"), Carrie Da Carious, Hyaness (a sergeant in the scorpion army involved in bringing torment with anger and fear), Syra (called himself "corkscrew"; twists the mind), Sheena (a scorpion spirit that plays with the emotions), Baca (establishes a root of bitterness; said, "I am lord of the [autism] kingdom"; eats away cells in the nervous system at and below the brain stem), Heckle (a slimy serpent that plays with the emotions), Holroc (an obstinate, stubborn, rebellious spirit who said, "I am the destroyer of the mind and much more"), Snerrol (a high-ranking spirit of autism), and Shamakober (brings dullness and confusion). See intellectual disabilities.

autoimmune disorders—Associated demons include Baltashar (lupus), Besetiosomo, Horus, Jason, Joba (causes food allergies and immune disorders caused by chemical exposure as well as infirmity/infestation in all the cells), Kalmar, Piner, Raynoid, Sam (scleroderma), Sundara, Thyrus, and Xanthian. See Horus.

automatic handwriting—One demon associated with this practice is Carmal, whose works include self-hypnosis.

Azbeltion—territorial spirit whose works include alcohol addiction.

B

Baal—historically, the Semitic and Phoenician god over productive forces of nature; a territorial prince from Ireland who works with Beelzebub; has manifested as a cow's head and an amoeba in the bloodstream; said, "I do it all"; is over all idolatry. Its works also include all infirmity, poverty, drug addiction, fear, lust, depression, miscarriage, infertility, mental fog, fear of failure, confusion, anxiety, tension headaches, fatigue, disunity, disorganization, rebellion, incredible itching, poor circulation, high cholesterol, damage to platelets, and torment with thoughts of rejection; has gained permission through Freemasonry in ancestry and Mayan ancestry; an incubus responsible for the person being molested as a child and miscarrying in adulthood; is a relationship thief and intimacy robber. See Beelzebub.

Baamop—entered through curses from oaths and pledges.

Baath—under Beelzebub; third in rank to Satan; its functions include rejection; manifested as a squirrel in the head; causes accidents; is cloaked in a black cape. In Irish tradition, Baath is the son of Magog, an ancestor of the Milesians, who are said to have conquered Ireland; Ba'ath is also an Islamic political party in Syria and Iraq. See Beelzebub.

Bacheen—territorial spirit whose works include bipolar disorder, fear, confusion, mood swings, a whirlwind of thoughts, depression, frigidity, and snoring; has manifested as a purple frog in the throat; associated demons include Balcar, Tamar, and Zaba. See Tamar and Zaba.

Backeraba—often enters from rejection from parents, usually the mother; in the kingdom of Raba, a high-ranking rejection spirit; its name given at creation was Living, and it now does the opposite; its works include self-rejection with condemnation because of sexual sin as well as urinary tract problems and chemical imbalance.

Balaam—Its works include confusion, pride, vanity, doubt, and nightmares; is a sleep robber; has manifested as a leprechaun; gained permission through involvement in Catholicism and Freemasonry.

Baphomet—related to the Knights Templar; its functions include wizardry; has manifested as a head with two faces with and without a beard, with the head of a cockerel, with the head of a man, with the head of a goat and the body of a man but with wings and cloven feet, and with the head of a goat; said during a deliverance session, "I like to ridicule"; doorway to its entrance was when the person became a 32nd-degree Freemason.

Barach—Its works include bulimia and alcoholism; manifested as a dark veil over the person's eyes; gained permission through unforgiveness; possibly another name for Barak.

Barak—territorial spirit over North and South America; its works include vitiligo, anger, lust, fear, fear of death, heart disease, tumors, obesity, gluttony, lethargy, fatigue, arthritis, kidney and vaginal cancers, addiction, hearing voices, and lupus; has manifested as a serpent in the blood, a worm in the blood, and a wolf in the stomach; gained permission through Freemasonry and Druid curses.

Beelzebub—territorial spirit that claims to be second to Satan, but is under Apollyon; its functions include doubt, unbelief, fighting, stubbornness, back pain, and religious legalism; is generally assigned to those in ministry; has manifested as a gold-and-purple dragon and a donkey in the emotional heart; is "almost beautiful"; shows up often as a blocker; has said, "I'm the highest of demons"; has manifested under the name Bezus.

Belial—causes ovarian, uterine, and lung cancers.

bipolar disorder—Daemon is a prince of the bipolar kingdom, which includes Balca (whose works include confusion), Nomad (a wandering, driven, pacing, restless spirit whose function is to make one homeless), Nemoid (a prince of relationship destruction and a pacing, driving spirit whose name may be a variation of Nomad, which is Damon spelled backward), Petanko (whose works include confusion), Petebius (whose works include foolishness), Sacanez (whose works include schizophrenia), Satyr, Veronus (which kills and destroys with hatred and is a prince under Daemeon and over Zaba in the bipolar kingdom), Winchell, Winton, and Zaba.

Blackwell—Its works include fear with threat and intimidation.

Blank—silences the mind.

Blargy—Its works include digestive disorders.

Blojo—causes bladder infection.

Blomco—causes digestive disorders.

Bozo—causes digestive disorders, acid reflux, stomach cancer, ulcers, and stomach infections.

Brain—Its works include cerebral palsy and muscle spasms; usually enters at birth or during pregnancy; trauma may be the source; associated with Pylar (an oxygen thief that cuts off oxygen to the brain), Randy (an outside spirit that controls the brain), and Ottowa (which causes aneurisms).

breast cancer—Spirits whose works include this type of cancer include Aaile (attacks the lymph glands of the breast), Arculias (attacks the left breast), Asmodeus (makes women suffer), Colial (linked to cancers of the breast and ovaries), Damulias (attacks the right breast), Ferna, George, Lukodius, Lukolias, Lukolidus,

Lymphaloma, Mayxze, Moxie, Optias (puts parasites and organisms into the body, inserts cancer cells, and causes blood cancers such as leukemia), Sheelak, Taile (attacks lymph glands in the breast), Verico (causes fast-growing breast cancer), and Woodstock.

bulimia—a function of several spirits, including Balsha, Barach (also causes alcoholism; gained permission through unforgiveness), Belthar (whose works also include gluttony), Eeyore (whose works also include depression, suicide, self-destruction, and confusion), Geldain, Gossbar (pronounced Goose-bar), Jim (whose functions also include worthlessness), Morphur, Mozambique, Ogedia, Red Swirl, Retella, Rupert, Shamia (an octopus of bulimia; its tentacles rob joy and peace, and its works include shame, dizziness, and lying), Spartacus (also linked to anorexia; manifested as a rat in the bowels), Tubar, and Zippulus (its works also include addiction to prescription drugs).

Burnstiller—one of the major spirits behind migraines; manifested as a hawk in the will.

bursitis—often a work of Sepheroff, which has gained access from rejection.

Butterworth—territorial spirit linked to digestive disorders.

C

Cali—See Kali.

Cameron—Its works include confusion and bipolar disorder; manifested as a beetle with pincers.

Cancer—part of a demonic trinity with Macon and Orion; its works include spiritual infirmity, false beliefs, perverting the Word of God, doubt, and unbelief.

Carpa—very powerful spirit that causes stomach nerves and ulcers; it also controls diseases and injuries of the central nervous system and spinal cord.

carpal tunnel syndrome—Spirits associated with this condition include Arrifamillo (its functions also include rejection, depression, fear, and worthlessness; manifested as a fly; permission was sexual abuse), Castile (also eats away emotions; manifested as a spider in the wrist), Emikild, Fangora (manifested as a spider with fangs in the wrist), Imikilot, James, Mark, Ronnie, and Tony.

Carrie Da Carious—a ruler of speech, confusion of speech, stuttering, and speech impediments; it also causes cleft palate and autism.

cataracts—a common function of Corbana and Kanoptic.

Centanoid—Its works include arthritis, fibromyalgia, complications of having Rh negative blood type; manifested as a parasite in the joints; was located in the blood.

central nervous system—Spirits associated with disorders of the central nervous system include Bin, Carpa (controls diseases and injuries of the central nervous system and spinal cord), Detimus (its functions include mind control), Holroc (an obstinate, stubborn, rebellious spirit that said, "I am the destroyer of the mind and much more"), Horuunda, Pycone, Sugarmort, Ulysses, Zilon (a serpent spirit with the venom of disruption in the central nervous system; also linked to neuropathy; manifested as a Japanese beetle; gained permission from trauma), Zorca the Great (causes mental disorders and neuropathy; manifested as a Japanese beetle).

Chentagua—territorial spirit whose works include fear, paranoia, and ulcers; manifested as a spider weaving a web of confusion.

chest—Demons associated with problems in the chest include Hairso (which causes pain), Maxze (whose works include chest pains), Mayla (a vulture of busyness), and Samhain (which causes pain).

cholesterol—Spirits associated with cholesterol problems include Andion (high cholesterol), Gingsu, Hamuth, Hectos, Jade, Jedda, Lepo, Mati, Nescar, Ohlzya, Pedrick, Peter (high cholesterol), and Rufus.

Chowa—causes deafness and ringing in the ears.

Chutus—linked to abandonment and confusion.

Clarparkae—Its works include traumatic fear of car accidents; associated with Bansadok (linked to fear of driving a car and fear of car accidents), Tamar (territorial spirit whose functions include mind control and manipulation, as well as fear of autos), and Viola (territorial spirit over I-35 bridge over Lake Lewisville in Texas that is linked to fear of driving and auto accidents).

clumsiness—Spirits associated with this condition include Par and Mesara (also known for causing accidents; manifested as a squid in the right leg).

clutter/hoarding—Spirits we often cast out when dealing with this condition include Felix (whose works also include gluttony and self-pity), Fillup (pronounced File-oop), Joslyn, and Kinx (a ruler of addiction).

Colash—Its functions include anorexia, eating disorders, and fear; manifested as an octopus.

colitis—often caused by Taegy, a constrictor that may also be known as Calous.

colon—Demons associated with disorders of the colon include Artify (stems from rejection; its functions include anger), Blargy (whose works include digestive disorders), Blomco (whose works include colitis and diverticulitis), and Calous (has manifested as a worm in the colon).

complacency—Spirits associated with this condition include Pishmar and Funk (whose works include indifference, listlessness, and lethargy).

compulsion—Spirits associated with this issue include Belanja, Danaris (its works include depression and OCD), Dingus, Gilmar, Horad, Hunter, Luther, Kaleno, Krulon, Olan, Orion, Philon, Phinon, Precep, Renece, Scabby, Seher, Steven, Stupido, Telmay, Trion, Trithon, and Tyron. See Orion.

compulsive behavior—See obsessive-compulsive disorder (OCD).

concupiscence—See Ammon, Belial, Hecate, and Sadona. We have also cast Libidinus, Moab, and Sarto out of people experiencing strong sexual desire. See also homosexuality, lesbianism, and masturbation.

confusion—See Orion (a high-ranking spirit that is a king of confusion), Abaddon, Abid (attracts spirits in others), and Absalom. Other spirits associated with confusion include Abash, Abednego, Abuki, Adar, Adelphi, Adon, Adonee, Aella, Aiers, Alantra, and Alestra.

congestion—a function of Jezreeca, a spirit that causes asthma/congestion and fills lungs with water.

contempt—a function of Zin, whose works also include man hating.

contention—a function of such spirits as Bluton, Eliad, Sesilus, Ceiltoia, Phalgm, Shadow Rock, and Tloom.

Cornucopias—brings mental torment.

covetousness—See Isis. Other spirits linked to covetousness include Cauthron and Grealth (also linked to greed).

Crab Fingers—Its works include female masturbation and yeast infection.

Crakeraba—territorial spirit; a strong prince of rejection, generally from the father.

criticism—a work of several spirits, including Ashtaroth, Cristendol, Fantanga, Hama, and Warrior.

cross-dressing—a function of Behemoth (whose works include sexual perversion), Bencai, Bodon (whose works include sexual perversion), Dark Desire (whose works include sexual perversion), Dartar, Embro (whose functions include lust), Googee, Hooker (whose works include sexual perversion), Jehosopher, Kadet, Megnon (whose works include sexual perversion), Sadolc, and Shally (whose works include inspiring fantasy through TV).

crossed eyes—caused by Curvacia, Jorge, Malcordonia, and Zilak.

Crusher—Its functions include oppression; causes brain damage; said, "I crush with oppression."

Curse of Cain—vagabond spirit; associated with Nomad, whose works include wandering, drifting, and homelessness.

cysts—We have found the following spirits associated with various types of cysts: Abuki (ovarian), Calipso (ovarian), Catatie (breast), Curster (various), Black Knight (various), Eleta (breast), Ensefel (various), Eulsies (uterine), Hippon (various), Lochtea (ovarian), Lorba (ovarian), Malak (spinal), Mamar (ovarian), Sesanna (ovarian), Tartar (uterine), and Zapa (various).

D

Daemeon—may be the same as Daimon, Damon, Damion, and Daemon; interchangeable for demon; a receiver of lies, focus thief, and relationship robber; a serpent spirit whose works include uncontrollable actions, foolishness, mockery, rebellion, perceptual distortion, confusion, ADD, rejection, acid reflux, anger, rage, hatred, and polycystic kidney disease; brings a cloud over the mind and heart; a prince of the bipolar kingdom. Damon destroys through the person's own words of condemnation; its name given by God at creation was Zekal, which means praise; Damon now causes sorrow and suffering.

Dagon—an ancient Philistine god; an incubus; its works include Freemasonry, false worship, nightmares, depression, sexual dysfunction through guilt, masturbation, incest, addiction to pain, sleep disorders, anger, confusion, addiction, and suicide; manifested as an ooze of ink and a beetle in the back, causing back, muscle, and joint pain.

Danaris—Its works include depression and OCD.

Daniel—unrelated to the biblical Daniel but is instead a territorial spirit over the Texas panhandle; works for Dumas; linked to false teaching and Freemasonry; an incubus and a serpent of fear; it steals joy and causes arthritis, osteoporosis, infertility, confusion, lust, doubt, unbelief, nightmares, and fear of the dark; entered a person through the hands of a doctor during a tonsillectomy.

deafness—a function of Chow, Chowa (also causes ringing in the ears), Dante, Drucell, El Wormo, Jamel, Rashti, Tefal, and Tremor.

deceit—All demons are deceptive—that's their number one work. Some spirits particularly associated with deceit include Aba, Abednego, Absalom, Aflack, Antichrist, Ashleay, Baruth, Bashtar, Beetlejuice (which also mocks), Bondao, Caiphus, Lying, Chism, Claudius (which distorts, clouds, and confuses), Colash, Ermonk, Harbinger, Heraba, Izzakabar (a ruler of deception), Janick, Kerah, Kira (also causes fear), Lamar, Leethawabie (entered through childhood imaginary friend), Madagascar, Oblivion (brings false words), Paos, Pit Bull (manifested as a five-headed beast with the faces of a pit bull with small horns all over its heads and the feet of a lion with long claws), Purnth, Racca, Satan (not the devil; sometimes pronounced Say-ton), Scooby-Doo, Shadak, Shadrach (came disguised as an angel of light), Shabia, Shamon El, Silvia, Thomasina, Tormencia, Tubal-Cain (a major Freemasonry spirit often with the high-ranking demons Baphomet and MaHa Bone; said about MaHa Bone, "He's one bad dude"), Twinkle, Zaba, and Uz (a lying spirit). See Tubal-Cain.

Deckersont—Its works include fibromyalgia, Graves' disease, and pressure or soreness in the back.

Delatoid—a dragon of the pit; its works include arthritis, fibromyalgia, Raynaud's disease, and depression; gained permission from anger.

delayed speech development—a work of Aneus, Ivy, Kremshaw (a host for Asperger's syndrome), Tempest, and Zorca the Great. See Tempest and Zorca the Great.

dementia—a demonic prince that causes Alzheimer's disease and memory loss; associated with Saradec (whose works include memory loss, forgetfulness, Alzheimer's disease, and dementia, and which gained permission through radiation treatment).

Demoncia—Its functions include personality change; associated with Apollyon, Juanita (whose works include Alzheimer's disease), and Kareenda (whose works also include Alzheimer's disease).

denial—a work of the strong prince Sopa.

depression—See Apollyon. Virtually all demons are linked to depression.

Devoshee—territorial spirit whose works include confusion and deception; a blocking spirit that often manifests as a dark cloud.

Devour—known for "ripping and tearing"; associated with Damus, Grenco (which devours), and Nismeth (which manifested as a panther and devours like a panther).

Dewayne—Its works include heart disease and a leaking heart valve; manifested as a hawk.

Deyon (pronounced Day-on)—a divider; its works include fear.

diabetes—The diabetes spirits are virtually always in the squid kingdom; these include Lutu (which manifested as a jellyfish with long tentacles in the pancreas), Abonia, Adam, Ahul, Archie, Ardie (linked to sugar imbalance), Ashteroth, Babel, Batshirra, Belial, Blutos, Bonai, Cain, Caraba, Carmella, Ceaver, Coch, Creighton, Crusep, Daglo, Darnelle, Denicka, Dimitri, Dinga, Ditak, Dominick, Eater, Eliac, Enoch, Eliah, Eshamog, Fereena, Flavion, Fondalar, Gabeon, Gail, Hectos, Hellectos, Homar, Icheby, Jarmin, Leopold, Malarkioni, Malbeensalmon, Melford, Molech/Moloch, Nassa, Nikera, Octo, Octopus, Olga, Raquasho, Ravi, Roto, Seth, Shagrin, Squid, Stoma, Tamar, William, Wu Toga, Zarin, Zaron, and Zortana. See Belial, Molech/Moloch, Tamar, and Wu Toga.

digestive disorders—a function of several demons, including Aaron (linked to acid reflux and choking), Abathar (constipation), Abaddon (candida), Achbak (IBS), Aguafur, Alon (ulcers), Alusha, Antilo (acid reflux), Apollo (acid reflux, constipation, and IBS), Apollyon,

Arachon (candida), Aranoid, Arethemus, Arragon, Artimus, Babel, Baydon (entered through fear), and Beatrice (manifested as a pig in the stomach). See Abaddon, Apollyon, and Aranoid.

discord—one of the works of Armuth, Crakeraba, Elloriah, Harmon, Ischqwa, Jagien, Plink (said when commanded to join as one spirit, "I don't join with anyone; I am discord!"), Salame, and Septune. See Crakeraba.

diverticulitis—one of the works of the demons Blargy (which is linked to digestive disorders), Blomco (whose works also include colitis and other digestive issues), Forsha, Leon, Saule, and Weasel. See Blargy and Blomco.

Donald—Its functions include TMJ and jaw misalignment.

doubt—among the works of Aberjinan, Absalom, Acton, Adian, Aella, Aeoro, Alpha, Closko, Danby, Raul, and Orion. See Orion and Absalom.

Down syndrome—a condition linked to Kremshaw (also a host for Asperger's syndrome), Shamakober (also linked to autism with dullness and confusion), Shockadula (associated with violence as well as Down syndrome), Snerrol (a ruler of autism), and Veritable (an autism prince). See Zorca the Great.

Draggulea—Its functions include manipulation, lying to control others, and anger; may cause bunions; manifested as a tall, skinny, beige, burned-looking creature in the mind.

Dragon—also known as Beelzebub, Satan, and the devil (Rev. 20:2); its works include Freemasonry. See Beelzebub and Komodo.

Dumas—a prince over the Texas panhandle; a peace robber and suppressor; its works include depression and nicotine addiction; manifested as a serpent in the vocal cords and a constrictor in the mind.

Duzzenorian—territorial spirit that causes headaches and migraines.

Dwayne—Its works include arrhythmia and poor blood circulation; manifested as an octopus.

Dysgraphia—a snake sent to confuse the brain; linked to learning disabilities; gained permission through alcoholism.

dyslexia—a function of Adamar, Araba, Blanche, Calipso, Chise, Delores, Edue, Gly, Gravya, Heztar, Lasteris, Liabus, Lodia, Micum, Oscar, Raiddple, Raymont, Tiaspe, Yaya, Zechadus, Zelda, and Zontar.

E

ear problems—a function of the demons Abeto (causes ringing in the ears), Adonata (causes ear pain), Akbar (causes ringing in the ears), Alexander (causes buzzing in the ears), Angelica (causes ear pain), Beckaltom (causes ear ringing/buzzing), and Borba (causes hearing loss). See Alexander.

Eastern religion—Kundalini is a yoga spirit that may position itself at the base of the spine; its works include guilt and shame. See Kali/Cali.

eating disorders—See anorexia, bulimia, and gluttony.

Eeyore—territorial spirit whose works include depression, suicide, confusion from gloom and despair, self-destruction, ADD, OCD, and bulimia; a focus thief that has manifested as a cockroach in the mind.

Egyptian gods—includes Ra, Osiris, Isis, Horus, Set, and Seth; among their functions are mocking, false voices with confusion and condemnation. See Horus, Isis, Osiris, and Ra.

Elamond—territorial spirit over Missouri, Kansas, Colorado, New Mexico, Oklahoma, and parts of Texas; says Sarcan is higher in rank.

Elizabeth—linked to cancer, painful female problems, and hepatitis.

Elsinor—said, "I sacrifice anything that's good. I rule the network. I keep everything linked and hooked up"; its functions include confusion and pain in the neck; manifested as a frog; entered through doubt. See Ezra.

El Donna—an incubus whose functions include bestiality, demonic sexual attacks on women (may have a doorway of sexual sins or abuse); associated with Janeesa, which said, "I'm like El Donna."

El Lobo—watchdog for the demonic kingdom; manifested as two yellow eyes.

El Wormo—Its functions include herpes, doubt, sciatic nerve damage, addiction, confusion, hypoglycemia, deafness, and ringing in the ears; manifested as a parasite in the bloodstream.

epilepsy—often a function of the demons Delbataba, Mephibosheth, Mishona, Mytos, Sitsizan, and Setsizon.

Epstein-Barr virus—See Gacio and MaHa Bone.

equilibrium—Disruptions in equilibrium are often works of Lawrence, Merado, Rula, and Tibop.

Errmacuse—disrupts with barriers, feelings of inadequacy and doubt; manifested as a panther in the mind.

evil eye—from the Egyptian curse. See Horus.

exaggeration—a function of many demons, namely Excel, Joppa, Mislo, Tetra, the Truth Choker, Vadvilim, and Zeus.

exhibitionism—Spirits whose works include flashing or exhibitionism include Bertha, Willsi, and Bakrae, an esteem robber whose functions include Freemasonry and rejection; may enter through gratification of exposure.

eye disorders—a function of Ahoraba, Apollyon (linked to growths on the eyes), Aral-Osiris, Asmodes, Baphomet (causes astigmatism), Caneya (causes warts in eyes), Cobra, Corbana (linked to cataracts), Curvacia (causes retina problems), Dorsey, Enasua/Lethal (manifested as an owl pecking at the eyes), and Horus. See Apollyon, Baphomet, and Horus.

Ezra—a strong prince of fear; its works include pride with arrogance, insecurity, depression, guilt, shame, restlessness, anger, bipolar disorders, and gum disease; often with Apollyon; works with Grapevine (a demonic prince of arrogance).

F

false anointing—a work of Delonavian, whose works also include anger.

false burdens—We often cast out a spirit called Noah whose works include deception, false responsibility, and false compassion; deceives people into thinking they deserve it and that God wants them to suffer; often rooted in unforgiveness of self.

false gifts—among the works of Adian, Alioeu, Baphomet, Beelzebub (false healing, prophecy, and tongues), Chinco, Orion, Lucifer, Satan, Bioratrice, Oblivion, Galendo, Sawyer (false tongues), Jezebel (false holiness), Zafari (false Holy Spirit and false prophecy), Leturu (deception and false discernment/trust). See Baphomet, Beelzebub, Jezebel, and Orion.

false religions—a work of Chinco, Mary, and Wrinkles.

false teaching—See Kali/Cali.

false tongues—Demons associated with this function include Adian, Babel, Babbling, Babylon, Bioratrice, Chinco, Dionysis, Galendo, Orion, Sawyer, Swadenkoala, Kikolekin, Psychobabel, and Sentar. See Orion and Psychobabel.

false words—a function of several demons, including Adian, Cesco (linked to false visions), Demeter, Harbinger, Oblivion, and Zafari (whose works include a false Holy Spirit and false prophecy).

false worship—a function of Celtic, Gaelic, Hema, and Ian.

family order—The following spirits are often cast out when there is disorder in a family: Jezebel (linked to disordered authority, especially in the family), Peta (whose works include division within the family; under Jezebel in rank), Para (whose mission is to divide and conquer and is also under Jezebel), Sultra (which we know little about), and Croucher (known for bringing strife). Also see Phillip, whose functions include deception, anger, and confusion as well as family dysfunction.

fatigue—Spirits associated with this function include Adboa, Apollyon, Arosay, Baal, Balanthal, Barak, Bocia, Bosea, Boshem, Carna (linked to sleep apnea), Crow, Decadus, Dizel, Dulsa, Enoch, False Shepherd, Fatai, Feddish, Gabeon, Hang, Helman, Hoard, Igabus, Jareeca, Jessica, Josa (pronounced Jo-say), Justin, Komodo, Kyra, Lawless One, Leer, Mertham, Michella, Molech, Mono, Morgan, Omar, Pain (opening may be heavy metal music), Parlay, Pemot, Pink (king of weakness), and Python. See Apollyon, Komodo, and Molech/Moloch.

faultfinding—a common function of Tarragon, whose works also include condemning and accusing others, deception, and justifying one's actions; manifested as a venomous serpent in the ears.

fear—Virtually all demons bring fear. Apollyon is the king of fear! Other demons that bring fear include Aaron, Abaddon (a ruler of fear), Abdullah, Abethor (manifested as a skeleton), Abiathar (manifested as a bird with a grip of fear on the heart), Abimalech, Abjucka, Abuki, Abuwontok, Acbar, Acbiel, Achel, Achilles, Achmad, Adalladon, and Agua (brings worry). See Aaron, Abaddon, Abuki, and Apollyon.

fear of death—Spirits with this function include Apollyon, Bangor, Barak, Bayschuer, Bicknet, Comacuse, Ezekiel, Freeby, Lanarvo, Mezhobic, Polimon, Prozl, Regatuda, Samaria, Trimp, Vakkai, and Voltar. See Apollyon and Barak.

fear of demons—This work is associated with Explent, Fuhrer (like Hitler; a scorpion of fear that brings fear of spiritual attack by demons), Horus, and Loab. See Horus.

fear of untimely/premature death—Demons associated with this function include Bangor, Barak, Bayschuer, Comacuse, Ezekiel, Freeby, Nayus, Polimon, Regatuda, Samaria, Shaboth, Trimp, Trojan, and Zodiac. See Barak.

Felix—This demon is often encountered when a person is dealing with fear, ostracism, and isolation.

female problems—We often encounter the following spirits when someone is dealing with female problems: Abuki, Aizar, Belial, Black Knight (cysts), Bolon, Caleb, Elizabeth, Hectos, Horatio, Lorba (ovarian cysts), Maya (fibroid tumors), Meriham, Mohim (pelvic inflammation), Orman (polycystic ovary syndrome), Pelah (caused hysterectomy), and Sadona/Sedona (female infirmity); Barak, Belchezk, and Scorpio are associated with cancer in the female genitalia. See Abuki, Barak, Belial, Elizabeth, Hectos, and Sadona/Sedona.

fibroid tumors—Demons linked to this issue include Belial, Connie, Drageier, Fivroid, Granchief, Jason, Maya, and Oxsaya. See Belial and Fivroid.

fibromyalgia—Spirits whose functions involve fibromyalgia include Abbadar, Acermon, Aranoid, Ash, Augnoton, Bantanavana (gained access from bitterness), Bartimus, Beelzebub, Boa, Bread of Life, Breath of Life, Canok, Centanoid, Charlotte, Cleophus, Cleoptile, Deckersont, Delatoid, Dicer, Ehab, Gelate, Genosite, and Genosito. See Aranoid and Beelzebub.

financial lack—Spirits associated with financial lack include Anaconda (a constricting spirit that stops financial blessing), Python (a prosperity thief that kills, steals, destroys, and devours finances), Carnivious (whose functions include gambling), and Mona (whose works include discouragement and fear of failure). See also lack.

Fivroid—Its functions include fibroid tumors on ovaries and heavy menstrual flow; manifested as a dog in the reproductive organs; gained permission through trichotillomania (an inability to stop pulling out one's hair).

foot conditions—often a work of Larkoploas, Rockalias, Ubetan, Oggun, Captu, Fardo, Faruluntar, Osabert, Lucifer (which causes ingrown toenails and foot/nail fungus), Rip (causes bone decay in heels), and Crollian and Dolcé, both of which bring pain.

forgetfulness—a function of Musta (also linked to herniated discs and neck problems) and Mindless. See confusion.

fornication—Spirits associated with sexual manipulation include Hakaran (whose functions include sex outside of marriage), Shonte, Hyacinth, and Malcan.

Frank—territorial spirit over Dallas and Lewisville, Texas; said, "I do all of it"; an incubus, it is an intimacy thief and relationship robber whose functions also include confusion, compulsion, gambling, arrogance, pain, anger, control, fear, shingles, depression, migraines, rejection, suicide, and spinal pain; an octopus; manifested as a constrictor in the central nervous system; gained permission from a Freemasonry curse; often with Moloch, MaHa Bone, and John.

Frederick—territorial spirit over England and Prussia; its works include confusion and unbelief; gained permission through Freemasonry; is a distributor of poison in the system; associated with Argon.

Frederick of Prussia—associated with Freemasonry curse.

Fumelles—Its functions include addiction to cigarettes.

fungus—Demons involved in causing fungi of the skin, nails, and feet, as well as pneumonia, tumors in the lungs, and appendicitis, include Beelzebub, Funk, Lucifer, Nimo (foot/nail fungus), and Roddessut/Rotisut. See Beelzebub.

G

Gacio—a chameleon in the feet; its functions include mononucleosis and Epstein-Barr virus.

gallbladder—demons that bring illness to this part of the body include Abularon, Cayman, Denemis, Donte, Gollum (an ugly, ugly spirit), Levesta, Loonda, Masshellert, Omadabar, Ralph, Spencer,

Tubal-Cain (manifested as a dragon in the stomach, ovaries, and gallbladder; said, "I have teeth"), and Yenda. See Tubal-Cain.

gastritis—frequently a work of Bozo, Genel, George, Sagitarius, and Senel.

genital warts—Dana and Higbiggler are both spirits linked to genital warts.

Glabboring—causes colon issues and obesity; manifested as an octopus in the colon.

Gladochifar—a boastful, proud demon from a long ancestry rule; an admiral in the chest that kills and destroys health; manifested as a serpent with the venom of self-doubt; said, "I do it all; I'm the keeper."

glands (thyroid)—Often attacked by Hiawatha (a spirit linked to Native American cultures; its works include glandular malfunctions, swelling, and edema) and Goratus (a violent spirit that attacks the pituitary gland); other spirits often called out when someone is delivered of thyroid issues are Lucidious, Rexpan, Rezpan, and Serge.

Glare—a spirit whose works include a look that "kills" with contempt.

glaucoma—a condition of increased pressure within the eyeball, causing gradual loss of sight. We have often cast out demons called Freddy and Kent in people with this condition.

Gloom—said, "I cover with darkness"; its works include confusion and spiritual blindness; a spirit called Hunsk said, "I rule Gloominess."

gluten intolerance—See Zucum.

gluttony—The following spirits have all been associated with gluttony: Aaron (obesity, gluttony, and comfort eating), Beautinay, Bejer, Belthar, Bioratrice (gluttony, sex, and food), Cacurus (to stifle anger), Casaab, Chebella, Cindilor, Crab, Facto, Fells (may be related to fear of disapproval), Felix (causes gluttony with self-pity; works with Zaba), Fellkum, Futh, Gail, Glabboring (gluttony and obesity), Glutanomous, Gorga, Hereford (manifested as a pig), Huntingdon, Jeremiah, Kilma, Klata, Lasuma, Marvin (gluttony and obesity), Masshellert, McKai, Median (also obesity), Merlot, Nayrabeeano, Nemroah, Nomad, Oblesq, Octavius, Ondilor, Oriell/O'Reily, Panad, Pisrala, Ruth (from self-hatred), Samuel, Sanabob, Seherama, Sela, Seleh, Serge, Shauman, Symie, Terrance (comfort eating), Tosjo, Trego, Tyshbedae, Warnof, Winchell (said, "I kill by overeating"), Woetasha, Woteige, Wretch, and Zelt. See Aaron, Jeremiah, Nomad, Oriell/O'Reily, Woteige, Zaba, and Zelt.

Goat—territorial spirit over Africa; its works include child sacrifice; works under Gorilla.

Goat Head—This is Baphomet.

Gorilla—the prince over the continent of Africa; has numerous witchcraft spirits under him; a territorial blocker from Africa; said during a deliverance session, "I was sent to kill him like I killed the deacon."

Graves' disease—Spirits linked to this disease include Deckersont (also causes fibromyalgia and pressure/soreness in back), Olaf, and Talon. See Talon and thyroid malfunction.

greed—Demons associated with this function include Anais, Aris, Cauthron, Donavan (brings anger), Grealth (also linked to covetousness), Hamold (manifested as a serpent of greed with many little snakes and eggs throughout), Isis, Karbel, Osgard, Ozgard, Picas (causes lust for things/being someone), Thaddeus (gained permission from rejection), and Zooka. See Isis.

grief—This is a work of the following demons: Beli, Berretan, Boraz, Carl, Cesna, Elwok, Enya, Ista, Megalopis, Panaross (entered from rejection), Somalo, and Wayshield.

gums—Demons often involved with gum issues include Angelica (causes gum disease or infection), Belenkie, Cruknop, Encranedahl, Ezra (causes gum disease), Impa, Mraddoscore, Rotaerrad, Rotherod (causes gum disease/deterioration; manifested as a beetle), Seddel, Taipae (causes erosion in the gums), and Zoopool. See Ezra.

H

hair loss—Demons connected to hair loss include Bahri, Closper, Haruke (causes trichotillomania), Magid, Shana, Tabu (causes trichotillomania), and Tempal (its functions include alopecia).

hallucinations—Spirits linked to hallucinations include Menah, Parnex, and Seman.

Handsel—territorial spirit over Southern California; a destroyer that destroys with sickness; clogs the liver; manifested as a serpent in the liver.

hand tremors—Demons we frequently cast out that are linked to hand tremors include Basquez, Beirg, Gonch, Othar, Pulbhlous, Roomis, Vernday, and Zothar.

Harry Potter—Its works include disruption, chaos, migraines, the occult, and witchcraft.

hatred—Demons with this function include Abaddon, Abelechia (brings self-hatred), Abisiam (stirs up self-hatred), Acrubus, Agladon, Agnuse, Ahmigihad, Al, Alamo, Alazon, Allela, and Allienivus. See Abaddon.

heartburn—Demons associated with this condition include Aaron, Aguafur, Antilo, Aranoid, Arasmus, Artimus (also causes acid reflux), Babel (linked to disease and acid reflux), Bin, Blargy (whose works include digestive disorders), Bozo, Brahma, Butterworth, Carpa (stomach nerves, ulcers; very powerful; controls diseases and injuries of the central nervous system and spinal cord), Cephias, Charqe, Daemon, and Dan. See Aaron, Aranoid, Blargy, Bozo, Butterworth, and Daemeon.

heart disease—Demons linked to this condition include Abuki, Abundance, Afib, Ahul, Albert (causes heart murmur), Alheman, Amarcus, Amoz (linked to arrhythmia), Anaconda, Apollyon,

Apollyus, Archibald, Arista (causes irregular heartbeat), Arthur, Aughty, and Corinthia. See Abuki.

Hecate (pronounced Heck-a-tee)—ruler of witchcraft and sorcery; a succubus/incubus whose functions include sexual impurity and perversion, hallucinations, alcohol and nicotine addiction, and hatred; works with Amolias, Amonias, Ceronis, Flubiac, Paine, Wadreamunco, and Waterenonca. See incubus and succubus.

Heckel—Its works include mockery and autism; manifested as a slimy serpent playing with the emotions; said, "I am not a bird."

Hecoli—Its functions include feelings of worthlessness; gained access from sexual abuse in childhood.

Hector—territorial spirit that backs up Dumas; an incubus that came from Las Vegas; its functions include sexual perversion, tension, back pain, guilt, and shame; manifested as a roach; destroys relationships.

Hectos—Its functions include all kinds of infirmity, including diabetes, female problems, and cholesterol issues.

hepatitis—Associated demons include Alons (hepatitis C), Baphomet (hepatitis A), Belial (hepatitis C), Caleb (hepatitis C), Carr (hepatitis C), Crowl (hepatitis A), Elizabeth (hepatitis C), Esther (hepatitis C), Haveen, Havoc, Hepo (hepatitis C), Jesshar (hepatitis C), Johan (hepatitis C), Jonah (hepatitis C), Klenorg (hepatitis C), Laron (hepatitis C), Luminous, Meshan, Meshorg (hepatitis C), Miskaile, Neff (hepatitis A), Nema, Plutonia (hepatitis C), Rake, Rickla, Samhain, Shana, Schnell, Tick (hepatitis A), Vazanore (hepatitis C), Wotah, and Yanza. See Baphomet, Belial, Elizabeth, and Samhain.

Hexus—causes to lie; linked to insanity, fear, addiction, and autism; a scorpion spirit; it said, "We control him."

high cholesterol—Demons we have cast out that are associated with this condition include Andion, Furtelant, Hamuth, Hectos, Jade, Jedda, Kahutu, Kantu, Pedrick (manifested as a leprechaun), and Peter. See Hectos and Peter.

Hiram Abiff—a leviathan that kills, destroys, and causes sickness; its functions include jealousy; linked to Freemasonry.

homosexuality—The following are some of the more common demons we have cast out in relation to this issue: Abnon, Alazar, Albert, Anon, Artemus, Arubia, Babel, Binah, Black Raven, Caldi, Candruas, Cantrol, Cervello, Eckimon, Elavar, Fornicashon, Frilel, Hank, Hecate, Herberta, Herod (lesbianism), Hinoth, Holol, Homo, Homos, Horalshka, Jefreo (lesbianism), Jopdah, Kackal (linked to AIDS), Keko, Kellentus, Kinsau, Laggot, and Savyor. See lesbianism.

hopelessness—Spirits associated with hopelessness include Adems, Agog, Angus, Argoso, Alastor, Azorian, Beldon, Buzzel, Calamari, Chicowski, Cobe, Coda, Costamogen, Daisha, Dominique, Drageier, Falon, Genocias, Gladys, Haman, Hexatar, Hosiah, Jahar, Kali/Cali, Karpesh, Lanton, Linear, Lorealbus, MaHa Bone, Malé (caused the person to have no will to live), Manaston, Manus, Meka, Mennom, Mitch, Morey, Moses, Narbesh, Navolian, Relon, Rhama, Sackon, Saltin, Saylic, Septune, Siphor, Sumsa, Sykula, Tallorous, Teron, Tolittle, Tonai, Tono, Trojan, Umalak, Watchu, Xanthan, Yacca, Zanntone, Zebiah, and Zolsher. See Kali/Cali, MaHa Bone, and Xanthan.

Horus—the all-seeing third eye of Freemasonry; always located in the pineal gland; its works include fear, anger, rejection, confusion, disorder, false hope/promises, depression, doubt, unbelief, bitterness, revenge, addiction, rape, nearsightedness, arthritis, acid reflux, autoimmune disorders, and IBS; works with Orion, Osiris, or Isis; permission gained through involvement in New Age religion, Unity church, and Freemasonry; manifested as a purple eye and a falcon; Heru is the Egyptian name for Horus.

humiliation—This is a work of many demons, including Anthrop, Blacksnog, Belittle, Fuqua, Godspel, Gudwaspi, Noestra, Patos (manifested as a duck), Piner, Ridicule, and Zorron.

Hysteria—said, "I came from hysterectomy." See fear.

I

Ichabod—means "the glory is departed" (1 Sam. 4:22); an incubus whose works include anger, fear, infirmity, cervical cancer, heaviness, and fragile X syndrome. See incubus.

Ignacius—Its works include fear and depression; manifested as a scarab beetle; gained permission through Catholicism and Freemasonry.

incest—Spirits whose works involve incest include Ammon, Azul, Celon, Dracon, Dvorcek, Ecala, Gogeth, Halibus, Hamish, Harpool, Heldini, Holul, Honnard, Hool, Iraneus, Laban, Luther, Mamool, Mary Magdalene, Moab, Oshime, Paipul, Papal, Papool, Papul, Paulus, Qubis, Sea Breeze, Shiam, Sinclair, Strider, Succoth, Vakkai, Voltar, Vorgon, Zander, and Zune.

incubus—from the Latin *incubare*, meaning "to lie upon"; a demon in male form supposed to lie upon sleepers, especially women, in order to have sexual intercourse with them. Other demons associated with this type of spirit include Able, Akmont, Alfatore, Ammon, Ananais, Androsep (entered through sexual abuse), Aperepus, Aphrodite, Balo (pronounced Bay-lo), Baruth, Bella, Benjamin, Bilbo, Bomulus, Celtic, Crab Fingers (its function includes masturbation in females), Dagon, Daniel, Delpha, Desiree, Diamonte, El Donna, Ezepahra, Finus, Hagar, Hector, and Herod. See Crab Fingers, Dagon, El Donna, and Hector.

infertility—Demons whose works involve infertility include Baal, Belatalmason (causes barrenness), Belial, Belsha (also linked to barrenness), Claudius, Culdone, Dane, Daniel, Dreyfus, Herod, Maranx, Mohon, Molech/Moloch, Raid, Sahiba, Salasal, Saritol, and Wil. See Daniel and Molech/Moloch.

Infidel—Freemasonry spirit whose functions include adultery.

infirmity—Spirits known for attacking with sickness include Adrian, Akbar, Alpha, Altura, Aphrodor, Athena, Babel, Bala (causes hernia and tumors), Baltashar (causes autoimmune disorders), Borishaba (its works include sickness of all kinds), Chadnoose, Garvor (linked especially to colon issues), Keri (its works include illness and death, and coughing), and Termination (over terminal diseases). See Woteige.

insanity—Demons involved in this type of mental illness include Balca (brings confusion and depression), Bartha, Impriss, Legion, Marty, Phillipson, Santibulon (linked to OCD), Shamon El, Snalcius, Willard, Winchell, Winton, and Zaba. See Legion, Shamon El, and Zaba.

insecurity—Spirits associated with insecurity include Abid, Aelon, Alexander, Amaly, Cable, Camen, Cameron, Cuma, Delinah, Demathus, Diana, Dido, Egore, Espont, Felix, Fibul, Flabie, Gaelic, Gordia, Gotha, Leeasuna, Maude, Onyx, Pithu, Pushan, Quan, Rashoal, Rona, Santibulon (causes OCD), Sardis, Satyr, Seaman, Selestia, Sharaba, and Zig. See Alexander, Cameron, and Satyr.

insignificance—A primary demon that makes people feel insignificant is Correctar, whose name suggests its function: It makes a person feel insignificant, brings condemnation, and tells the person they can't do anything right.

insomnia—Spirits that can rob people of sleep include Comachan (a driving spirit that causes restlessness), Cordfornlesse, Egles, Falek, Flabashan, Garnet, Iclama, Masshellert, Seman, Shectphar, Shevellert, Steven, Tum, and Xavier.

insult—A spirit associated with having a sharp, critical tongue toward others is Kapont.

intellectual disabilities—a function of Carrie Da Carious, Nangeeshanwong (also linked to disorder, ADD, Taoism, and Buddhism), Richard, Shockadula (causes Down syndrome), and Thomas.

intellectualism—linked to Germblati, whose works include false doctrine.

Interna—located in the stomach; its works include destruction and all sickness, particularly diverticulitis, hypertension, asthma, and ulcers; manifested as a squid.

intestinal problems—associated with Bruno (a leviathan), Meck (causes bleeding; gained permission from doubt), Shehan (brings cancer), Testaphile (its functions include lactose intolerance and intestinal blockage), and Zefna (causes pain; gained permission from drug use). See colon.

intimacy thieves—These include Albert, Amalek, Angie, Archer, Arturo, Ashteroth, Baal, Barrabus, Beelzebub, Buttercup, Cheryl, Clammer, Cloarol, Crymore, Delphi, and Dorcus. See Baal, Beelzebub.

Ishtar—territorial spirit; a relationship robber whose works include guilt, whoredom, fear, rejection, abandonment with confusion, suicide, remorse with guilt, profanity, and devious thoughts; gained permission from Druid ancestry; works with Ashdar, Aschtart, Astarte, Ashtoreth, Astar, Hagar, Kali/Cali, Queen of Heaven, Shalabar, Shalamar, Simeramus, Tomar, Turnstile, Venus, Zacar, and Zomar.

Isis—Egyptian goddess who is the wife and sister of Osiris; works under Osiris; linked to the all-seeing eye of Freemasonry; its works include anger, rage, revenge, poverty, mockery, heart disease, distraction from the purposes of God, fear, guilt, shame, and strife.

isolation—a function of Agess, Asa, Chase, Chikkeewa, Crymore, Edemagar, Elgir, Felix, Hondu, Islandic, Jamul, Janessu, Leper, Leuis, Lock, Lyric, Micasay, Michael, and Morpheus.

itching—See Baal. We also have cast out a spirit called Suswaney that causes itching and gained access through rejection.

J

Jabez—unrelated to the biblical Jabez; a territorial spirit over Indiana; occupies the mind; is a peace robber; its functions include turmoil and anger; gained permission through Amish religious practice.

Jachin—a controller and protector of the demonic kingdom; steals sanity; its works include mockery, depression, bipolar disorder, headache, and pressure in the forehead; has manifested as a hawk in the hypothalamus; gained permission through Freemasonry.

Jack—is the Jackal; a joy robber that said, "I jack her joy"; linked to confusion, hardening of the arteries, and heart disease.

Jackal—a territorial spirit of mockery and hatred whose functions include pornography, blasphemy, and questioning God's Word; mocks/mimics spiritual gifts, especially prophecy in dreams and visions. The jackal (the animal) has long been the subject of superstition about death and evil spirits. The ancient Egyptians believed a jackal-headed god called Anubis guided the dead to those who judged their souls.1 Such beliefs were probably encouraged by the jackal's cleverness, nocturnal habits, eerie howling, and scavenging.

Jackson—a civil war spirit and benefits thief whose works include suicide, ADD, migraines, fear, depression, and control; has manifested as an armadillo and a lizard.

Jacob—a territorial spirit over High Island, Texas; linked to false hope/assurance, pornography, fear, anger, bitterness, disorders of the thyroid and metabolism, poor self-esteem, nightmares, arachnophobia (fear of spiders), rejection, and TMJ; comes in dreams with a smothering sensation; a succubus in the emotional heart and thoughts; its twin is called Israel and is linked to hepatitis C, liver damage, confusion, ovarian and uterine cysts, suicide, depression, bipolar disorder, and hormone imbalance.

Jaha—Its works include rejection.

Jahamm—Its works include rejection.

Jahar—Its functions include depression and hopelessness.

Jaharigan—Its functions include poverty; has manifested as an eel in the stomach.

Jahary—linked to alcoholism; has manifested as a serpent with venom in the mind.

Jahaya—Its works include rejection; has manifested as a serpent everywhere in the body.

Jahaz—Its functions include torment.

Jahbulon—Its works include Freemasonry curses.

Jambres—linked to depression; manifested as a viper with venom of depression and despair. Jannes and Jambres are the names of the Egyptian magicians who resisted Moses (2 Tim. 3:8; Exod. 7:11, 22). According to the Jamieson-Fausset-Brown Bible Commentary, Jannes is from the Abyssinian language and means a trickster, and Jambres means a juggler.2

Janeesa—linked to sexual torment; said, "I single one out for sexual abuse and torment" and "I'm like El Donna"; a dark figure with a cape riding a black horse and carrying a shield.

Jannes—territorial spirit over Syria; its function is described in 2 Timothy 3:8 (MEV): "Now as Jannes and Jambres resisted Moses, so these also resist the truth, men of corrupt minds and worthless concerning the faith."

Jasarus—linked to fear, Freemasonry, and enlarged prostate; manifested as a rat in the genitals.

Jasbar—territorial spirit over Oklahoma whose works include anger and angry outbursts; manifested as a lizard in the throat.

Jasbeth—Its works include fear and headaches; manifested as a constrictor in the head.

Jasimine—territorial spirit over Greece whose functions include sexual torment, lust, frigidity, sexual perversion of all kinds, and procrastination; involved in causing ovarian cysts, colon cancer, and fibromyalgia; blurs vision; manifested as an octopus; wanted to be known as king; gained permission through pornography.

Jasmal—territorial spirit whose works include confusion; manifested as a bee buzzing through the mind.

Jason—territorial spirit over the Eastern coast of the United States; its works include all fear, anger, sadness, doubt, guilt, and shame; a commander that manifests as a spider linked to infirmity, namely diabetes, hypoglycemia, heart disease, fibroid tumors, nerve damage in the hands, asthma, and arthritis.

Jasper—territorial spirit over Scotland, Mississippi, and Johnson County, Texas; linked to guilt, shame, death, confusion, unbelief, bestiality, and cancer; may be located in the reproductive organs; manifested as a seat in a high place and a brown bear; gained permission through Freemasonry, and in Mississippi entered through abortion; a reminding spirit that said, "I'm here to pass along the will of my master."

Jeffrey—territorial spirit over Texas (under Sarcan); destroys with lust; brought tightness in the chest; linked to heart disease and Freemasonry; associated with Marcus and Jedadiah (a big-time lust spirit whose works include poverty). See Sarcan.

Jehogah—territorial spirit over Hurst, Texas; linked to depression and jealousy; over Damon and a brother to Cameron, which is a territorial spirit over Fort Worth, Texas; works with Apollyon. See Apollyon, Cameron, and Damon.

Jehosaphat—territorial spirit named Splendor at creation that now does the opposite; its works include havoc, criticism, torment with confusion, frustration, ruination, control, rejection, unworthiness, control, manipulation, lust, anxiety, and fear of schizophrenia; a dragon spirit from Mormon ancestry; affects breathing; linked to migraines and pain in the back and shoulders; alters metabolism; kills with cancer; works with Woteige. See Woteige.

Jehosopher—Its functions include sexual fantasies and fetishes; manifested as a spider in the brain.

Jephazel—named Jacob ("he is loved") at creation; now linked to suicide; manifested as an octopus on the skullcap.

Jeremiah—name given at creation to a territorial spirit whose works include hurt, confusion, warts, cysts, hypertension, pain, discomfort, depression, disordered eating, insecurity, and choking sensations; manifested as a bullfrog.

Jeremy—territorial spirit most likely related to Freemasonry, confusion, and depression; a serpent spirit that caused a hole in the heart, heart palpitations, disordered eating, anxiety, and panic; manifested as a cockroach. The name it was given at creation is Jeremiah.

Jerub—manifests as a frog; causes wart growth on the eyes. Jerub Baal is the name Gideon's father gave to him after he destroyed the altar to Baal. The people were angry with Gideon for destroying their altar, and Gideon's father told them not to harm him, saying, "Let Baal contend with him" (Judg. 6:32, NIV); Jerub Baal means "let Baal contend." It is basically saying if Baal is so strong, and if he's even real at all, let him fight Gideon himself.

Jezebel—territorial spirit that disrupts order of the home, destroys families, robs relationships, challenges true authority, mocks the message of God, destroys through dissension, challenges truth with cunning deception, and presents a false holiness; its works include rebellion; a know-it-all that seeks to rule; its greatest enemy is true spiritual authority. Permission came through a soul tie. Its functions include anger with hatred, lust, frigidity, control, confusion, and chaos; manifested as a lumpy worm in the mind; has caused tumors, hypoglycemia, migraines, and multiple sclerosis.

Jezreel—territorial spirit that affects the tongue and swallowing; causes mouth disorders and speech development delay; its works include control, desecration, lesbianism, violence, and sadness; an incubus that floats and destroys; manifested as a beetle in the mind; may be the same spirit as Jezareel. See incubus.

Job—territorial spirit that oppresses Indiana; a scorpion captain and a sleep robber, it brings anxiety, panic, misery, suffering, mental anguish, fear, infirmity, addictions with infirmity, caffeine addiction, headaches, deception, heart disease, diabetes, and depression;

the king of all feelings, it had an evil face and was riding a horse with armor; over Fumar, Nic, and Rojo.

Jocleen—Its works include perversion, attacks on self-esteem, condemnation, and mockery; linked to Freemasonry.

Jolt—a leviathan that brings anger/rage toward children, destroying family and marital relationships; also brings self-condemnation. See leviathan.

Jonah—Its functions include lust with filth, pornography, sexual perversion, rejection, dissatisfaction, unthankfulness, and unforgiveness; kills and destroys emotions; manifested as a liver beetle and causes diabetes and hepatitis C; also manifested as a wolf.

Jonas—Its works include anger, strife, rebellion, and sexual attraction to men; gained permission through embarrassment in childhood, and anger; manifested as a bird in the reproductive organs and as a knight.

Jonathan—territorial spirit and an oracle; its works include false prophecy, hatred, emotional hurt, confusion, self-condemnation, and an imaginary lover; an incubus and a scorpion spirit, it causes tumors in the uterus, papillomas (benign tumors such as warts), and bacteria/viruses in the blood; the doorway to its entrance was sex out of wedlock. See Anthwerp, which may be another name for this spirit.

Joshua—high-ranking territorial spirit over Kingsport, Tennessee; steals courage; a scorpion of fear whose works include anger, condemnation, witchcraft, and confusion; manifested as cat eyes and bats' eyes; entered through spells and incantations; falls in rank under "Sammy," which is likely Samhain.

Judas—territorial spirit linked to addiction, guilt, shame, rejection, rebellion, mockery, depression, and poverty; manifested as a roach in the tummy; its works also include rebellion, control, headaches, Raynaud's disease, Barrett's esophagus (which is linked to chronic heartburn and can turn into cancer of the esophagus), colon and uterine cancer, and other colon disorders; manifested as a lizard in the head; gained permission through Catholic ancestry and bad financial stewardship; rang bell in attempt to call other territorial spirits for help.

judgmentalism—A primary spirit we have cast out in relation to judgment is Hama; its name given at creation meant "harmless," but it now causes emotional harm through words; it is also linked to criticism. Other demons we have cast out in relation to this issue call themselves Chintar, Cristendol, Empire, and Joab.

K

Kaballah—a serpent spirit that ruins with alcohol; it gained permission through childhood abuse. Other variations of this name are Kabbala, Cabbala, Cabala, and Qabalah.

Kabbala—The primary demon associated with this form of Jewish mysticism is Baal, which brings doubt, confusion, and false healing gifts; it gained permission through kabbalah studies.

Kali (or Cali)—The East Indian goddess of death, this is a demonic ruler connected with the curse of death and destruction; comes in by reading books on Eastern religions; a scorpion spirit of death whose works include nervousness, depression, suicide, and abortion; a fire god, it is linked to kidney stones that caused burning pain (in one case it manifested as a ball of fire), child abuse, incest, and destruction through infirmity; it has manifested as a beetle in the stomach and causes Lyme disease and all illness, including end-stage renal disease.

Kama—Its works include lust.

Keltip—Its functions include defilement; manifested as a tiger in the will; gained permission through childhood sexual abuse.

Ketev—a demonic spirit whose works include bitterness and destruction. Historically, the twenty-one days from the seventeenth of Tammuz to the ninth of Av represented a notable time of bitterness and destruction for the Jews; according to the rabbis, the demon that prevails during this time is also called Ketev.3

Keywor—linked to bedwetting; causes physical pain in the neck.

kidney diseases—Demons associated with various kidney diseases include Akeem (kidney stones), Apollyon (kidney failure), Barak (cancer), Caleb (kidney stones and kidney failure), Daemon (polycystic kidney disease), Deckamon (kidney failure), Garvin (posterior urethra), Halla (kidney failure), Jessuba (kidney failure), Kali (kidney stones), Labadesh (kidney failure), Laven (kidney failure from diabetes), MaHa Bone (kidney stones), Nakata (kidney infection), Pluto (kidney failure), Renny (kidney failure), Sarcheem (manifested as an eel in kidneys/bladder; entered from lupus), Shular (kidney failure), and Temparnium (kidney malfunction). See Apollyon, Barak, Daemon, and Kali/Cali.

Komodo—an incubus whose works include depression with fatigue, weariness, and procrastination. See also O'Reilly and Sally. Able to grow up to ten feet long, the Komodo dragon is the largest lizard in the world. They are largely restricted to a few small islands in Indonesia, where they rule supreme. They can run almost as fast as a dog for short stretches, but they typically ambush their prey. Once bitten, their prey is brought down shortly by the deadly bacteria in the Komodo dragon's mouth. See incubus.

Konga—territorial spirit that has manifested as a huge pterodactyl; said, "I go anywhere I want" and "I'm the king."

Kundalini—yoga spirit that dwells at the base of the spine; always gains access from practicing yoga; is sometimes a nest of serpents; its works include guilt, shame, and religious control; works with Virgo and Sagitarius. There are common side effects, or demonic symptoms, reported by those who have invited these demons: involuntary jerks, tremors, shaking, itching, tingling, crawling sensations especially in the arms and legs, energy rushes or feelings of electricity circulating through the body, heart palpitations, intense heat (sweating) or cold, visions or sounds, periods in which particular emotions become dominant for short periods of time, depression, pressure inside the skull, headache, and involuntary suspension of breath.

Kyle—Its works include rejection, feeling unloved, suicide, and hopelessness; manifested as a scorpion in the emotions; gained permission through masonic involvement.

Kyme—linked to alcohol addiction; manifested as a porcupine in the mind.

Kyra—Its functions include fatigue.

Kyro—a protector of the demonic kingdom; manifested as a wolf.

L

lack—The following demons are associated with lack: Mimilo, Punta, Vernon, Olet, and Lackabus (an informant, raven, messenger, spy, secret agent; it gathers and passes information). See financial lack.

lactose intolerance—A common demon we encounter related to this issue is Testaphile, a blocking spirit whose works also include intestinal blockage and who manifested as armor.

Lance—a scorpion spirit whose works include addiction, pleasure through drugs, confusion, suicide, and frigidity; manifested as a goat with horns; gained permission through Metallica's music; worked for Absalom.

Lancelot—a territorial spirit over Britain; its works include fear of failure, addiction, and self-destruction.

Larificas—Its works include sexual perversion; was located in the stomach; gained permission from ancestral incest.

learning disabilities—Spirits associated with this issue include Aceus (ADD; gained permission from cocaine use), Araba (dyslexia), Baphomet (ADD), Bo (dysgraphia), Ezelle (ADD), Backeraba (ADD), Bajmar (ADHD), Barnabus (ADD), Beelzebub (ADD; learning difficulties and disabilities [LDD]), Bennett (ADHD), Bermist, Blanche (dyslexia), Bodosom (ADHD), Calipso (dyslexia), Cardo (ADD), Ceph (ADD), Cornell (ADD and confusion), Daemeon (ADD), Daimon (ADHD and dyslexia), Delbown (ADD and LDD), Delores (ADD and dyslexia), Demus (ADD and dysgraphia; manifested as a snake sent to confuse the brain; gained permission through alcoholism). See Baphomet, Backeraba, Beelzebub, and Daemeon.

Legion—territorial spirit over marshes/lowlands and Little Rock, Arkansas; its works include idolatry, control, rebellion, gossip, rejection, and deceit; it is a destroyer of anointing and a serpent of confusion.

Legionnaires' disease—associated with a spirit called Ledsi.

lesbianism—The following spirits are associated with lesbianism: Babel, Baphomet, Binah, Cantrol, Gamleel, Italiana, Jefreo, Kifus, Kin, Kinsau, Lemnich, Liason, Mezza, Musswal, Pegus, Prevah, Ramon, Sabel, Savyor, Selenco, Snogg, and Tasha. See Baphomet and homosexuality.

leviathan—This is not a demon name; leviathan is a type, like a serpent or scorpion spirit. It is the king of the children of pride, and its works include mourning, spiritual darkness, arrogance, and spiritual pride (using logic, rationalization, and justification to know the things of God). It is also the king of doubt and blocks the mind, hinders spiritual growth, distracts and disturbs concentration during Bible study or prayer, causes weariness/sleepiness in worship services, and smothers the breath of God with pride and arrogance. It is linked to the misappropriation of gifts and talents. A huge serpent coiled in the abdomen; dislikes Psalm 74:13–14 (NKJV): "You divided the sea by Your strength; You broke the heads of the sea serpents in the waters. You broke the heads of Leviathan in pieces, and gave him as food to the people inhabiting the wilderness"; causes brooding, melancholy, depression, gloominess, irascibility, mental dejection, mania, and digestive problems; in the lungs, it robs spiritual breath (Job 41:1). Associated with Bohemus, Buckley, Cain, Calp, and Doubtking. In Jewish folklore, Rahab is the name of a sea demon, a dragon of the waters. Known as the "ruler of the sea," Rahab is responsible for shaking the waters and producing big waves; he is also responsible for the roaring of the sea. This name originally designated the primordial abyss, the water dragon of darkness and chaos, and so is comparable to Leviathan and Tiamat. Rahab later became a particular demon, an inhabitant of the sea, especially associated with the Red Sea and sometimes associated with Leviathan.[4] See Rahab.

Lilith—territorial spirit whose works include guilt, shame, fear, headaches, and lust; manifested as a beautiful woman. In Jewish folklore, Lilith is associated with a class of Mesopotamian female demons called lilītu, which is often translated as "night monster."[5] Its evil especially targets children and women in childbirth. Lilith appears as a screech owl in the Bible (Isa. 34:14).

liver issues—Spirits associated with disorders of the liver include Abigail (cancer), Ariel (cancer), Baphomet (hepatitis A), Chala, Clabence (from alcohol abuse), Crowl (hepatitis A), Eggthus, Herbocius, Jiad, Laven (from diabetes), Liver Beetle (cancer; manifested as a snake; gained permission through stress), Lucifer (cancer), Nicean, Polymus, Rackon, Scorpio (cancer), Thoran, Tick (hepatitis A), Vincent (cancer), and Warrior (cancer). See Baphomet and hepatitis.

Logarith—Meaning "God's reason," it was the name given to Abaddon at creation. Now a demonic king that manifested as a gargoyle-looking creature, he said, "I am the king of fear," and he brings violence and destruction; works with Yaba; its works include pride, bipolar disorder, and fear in the mind. His name is used interchangeably with Apollyon.

loneliness—Demons associated with loneliness include Annanias, Bangle, Chase, Colly, Crabby, Declongie, Felix, Formadian, Fred, George, Higbiggler, Iaoli, Joshamath, Keith, King, Michael, Negreel, Osiris, Phiton, Psykilion, Rathana, Rosemary, Oxsaya, Shaltaie,

Shata, Sindle, Tension, Tippan, Tishtog, Tomius, and Zanil. See Osiris.

love (false)—Spirits associated with false love include Androimoda, Ashtaroth, Asmodeus, Diana, Hecate, Rosemary, Tamotha, and Venus. See Ashtaroth and Hecate.

love quenchers—See relationship robbers and intimacy thieves.

Lucifer—Many spirits claim this name, but they are not the anointed cherub; a liar, a deceiver, an antichrist spirit, a peace robber, and a gift/ministry robber; a destroyer with deception; demanded, "Who are you?" during a deliverance session; a cause of migraines and a producer of pain, fear, and doubt; associated with rheumatic fever and heart murmurs; said, "I organize and communicate between here and the heavenlies"; manifested as a big black panther, a dog in the heart, and a wolf in the mind; is behind all fear and all addiction; gained permission from Freemasonry in ancestry; brings torment with guilt from sexual fantasy/perversion; linked to heart damage due to hypertension as well as ingrown toenails, foot/nail fungus, liver cancer, depression, anxiety, and panic; a serpent spirit and a dragon.

Lucifer (not Satan)—said his territory "is anywhere I want" in the world; encountered once trying to protect the kingdom of a satanic ritual abuse victim; said, "She is my bride; she belongs to me"; claimed to be the anointed cherub and not afraid of Michael; said he did not need permission to access the woman receiving deliverance and that he would obey the command to leave my home but not to leave her. He did, however, obey the commands when she confessed, "I am redeemed by the blood of Jesus Christ." It was an extremely rare encounter.

Lucifer (not Satan)—territorial spirit over Georgia; a destroyer through sex.

Lucifer (not Satan)—territorial spirit over southern Oklahoma.

lung conditions—Demons associated with lung issues include Agra (asthma), Anmus (lung infection), Athrop (asthma), Azeta (asthma), Azbel (asthma), Azlon (bronchitis), Azmil (asthma), Balcat (asthma), Bandoor (asthma), Baphomet (emphysema), Becola (from smoking), Beelzebub (asthma), Beine (asthma), Belgar (asthma), Belial (cancer), Bernardi, Boabar (asthma), Bolathaz (asthma), Boli (asthma), Brock (emphysema), Chester, Cheznel (allergies/asthma), Cilie (cancer), Cromesh (pneumonia), Cruxlan (bronchial tube problems), Cyrus (asthma), Deptamler (asthma), Derbine (pain from smoking and pneumonia), Elcon, Elmir (asthma), Emalt (emphysema), Emphessia (emphysema), Gamreeth, Ghico, Gormania (a constrictor cutting off the breath), Jaboc, Jason (asthma), Jehosophat, Jezreeca (asthma/congestion), Kattamu (pulmonary fibrosis), Kelzar (bronchitis, asthma), Lectrose (asthma), Lee (cancer), Lio, Macon (emphysema), Mayca (shortens breath), Merdon (asthma), Meriham, Mertham (asthma), Mesople (asthma), Miah (asthma), Monai (asthma), Montaba (cancer), Muco (coughing, vomiting; gained permission through interferon), Mur (asthma), Musalex (bronchitis), Myront, Nic, Octos (coughing, congestion), Ontak (asthma), Osiris (emphysema), Ra (cancer), Rahab (bronchitis), Reja, Riley (damage from nicotine), Rufka, Sancor (cancer), Shanar (asthma), Shibboleth (emphysema), Shincole (asthma), Shincole (asthma), Solon (asthma; gained permission from fear), Syrius, Tagasus (affects bronchial tubes), Talon (emphysema), Tapazoid (lung consumption; a bacteria in the lungs), Tarantus (asthma), Teryalpem (asthma), Tilanjia (asthma), Toopé (pronounced like toupee), Tora, Tresbache (asthma), Tubal-Cain (emphysema), Whezomer (asthma), Worker (asthma), Yakast (pneumonia), Zar (asthma), Zeparia (asthma), Zinueos (asthma), and Ziro (allergies, asthma, and bronchitis).

lupus—Associated demons include Anmus, Baltashar, Barak, Kilazimine, Macurtle, Meshawa (gained permission from anger), Navian, Sarceem, and Sarcheem (an eel in kidneys/bladder).

lust—There are too many to list, but chief among the spirits associated with lust is Marcus; others include Jeffery, Moab, Hecate, Abacus, Abaddon, Abar, Abid (attracts lust spirits in others), Able, Abylonius, Acermon, Adias, Adic, Agneau, Alacot (masturbation), Alatro, Alcon, Alecia, Alee (a succubus), Allenorgal, Alsce, Amilech, Anach, Annus, Anser, Anton, Analee, Anthwerp (sex addiction), Antwon, Apec, Aramus, Armand, Aro, Arthur, Aruall, Asmodeus, Asna, Astorik, Atruea, and more. See Abaddon and Marcus.

lycanthropy—a psychiatric state in which the patient believes he is a wolf.

lying—All demons lie, but spirits frequently associated with this function include Barbossa, Caiphus, Cleo, Pipytheus, Pytho, Belial, Disquias, Embrine, Melco, Melson, Mislo, Pytho, Wrinkles (false religion), Zieteas (lies, confusion, distraction from truth; slightly twists the truth), Uz, Charleston, Mitre (gained permission from shame), Ramodon, Saan, Syth, Tony, Xavier, and Zeno.

Lyme disease—Associated demons include Abula, Baphomet, Habecka, Malek, Zenim, Ukum (desecrates with sickness; manifested as a mutated leech located in the adrenal glands), Shosho (the Borrelia bacteria appears as a serpent through a microscope; is with Habecka, a serpent with venom and constriction); Abuki (causes "dog tapeworms" in people, damages ovaries, and causes other female problems), and Havila (a squid spirit in the bladder, kidneys, and bones; in the bones with arthritis). See Abuki and Baphomet.

Lymph—territorial spirit over the United States; causes pain.

Lympha—brings perverted thoughts; gateway was abortion; manifested as an alligator.

Lymphaluma—linked to breast and liver cancers; manifested as a snake in the breast.

lymph glands—Associated spirits include Oseol, Seclosium, and Taile.

lymph nodes—Spirits associated with problems with the lymph nodes include Bosea, Bocia, Bozo, Blomco, Butterworth, and Blargy.

M

Macabe—describes himself as a Maccabee but has no connection with those ancient Jewish martyrs; its works include anger, headaches, and TMJ; manifested as a serpent in the head; permission was ancestral Freemasonry.

MaHa Bone—may be the highest ranking of the Freemasonry spirits; will usually have others in his kingdom, including Samhain, Baphomet, Horus, Isis, Osiris, Ra, and Baamop. See Baamop, Baphomet, Horus, Isis, Osiris, Ra, and Samhain.

Man-Hating—brings contempt; works with Jezebel and Zin. See Jezebel.

mania—a ruling prince of depression and mental illness; large kingdom of destruction through depression; associated with Maduba and Mia.

manic depression—associated with Jezebel (linked to bipolar disorder), the Mason, Manny, Marty, Split, Winton (brings bipolar spirits), and Wrench (linked to bipolar disorder). See bipolar disorder and Jezebel.

manipulation—Demons associated with this practice include Aflack, Astor, Azoria, Bunion (whose works include lying to control others), Camon, Carpus, Dragulae, Guardian, Jezreel, Kyeshe, Lothor, Magnor, Mardia, Mari, Matuis, Mezwich, Tyra/Rebecca, Sheba, Sharon, Starak, and Turk. See also witchcraft and Zor.

Marcus—a chief of lust; also associated with unbelief and abandonment.

marijuana—Demons associated with marijuana addiction include Felix (whose works also include nicotine addiction) and Selbek. See Felix.

martyrdom (self)—Bianca is a demon whose works include anger and self-persecution.

Mason—Its works include fear of breaking down at railroad crossings, control, manipulation, doubt, unbelief, infirmity, headaches, rejection, confusion, and dizziness; linked to Freemasonry spirit; manifested as a mason jar; said, "I call that which is as though it were not."

Mason, The—Its works include fear and witchcraft; gained permission from membership in the Rebekah Lodge (part of the Odd Fellows fraternal organization).

Masonic curses—These are the most common curses apart from ancestral curses; affect health in many areas. Associated demons include Baphomet, Antichrist, Micha, Macha, Shibboleth, Jachin, Tubal-Cain, MaHa Bone, Malachi (brings depression), Hiram Abiff (brings sickness), Azy (covers with blackness), Micah, Joppa, Jahbulon, and the Knights Templar, Grand Wizard, Sashqua (fear), Macon (the prince of disease), Hecate (a ruler involved in female witchcraft, sorcery, and the underworld powers), Diana, Rosemary, Venus (involved in witchcraft, supernatural sex desires, sexual false love), Frank (may be from gold, frankincense, and myrrh; Frank rules in the bipolar kingdom under Tamar), Lucas (brings jealousy; said, "I see swords and blades"), Jezebel (linked to witchcraft, manipulation, and female dominance, and destroys proper order in the home), Evil Eye, Third Eye, Ra, Attuor, and Horus (causes injury and harm and is associated with jealousy and witchcraft). See Antichrist, Baphomet, Evil Eye, Hecate, MaHa Bone, Rosemary, Third Eye of Freemasonry, Tubal-Cain, Venus, and witchcraft.

Masonic Rosicrucians—The full name of this body is Societas Rosicruciana in Civitatibus Foederatis Masonensis, which is Latin for "the Masonic Rosicrucian Society in the United States." The governing body is the High Council, headed by a Supreme Magus who serves for a three-year term. The state body is the college, headed by a Chief Adept who serves for life. As a rule, there is no more than one college per state. A college may contain a maximum of seventy-two members. Members are Christian, Trinitarian Master

Masons who have distinguished themselves by exceptional scholastic achievement, research, or educational ability, or by unusual service to the Masonic fraternity. The Rosicrucian is a legendary and secretive order dating to the fifteenth or seventeenth centuries. It generally is associated with the symbol of the rose cross, which is also found in certain rituals beyond Craft (or Blue Lodge) Freemasonry. The Rosicrucian Order is viewed by many modern Rosicrucians as an inner worlds order, comprised of great "Adepts." When compared to human beings, the consciousness of these Adepts is like that of demigods.[6]

masturbation—Associated demons include Ballerdell, Blessedness, Culdone (also linked to infertility), Doozhan, Dumas (territorial prince that has manifested as a constrictor in the mind and brings depression), Eros, Gerithian, Jacque, Lechar, Levan, Meshal, Morbar, Molech, Reich, Rycher, and Seth. See Dumas, Molech/Moloch.

menopause—Related spirits include Harold (linked to hot flashes) and Joshishe (involved in early menopause).

menstruation—Demons involved in problems with menstruation include Anchor (brings torment and disorders of the menstrual cycle), Ammon, Belial, Cudulla, Harold (hot flashes), Pushan (PMS), Scropola, Serf, Tabitha (cramps), and Vegamarian (PMS). See Ammon and Belial.

Mercury—territorial spirit that said, "I travel in and out of the churches" and "I've got my business; you've got yours. Leave me alone."

Meriham—territorial spirit assigned to the family; under Jezebel; involved in man-hating and family disorder.

metabolism—Demons that affect the metabolism include Quazar (a spider of pain and lies, located in the thyroid), Lectern, Gibforth, Mixonella, Methastophalis, Partain (linked to metabolism disorder, a parasite in the colon, and polyps), Relos (its works include fear and overactive metabolism), Shushum, Washton (said, "I hold on to weight by slowing her metabolism"), and Ugo.

Metalica—Its works include suicide, pain, and addiction; manifested as metal taste in the mouth; may be related to the spirit Mercury. In ancient mythology, Mercury was a messenger-god associated with wealth, business, and storytelling/communication.

Mephistophales—Its works include confusion, doubt, and unbelief; manifested as a puppet with a mustache in its head; said, "I herd them all together" and "Just let me go"; gained permission through Freemasonry.

Micah—territorial spirit over the United States; its works include anger and isolation; also linked to headaches from tightening jaws and to sciatica; said, "I'm the big cheese"; manifested as a pterodactyl in the central nervous system and a beetle in the mesenteric vein. (The superior mesenteric vein is a blood vessel in the portal venous system that helps blood travel from the intestines to the liver.[7])

Micha—said, "I'm the librarian; I arrange the knowledge in his mind"; its works include separation/isolation through anger, rejection, sleep disorder, asthma, and allergies; a controller of thoughts with guilt and shame; manifested as an octopus and a bird in the head, causing a throbbing heart; gained access from reading false knowledge and Freemasonry curses; in a ruling trinity with Azy and Osiris. See Osiris.

Michael—means mighty; brings confusion; reports to Beelzebub; a prince in the bipolar kingdom linked to mental illness, depression, anxiety, schizophrenia, rejection, addiction to marijuana, pride, doubt, migraines, back problems, solitude, instability, learning disabilities, ADD, sexual perversion, cellulitis (bacteria), misery in the stomach, acid reflux, and salivary gland malfunction; a worship robber that has manifested as an alien, an octopus, a robin, a beast, a pterodactyl, a cockroach laying eggs, and a bug in the bloodstream; associated with Brock and Fumar; said, "I help the kingdom" and "I'm with El Wormo." See Beelzebub.

migraine headache—Associated demons include Abe, Abendiah, Abrahm, Adoff, Afar, Altheel, Angelika, Archibald, Argol, Azur, Azwrath (gained permission from anger), Bedestria, Bonacel, Meson, Drauness (brings drowsiness/sleepiness; gained access from an epidural), Bazel, Bombay, Bonton, Burnstiller, Cameron, Castro, Caten, Cleophilus, Creno, Donjere, Ebadia, Gibleh, and Zenus. See Baphomet, Burnstiller, Cameron, Duzzenorian, Jasbeth, and Michael.

mind control—The following demons are often involved when a person is dealing with mind control: Alato, Artyza, Blan, Captaintio, Coma, Cumnus (mind control; entered from Mahikari studies in Japan), Detimus, Green Hornet, Green Phantom, Karathon, Karpay, Louver, Meganosis, Megara, Moshabiek, Negaera, Nethanan, Oberion, Oratory (entered by curses; the third eye may be involved), Rapunzoe, Repnual, Seridiah, Shrim (transcendental meditation), Tamar (gained permission from a therapy group), Tisiphonel, Trasharaba, Tysel, Uleses, Verono, Veronu, and Voodoo (entered through rituals). See Tamar.

miscarriage—Demons associated with miscarriage include Anuthem, Baal, Beil, Belshazzar, Chlandry, Dane, Donasu (from rejection), Elizabeth, Eric, Halibus (tubular pregnancy), Iyon, Lodibar, Mohon, Molech/Moloch, Peptis, Phfrink, Rafael, Raid (also linked to infertility), Sar, Thorn, Torok, and Will. See Baal, Elizabeth, and Molech/Moloch.

misogyny—a woman-hater; often enters through hurt or disappointment from a woman; has gained permission from being given up at birth.

mitral valve prolapse—This heart condition is among the works of Baphomet, Elloriah, Hanka, Seth, and Tecumseh. See Baphomet.

Mitre—Its works include lying and shame; gained permission from pornography.

mixed messages—See Psychobabel.

Moisee—a witchcraft prince; associated with Witchdoctor (a friend of Moletha, sister to Tobitha, and patient of Keeshba).

Moishee—also associated with Witchdoctor; its functions include arthritis and fibromyalgia; manifested as a snail in the bone; gained permission after the person consulted a root doctor.

Moisheeba—a witchcraft prince over rage; also over Oisheeba, a prince of darkness.

Moitatri—Its functions include lust.

mojo—a voodoo curse; connected to witchcraft.

Moksheen—territorial spirit that brings a cloud of confusion; gained permission through Dungeons and Dragons game.

Molan—a serpent of rejection in the mind.

Molar—Its functions include eye problems; associated with Potato, a spirit whose works include depression, hypertension, and doubt.

Molech/Moloch—territorial spirit whose functions include child sacrifice, abortion, confusion, and physical abuse; its functions include abortion, female disorders, self-mutilation (cutting), death, suicide, destruction, sacrifice, self-condemnation, financial suffering, selfishness, lack of self-control, hypertension, fatigue, fire, child abuse, kidney stones, masturbation, dysmenorrhea, hysterectomy, fibromyalgia, and confusion; is a moth that eats away at self-esteem; said, "I destroy everything"; linked to Molech worship; is virtually always with Belial, Elizabeth, and Sedona. See Belial, Elizabeth, and Sadona/Sedona.

Molecha—a brother to Molech; functions include abortion and violent thoughts.

Moleesha—territorial witchcraft spirit in Indianapolis; linked to Druids.

mononucleosis—See Gacio and Rapscallion.

Mortae—said, "I am like Woteige; you've never seen me before"; its functions include premature death; gained permission after the person attended the Festival for the Dead in Argentina; manifested as a multiheaded serpent like Medusa attached in the center like a skullcap on top of the head; associated with Medusa (whose functions include memory loss; is similar to an octopus spirit but claims, "I'm worse than an octopus"). See Woteige.

multiple sclerosis—Demons associated with this illness include Kingway and Tekus.

N

nail-biting—influenced by Speed Demon (a prince that gained access from a 32nd-degree Freemasonry curse), Grith, Clotuser, and Dong (gained permission from fear).

neck problems—associated with Micah, Purple (a spirit that brings tightness in the neck), Hero, Elsinor (causes neck pain), Keywor (causes pain in the neck), Musta (pronounced Moo-sta; linked to herniated discs), Targo (brings pain), Timothy (brings pain), Hanara (linked to nerve, muscle, and disc damage in neck and back), Moulder, Joppa, Jehosophat, and Praterand (gained permission from unforgiveness). See Elsinor, Keywor, and Micah.

Nephasin—linked to occultic "hum" dreams; manifested as a gargoyle.

Neptune—a leviathan king; ruler of disorder; associated with Jezebel; an intimacy thief; brings fatigue and attacks self-esteem.

nightmares—Demons linked to nightmares include Abe, Alazon, Alchemist, Argyle, Arieba, Arno, Ashkurha, Bagang, Balaam, Baphomet, Belshar, Bobul, Bodosom, Bomanna, Bomulus, Bougaba, Calaba, Captain Lorio, Carlousma, Cassius, Chello, Chino, Chronicle, Cindy, Clophus, Dagon, Dampper, Daniel, Defor, Dominique, Donada, Dorna, Edom, Ela, Ephraim, Esason, Ezriel, Felix, Gage, Garmon, Gliddarde, Hait, Hanner, Heller, Hero, Ilia, Iris, Joya, Keldock, Kia, Klon, Klota, Lacrae, Lavada, Lemores, Lierettes, Lifandice, Lishou, Lobos, Lona, Luraan, Lusash, Malo, Mandermoth, Marcos, Masshellert, Merin, Miyndo, Molocka, Nectar, Nephasin,

Nexus, Olmec, Orkwright, Oxsaya, Perez, Poindexter, Pontus, Pribius, Prozel, Punjab, Quantro, Ralph, Ramiat, Ratcliff, Rei'al, Rison, Saboa, Samhain, Sara, Sartish, Sartoohe, Sasha, Seylon, Shectphar, Sierra, Sitsle, Sleeper Inkwell, Solo, Sodor, Syth, Tempest, Tempka, Tibu, Timok, Trazor, Troman, Tyberius, Uripedes, Valshious, Victor, Wonderful, Yetho, Zaccariee, Zarthros, and Ze. See Baphomet, Dagon, Daniel, Felix, and Samhain.

Nimo—Its works include suicide; associated with Asmodaus Suron, which brings fear, hopelessness, anxiety, migraines; manifested as a slug spitting pain; works with Juron.

Ninety-Nine—manifested as double nines in Osiris; part of the Egyptian kingdom. See Osiris and Horus.

Nismeth—a devouring prince; manifests as a panther and devours like a panther; associated with Devour (known for "ripping and tearing") and Grenco (devours).

Nomad—aims to make a person homeless; a wandering, driven, pacing, restless spirit; influences people to move from church to church; is Damon spelled backward; its works include gluttony and confusion (an eagle); robs acceptance; an excellent gatekeeper; associated with Jarthor and Nemoid, a prince of relationship destruction; another pacing, driving spirit; drives the addiction kingdom; also the territorial prince of the homeless.

nomadic—Demons linked to nomadic, wandering behavior include Gretchen, Gypsy, Impa, and Nomad. See Nomad.

Nunscé—territorial spirit over the southern portion of the African continent; is fed with fear; has manifested under the name Gorilla. When asked if he knew John Karl Davis (an African missionary friend), the demon said, "Yes, and I don't like him!"

O

obsession—Demons whose works are associated with obsession include Krulon, Precep, Steven, Scabby, Seher, Telmay, and

Trithon. See addiction, obsessive-compulsive disorder (OCD), and compulsion.

Obsessive—Its works include poverty and fear of rejection; worked for Ezra.

obsessive-compulsive disorder (OCD)—Demonic spirits that influence OCD include Belanja, Danaris, Dingus, Gilmar, Horad, Hunter, Kaleno, Krulon, Luther, Olan, Philon, Phinon, Renece, Steven, Stupido, Trion, Trithon, and Tyron.

One-Eye—linked to the occult and Isis, the Egyptian goddess, as well as Osiris and Horus. See Horus, Isis, and Osiris.

oppositional defiant disorder (ODD)—Spirits that influence this behavior include Dillon, Lunar, and Manchester, and they bring confusion and anger. ODD is a pattern of negativistic, hostile, and defiant behavior in children lasting at least six months during which four or more of the following are present: (1) loses temper, (2) argues with adults, (3) actively defies or refuses to comply with adults' requests or rules, (4) deliberately annoys people, (5) blames others for his or her mistakes or misbehavior, (6) touchy or easily annoyed by others, (7) angry and resentful, and (8) spiteful and vindictive. The disturbance in behavior causes clinically significant impairment in social, academic, or occupational functioning.

oppression—strongly linked to unforgiveness; spirits associated with this include Headi, Lamitha, Palo (which gained permission through kabbalah), and Ralph, a prince of oppression.

oral sex—Demons we frequently cast out related to this issue are Jasmine, incubus, and succubus. See incubus and succubus.

organism—Its works include female lust, masturbation, and sexual promiscuity.

Oriell—Its works include food addiction, gluttony, and fear of water; gained permission through Freemasonry. Another name may be O'Reily.

Orion—named Daystar at creation; a proud, beautiful, intellectual spirit. Its works include confusion, irascibility, mental dejection, sleep apnea, heart disease, diabetes, spiritual pride, fear, suicide, and false spiritual gifts; it has manifested as a squid in the pancreas; gained entrance through false worship in ancestry; also known as Purple Shield, which said, "I am the ruler of the belt and sword." Numerous spirits ending with "on" are in his dominion: Byron, Dargon, Darion, Demon, Juron, Keron, Kiljon, Kilron, Maxon, Nexon, Olon, Orhon, Pejon, Philon, Phinon, Rayon, Similon, Suron, Taron, Trifon, Trion, Trithon, Tyron, Zaron, and Zeron.

Osiris—the ancient sun god who is the husband and brother of Isis; a territorial spirit linked to Freemasonry, the third eye of Freemasonry, the all-seeing eye, anger, envy, jealousy, distraction from the purposes of God, and rejection; an excellent gatekeeper that works with Isis; gained permission from occult activity in ancestry; said, "I see the moon" and "What a show this family has been!"; a ruling prince, it has manifested as a purple, pulsating light; in a trinity with Azy and Micah; a spider that said, "I plant thoughts"; involved in all addiction; its works also include revenge, torment, rebellion, heart disease, unforgiveness, confusion, fibromyalgia, arthritis, abandonment, fear, rage, depression, loneliness, migraines, damaged eyesight, and diabetes; has manifested as a sun in the neck and throat. Other names of Osiris include Asar Tem Ka Kha, Ap-Uat, Ptah Tettet, Seb, Heru, An-Her, Anpu-Khent-Neter-Seh, Nut, Shenthit, Heqtit, Neshnet, Net, Serqet, Maat, Ahit, Meskhen, Amseth, Hapi, Neteru Qerti, Aturti Rest Meht, Amkhiu, Nu Asar, Anpu, Aaron, Agess, Dogger, Explent, Garvor, Islana, Betcatacon, Roi, Klodo, Negress, and Phillipe. See Isis and Micah.

Ovacon—Its works include ovarian cancer and bestiality.

ovaries—Demons involved in diseases and disorders of the ovaries include Abuki (cysts), Belial, Calipso (cysts), Colial (linked to cancers of breasts and ovaries), Farrell, Jasmine, Katasha (cancer), Kitel (cancer), Lorba (cysts), Lochtea (cysts), Mamar (cysts), Opa (cancer),

Orman (polycystic ovarian syndrome), Pentoulle, Scorpio (cancer), Sedona, Sesanna (cysts), and Tubal-Cain (said, "I have teeth," and manifested as a dragon in stomach, ovaries, and gallbladder).

P

Pace—Its works include restlessness.

Pacer—a driving sleep robber, its works include unrest; manifested as an eagle in solar plexus. Associated with Hamb, whose works also include restlessness, pacing, and driving. See Sarcan.

pancreas—Disorders of the pancreas are often linked to Boice, Gena (causes diabetes; manifested as a sparrow), and Mikal (look for squid). See diabetes.

paralysis—Huntington's chorea or paralysis with or from strokes often involves Hundageer and Par.

pedophilia—often the work of Lackla.

peptic ulcers—often the work of a demon named Palsy.

perceptual distortion—associated with Bashtar, Caanan, Daemeon, Hyperbole, Jeikyll, Pharoih, and Pordo. See Daemeon.

peritonitis—often the work of Darkama, Dygreenima (peritonitis; manifested as a black bird), and Ioma.

Peter—Though the name means rock or wealth, this demon does the opposite; it is a scorpion spirit and a commander of fear whose works include rejection, confusion, anger, false words from God, guilt, shame, suicide, deception, doubt, unbelief, stress, depression, and sleeplessness; a ministry robber, it is associated with bondage of all kinds and all physical pain. It said, "I make her tired," during a deliverance session; has manifested as a mouse and an imaginary childhood friend; and is linked to high cholesterol. It is also known as Pete.

Philemon—a spirit whose works include ambition, pride, depression, and rejection; a serpent in the mind; has manifested as a horse; gained permission through Freemasonry.

Phillip—Its functions include deception, anger, confusion, blasphemy; panic/anxiety, family dysfunction, and rejection; has manifested as a canopy blocking a man's praise and prayer, a dragon, and as a blue snake with venom in the mind and belly.

Pig—associated with food addiction, sexual appetite, and gluttony; under Woteige; gained permission through Mafia heritage. See gluttony and Woteige.

Pink—king of weakness, fatigue, pain, affliction, restlessness, embarrassment, humiliation, and poverty; a blocker; part of Orion's kingdom; a pink swirl; said, "I'm here to annoy you"; one source may be heavy metal music; gained permission through ancestral witchcraft.

pituitary gland—Demons that attack this part of the body include Farrell, Goratus, Hell, and Rezpan.

plantar fasciitis—often the work of a demon called Amphibole.

Poindexter—strong mockery spirit with humor and deception; usually with the Jackal; manifested as a fish; its name at creation was Clove, which means joy; its functions now are anxiety, fear, doubt, unbelief, nightmares, fear, IBS, and revenge.

Pokémon—See Xzen.

pornography—Demons whose works include pornography include Absalom, Ashera, Ashtoroth, Beliff, Belshazar, Bomulus, Bueal, Cirius, Clyde, Corneo, Crustifix, Dagger, Darben, Diamonte, Erli, Fastiggle, Glok, Hagar, Herron, Isaac, Isis, Jacob, Jake, Jasmine (oral sex), Jeppeth, Jenoch, Julio, Krol, Kroma, Kryon, Lackla, Lars, Lugerious, Lyle (from ancestors; the pornography spirit often manifests with pain beneath the left shoulder blade), Maquina, Marshall, Mashawn, Mitre, Monarch, Muusel, Pantasia, Pillar, Raunelb, Retralia, Snogg, Spearnach, Swest, Tipton, Totem, Viceroy, Wart, and Xzlima. See Absalom and Isis.

prejudice—one of the works of the following demons: Edemagar, Ekbah (an African spirit), Jundy, Klla, Penurial, Superiority (a demonic prince), and White Peak (a KKK and Freemasonry spirit).

premenstrual syndrome (PMS)—often the work of Belial, Eater, and Galaza. See Belial.

prostate cancer—Associated demons include Leuctia, Melanomis, Tarver, Zel, and Zenama.

prostatitis—Demons associated with this condition include Abar (entered from lust), Abaddon, Alazon (also linked to hatred and nightmares), Assyrian, Brez (also involved in problems in the urinary tract), Garvin (also linked to kidney diseases), Jasarus (its works include enlarged prostate), Leuctia (also connected to prostate cancer), Pleegel, Preminarius, Proeil, Scepter, Shimrah, Spoonge, Zel (also linked to prostate cancer), and Zimion. See Abaddon and Jasarus.

prostitution—This is among the works of Borechon, Boricon, Bymas, Trymas, and Valentine.

psoriasis—Demons often linked to this condition include Noestra and Timbra.

Psychobabel—Its works include mixed messages, confusion, and distraction; works with Babel (which is linked to disease and acid reflux) and Aguafur (which is associated with heartburn, digestive disorders, and acid reflux).

Q

Quantum—Its works include all addiction; manifested as a boar in the emotional heart; caused pressure in the head.

Quarro—Its works include rejection.

Quartz—territorial spirit; its works include fear and unrest.

Quasar—Its works include divorce and relationship robbing.

Quatar—said, "I'm not the prince; I'm the queen"; entered through Queensrÿche's music; may be spelled Katar.

Queen of Heaven—a manifestation of Ishtar. See Jezebel.

Quiznor—Its works include doubt with questions.

R

Ra—the Egyptian sun god in Osiris and Horus' kingdom; also known as Reneth; punishes with unhealthy self-esteem, frustration, and poverty; manifested as a sun swallowed in darkness; an incubus whose works include rape; an intimacy thief and relationship robber that kills life. Its functions also include restlessness, sleeplessness, hypertension, heart disease, and lung cancer. It said, "I am every-where; all is mine." See Osiris and Egyptian gods.

Ra—territorial spirit whose function includes oppression; said, "I roam where I want." When I asked, "Are you the Egyptian sun god?" he said, "I know him!"

Raba—high-ranking rejection spirit; said, "It's us—all of us"; linked to usury/making a profit from the misfortune of others.

Raddple—Its functions include ADHD.

Radooma—Its functions include rejection; has manifested as a winged serpent.

rage—a work associated with Abethor, Alyon, Anchulon, Angemon, Angora, Armtoken, Ashron, Axium, Balthazar, Baphomet, Barclay, Belsha, Beneniah, Bob (gained access when the person was lied to), Boll Weevil, Bull, and Caldronis (its functions include cutting). See Baphomet.

Rahab—strong prince of rejection; a reminding spirit; said, "I'm one of the smaller ones; I always get left behind"; its functions include anger, pride, bronchitis, self-righteousness, haughtiness, self-impor-tance, arrogance, self-deception, ego, and control; has manifested as a leopard and a snail; in Raba's kingdom. "In medieval Jewish folk-lore, Rahab is a mythical sea monster, a dragon of the waters, the 'demonic angel of the sea.' Rahab represents the primordial abyss, the water-dragon of darkness and chaos, comparable to Leviathan and Tiamat. Rahab later became a particular demon, inhabitant of the sea, especially associated with the Red Sea."8

Rahab—territorial spirit whose functions include blame and control.

Rapscallion—Its functions include mononucleosis, fatigue, and autoimmune disorders; gained access from childhood molestation; also enters through mononucleosis, herpes, and Epstein-Barr virus.

rebellion—I have collected pages of names of demons associated with rebellion. That's because all demons are rebels. Some that I encounter repeatedly include Abbadar (whose functions also include anger), Absalom, Acknon, Aerostar, Agabod, Alexander, Allah, Allor, Alzer, Aperapus, Aral-Osiris, Archeus (whose works include pride), Aris, Ashteroth, Augustborn, Axium, Azwrath, Baldasado, Ballismma, Beja, Bodosom, Buscam, Buttress, Cissor, Claptula, Clatics, Cleo, Clovis, Colossus (gained access from anger and rejection), Dahagatharh, Dancer, Dar, Dichon, Dio, Disquias, Druler, Elijam, Filimou, Helic, Ito, Jada, Jeffis, Jezebel, Jonas, Kedash, and Kemar. See Absalom, Alexander, and Jezebel.

Reiki—Its functions include pain; manifested as a bug in the will; entered from "fingers" in a Reiki session (a New Age healing technique); linked to metaphysics.

rejection—I have pages of names of demons whose works include rejection. This is one of the most common attacks made against people because it opens the door to so much other oppression. Some demons I encounter often include Abara, Abaddon, Abelechia (linked to self-rejection), Abisiam (linked to self-rejection), Abiuihanahee, Abknon, Absalom, Achan, Adji, Adolfo, Adolphus, Adul, Agash, Akbar (linked to fear of rejection), Akir (entered through abandonment), Akraba (a ruler of rejection; brings guilt), Alantra, Albacon, Alcazar, Alexander, Alfie, Alfreus, Alikila, Alito, Aljazar, Allah, Alleycat, Alonon, Aloregon, Amadeus, Ama-Molech, Amber, Amos, Anadon, Andoia, Andrew, Angelica, Annais, Anostosh, Anra, Apollyon, Apollyus, and Araba. See Alexander and Apollyon.

relationship robbers—These include Abozar, Acez, Anostosh, Aramais, Arturo, Azusus, Baal (a relationship thief and intimacy robber), Baresh, Besaida, Caleb, Cheryl, Corpius, Cynthor, Delphi, Esop, Frank, Frederick, Gaddori, Genios, He-She, Heron, Howard, Intimacy Thief (causes strife and destroys marriages), Lambasill, Midra, Mordechia, Shalatar, Slayer (kills relationships), Theresa, and Yoguf.

religious abuse—a particular function of Lalac, Radish, and Tadish.

resentment—a common function of the spirits Aswan (from abandonment), Bantanavana (linked to fibromyalgia, which is almost always rooted in bitterness and unforgiveness), Belgar (linked to asthma), Camo, Gulti, Horab, Jularee (its functions also include bitterness), Kalana, Karl, Labyamo, Laza, Lazo, Malo, Naldol, Parham/Paddy, Pocure, Red Dot, Rezna, Vishnu, Zellinimus, and Zephius.

Risellen—Its works include rage, fear, arthritis, and hypertension; works for Risnofin; works with Osiris and Isis.

Risk—steals hope.

Risnan—Its works include desire for tattoos and rebellion; manifested as a flea.

Risnofin—Its functions include anger, rage, and suicide; manifested as a serpent in the feet.

Rosemary—territorial spirit whose works include loneliness.

Rosemary—a seducing spirit whose works include false love, inappropriate sexual desire, eye conditions, fatigue in the eyes, eye strain, headaches, and fear of isolation; manifested as a serpent in the emotions; gained permission through going to psychics; said, "I'm the queen; I'm the high one"; claims power through the Catholic Church and the rosary.

Rufus—Its works include fear of betrayal, arthritis, hypertension, thyroid disorders, high cholesterol, nervousness, headaches, and torment; manifested as a jaguar and a roach in the head; gained permission through Freemasonry in ancestry and unforgiveness.

Rycher—Its works include masturbation.

S

Sabel—lesbian spirit whose works include torment and inordinate desires; located in the brain and affects chemical releases; a serpent of sexual perversion; gained permission through childhood sexual abuse.

Sacanaz—a damnable seed spirit whose works include schizophrenia, vile blasphemy, and pain; associated with Carnavan.

sacrifice (human)—a function of Tamuz (linked to Satan worship), El Lobo (a wolf/werewolf), and Myazoma (associated with worship of Lucifer and pagan sacrificial rites). See Molech/Moloch and Molecha.

Sadona (or Sedona)—Belial's twin; linked to problems with female organs, Bartholin's cysts, and endometriosis.

Sagitarius—Its works include sorrow, rejection, sexual perversion, and gastritis.

Sally—a prince that prevents relationships; its works include insecurity, rejection, heaviness, torture, fatigue with depression, and hypoglycemia; a succubus that manifested as a salamander in the thyroid.

Samhain—a ruler of the bipolar kingdom under Tamar; its works include hatred, lust, self-gratification, masturbation, eating disorders, hypertension, anxiety/panic, doubt, unbelief, and ringing in the ears; manifested as a serpent with the venom of fear, a raven to sabotage life, a salmon, and a grackle. See Tamar.

Samhain—territorial spirit in Ireland; the spirit worshipped by the Son of Sam cult; its works include murder, torture, turmoil, havoc, and chaos. Works with Bladeromain, whose functions include violence, chaos, and murder; sometimes enters through abortion; if Bladeromain is already present, it might be responsible for abortion. It said during a deliverance session, "This spirit does not like you. He says terrible things about you. He doesn't like you because you force him to truth and because you are honorable…He hates you!" He often expresses his disgust with me, saying, "I am havoc."

Samhain—a strong prince that kills with misery and chaos; its works include suicide, anger, mockery, fear, sexual arousal, wantonness, greed, incest, pornography; bipolar spirit; manifested as a ball of fire; co-prince with Bread of Life (both worked for Devoshee); Samhain said, "I am a turtle that slows the mind."

Sarcan—territorial spirit over Texas that claims to be higher in rank than Elamond, a commander in Satan's army who is third under Rasha, Xanthan, and Beelzebub.

Sartoohe—a sleep robber that brings nightmares and fatigue.

Satan—Many demons call themselves Satan, but he will not show up at your deliverance session. Any demon using his name is lying.

Satan worship—a function of Baphomet, Goat, Mazoma (a reminding spirit), Samhain, Tammuz, and Warloc. See Baphomet and Samhain.

Satana—a succubus whose works include ecstasy and getting high.

Satyr—a succubus that manifests during bipolar highs; its works include condemnation, headaches, confusion, and sexual perversion; entered through childhood abuse; manifested as a half man/half horse.

scoliosis—We frequently encounter the following demons in relation to this issue: Dramadis, Gravel, Jac (pronounced Jase), Lamech, Regatuda, and Slayta.

seduction—a function of many spirits, including Absalom, Catrana, Katrina, Pussywillow, Ouarura, and Tiaus. See Absalom.

Seguekirk (pronounced Si-gay-kirk)—Its works include anger and fear of being ostracized, excluded, and shut off.

seizures—a function of Artrial, Cappinicus, Delbataba, Manaston, Mephibosheth, Mishona, Mytos, and Sitzizan.

self-mutilation—The following demons are often involved in this practice: Abollanod, Barskolemue (cutting), Caldronis (cutting), Cyleem, Danaska, Delevis, Dinonakta, Tom (trichotillomania, a hairpulling disorder), Darnus (cutting), Johad (cutting), Malco (cutting), Orkwright, Paul (cutting), Rascald (cutting), and Zothar (cutting).

sensuality—Demons that are especially known for this work include Haveta, Malayshay, and Petulia.

Shamon El—a territorial death demon; its works include infection. See Zaba, anorexia, bulimia, and gluttony.

Shockadula—territorial spirit; said, "I can't get inside her. I own her son; he's mine." Often associated with birth defects, Down syndrome, and anger with violence.

sinuses—one of the works of Igneous (entered from nicotine addiction), Marsar (its works include sinus headaches; manifested as a caterpillar in the eyes/sinuses), Precep, Sid, Smittym, and Tagasus.

sleep apnea—Demons associated with this condition include Bophometh, Burké, Carna, Chalie, Evlar, Garvin, Laryra, Oxford, Saymore, Shiraz, Slowia, Tamar, Tisu, and Zondondra. See Baphomet and Tamar.

sodomy—Its works include humiliation and sexual perversion; associated with Boshem and Zaba (whose works include anger, rage, and fear).

Spartacus—functions include anorexia and bulimia; manifested as a rat in the bowels.

Spider—a spirit whose works include gossip, temptation, and tension. Associated with arachnophobia (an inordinate fear of spiders), Amerato (which brings depression in the mind, causes osteoarthritis, and said, "My venom is hatred"), Arachnid, and Arachne (who said, "I create the web"). In Greek mythology, Arachne was a mortal woman who defeated the goddess Athena in a weaving contest. Ashamed for besting a goddess, Arachne hanged herself, but

Athena loosened the rope, which became a cobweb, and changed Arachne into a spider.[9] See Kali/Cali.

Squid—a ten-tentacled demon linked to diabetes. See Woteige.

Squird—Its works include all addiction; manifested as a life raft in the mind; said, "I keep him afloat."

Squix—a ruler of the evil eye.

succubus—a sexual arousal spirit in female form that comes to men in the night to have sexual intercourse with them, much like an incubus does to a woman. See incubus.

Syrus—a devouring spirit of depression whose works include wanderlust, mind control, and addiction; part of a vast kingdom; manifested as a wolf; gained permission through tuberculosis in ancestry.

T

Taby—Its works include migraine headaches. He said, "I am a bull; I plunder with pain." I used the two-edged sword of the Word of God on him, and he responded, "That's not fair." A spirit called Tordo was with him.

Talon—creates metabolism disorder and thyroid malfunction; is a ruler of physical pain and a strong controller; was located on the back with talons, but it also can be in the central nervous system as a serpent or in the mind with claws (like a vulture). It said, "I pierce the mind and drain"; its works include depression and mental anguish. Duece is a twin of this spirit; it is a ruler of the bipolar kingdom whose functions include depression. It manifested as a vulture, a falcon in the chest, a hawk in the central nervous system, and as a constricting serpent wrapped around the head causing headaches; its works include eating disorders with fear of germs, fear, mockery, anger, pacing, sleeplessness, goiters, nausea, emphysema, and fibromyalgia; gained permission from anger and from people in the person's ancestry prostituting the Word of God.

Talon (pronounced Tay-lon)—a restless, driving, pacing territorial spirit whose works include thyroid malfunction, rejection, abandonment, and schizophrenia; manifested as a serpent in the nervous system at the base of the skull.

Tamar—territorial spirit whose works include mind control (mind over matter), manipulation, rejection, fear of auto accidents, sleep apnea, misery, doubt, unbelief, diabetes, stress, PMS, and ulcers in the mouth; manifested as a mole in the pancreas, a centipede in the nerves, and a spider in the mind; gained permission through a therapy group; a twin to Jango.

Tempest—a whirlwind from an ancestral curse that goes back eighteen generations; claims to be a basilisk and stronger than a tiger; its works include anger, rage, rebellion, fear (also of authority), night terrors, sleepiness in spiritual situations, delayed speech development, torment, and rejection; manifested as a bear in the chest.

Tenacious—a blocker with power and strength; a serpent that kills/breaks the spirit.

terror—Spirits known for this function include Aggdu, Baltashar, Baphomet, Betainment, Crucible, Fang, Limitation, Restriction, Ricla, Oxus, Smith, Tara, Tied Feet (oppresses, holds down, holds back), Toomeeth/Geeoma, Washash (accesses through dreams), and Wrewrazy (brings confusion). See Baphomet.

testes/testicles—See Belial. Other spirits linked to issues with this area of the body include Lustaraba, Myra, and Zenama, all of whose works include cancer.

Third Eye of Freemasonry—See Horus, Isis, Osiris, and Ra. The third eye, also known as the all-seeing eye, is referenced in many ancient civilizations and is known among Freemasons as the Eye of Providence. According to some accounts, it was worshipped as the solar eye, also known as the Eye of Ra or the Eye of Horus in Egyptian mythology. It also has been linked to the Eye of Jove, or Jupiter, in Roman mythology and the eye of Phoebus, or Apollo, in Greek mythology.

Thor—the mythical god of thunder, lightning, and storms, Thor is a territorial spirit over Norway whose works include depression, fear from threat, hopelessness, anger, rage, confusion, low self-esteem, allergies, and back problems that require surgery; manifested as a monkey on the back and a bird in the thyroid.

thyroid malfunction—Demons associated with disorders of the thyroid include Aloza (a destroyer of thyroid glands), Amar, Anius, Bledsoe, Cusho, Druel (causes hypothyroidism), Ducala, Felic (causes hypothyroidism), Gibforth, Gibon, Helter, Hepsa, Hormann, Jareeca (causes fatigue), Jarvis, Kasar, Lectern, Leezer, Leer, Leopold, Lesis (a keeper of the gate for thyroid demons), Ludwigg, Lurge, Machelle, Mahor (causes Graves' disease), Mosic, Perilus, Quazar (causes metabolism malfunctions; manifested as a spider in the thyroid), Relos (causes overactive metabolism), Rufus, Sally, Selsius, Shata, Shelob, Sit, Slut, Stonewall, Talon (causes metabolism disorders), Talon (pronounced Tay-lon), Tonsu, Ugo, and Vola (causes hypothyroidism).

Tourette's syndrome—a condition often linked to Cul, which refers to a passageway, as in a cul-de-sac, an entrance with no way out except to backtrack. The doorway to Cul was alcohol abuse in ancestry. Other demons associated with Tourette's include Dakota, Denothropy, Ze, and Zenatar.

trichotillomania—compulsive hairpulling is a work of the following demons: Creet, Fivroid, Haruke, Jeed, Mikatral, Tabu, Timeron, and Vinedine. See Fivroid, compulsion, and rejection.

Tubal-Cain—a major Freemasonry spirit, it is a destroyer of hope whose works include masturbation, abortion, depression, betrayal, arrogance, destruction, and impotence; keeps a person from being submissive and twists thoughts away from God; said, "I have teeth"; manifested as a dragon in the stomach, ovaries, and gallbladder and caused infirmity in the chest from oaths that were like a spear to the chest. A wolf spirit that often manifests with two red eyes, it is a devourer whose functions also include lust, sexual abuse, selfishness, a curse on the stomach, cancer, diabetes, hypoglycemia, failure, fear, doubt, unbelief, rebellion, anger, bitterness, violence, death of the mind, paranoia, and self-hatred. It has also manifested as bull destroying the mind and a vulture in the mind.

U

Umbra—a shield that blocks God's light; keeps a person hidden from others and their talents. The sun is the only body in the solar system that shines with its own light. All the others, including Earth and the moon, reflect the sun's light. They also cast shadows. When in the course of their orbits the moon's shadow falls on Earth, or vice versa, it is known as an eclipse. There are two parts to these shadows. The umbra is a central cone of darkness, which tapers away from Earth or the moon, while the penumbra is an outer cone of partial shadow that diverges instead of tapering.

unforgiveness—This gives demons legal permission to torment believers. Holding on to unforgiveness will hinder deliverance, so this is a big issue. These are just some of the demons whose functions include unforgiveness: Aachen, Ababba, Abaddon, Amalek, Aranish, Ben, Buser, Casseopia, Caylor, Ceiltoia, Centric, Christian, Creighton, Damus (gained access from rejection), Derek, Epod, Esau, Estrella, Harson, Hate (pronounced Hay-tee), Hedley, Hezbollah, Horab, Jabel, Jareel, Jath, Joel, Jonah, Joss, Kalana, Kenrod (linked to unforgiveness of self), Kodu, Laza, Lazo, Loche, Madlin, MaHa Bone, Methdon, Morash, Mossha, Nahum, Nequa, Obadee (linked to unforgiveness of self), Obar, Okmulgee, Omer, Osiris, Osmos, Ostuce, Pestisese, Plebus, Pradylis, Ragul, Resgar, Rostarifin, Rufus, Rumpelstiltskin, Schustamaya, Scyune, Shenta, Spinx (linked to unforgiveness of self), Staste, Talcum, Trana, Valiant, Wanna, Wormwood, Xenon, Yavo, Zachariah (associated with fear of unforgiveness), and Zumba. See Abaddon, MaHa Bone, Osiris, and Wormwood.

urinary tract—Demons linked to disorders in the urinary tract include Amethyst (urinary tract infection), Belial, Bisimo, Blojo,

Brez, Charles, Diana (bladder issues), Garvin, Hadar (bladder collapse), Jella, Lato (bladder issues), Papataus, Piries, Portia (bladder issues), Preskklo, Polymus, Rasham, Smulith (weak bladder), Stony, Sudo, Terrance, Tramella (urinary tract infection), Uri (irritation, pain, frequent urination), and Viath. See Belial and Blojo.

uterine conditions—Demons associated with disorders of the uterus are Arcolias, Bedough (cancer), Belchezk (cancer in genitalia), Belial (cancer), Blargy (tumors and cancer), Elizabeth (cancer), Eulsies (cysts), Kitel (cancer), Molech/Moloch, Pentoulle, Scorpio (cancer), Sedona (cancer), Tartar (cysts), Peptis (cancer), and Zenama (cancer). See Belial, Blargy, Elizabeth, Molech/Moloch, and Sadona/Sedona.

V

varicose veins—one of the works of Astoroth, Khan, Leonal, Tokia, and Ziegler.

Venus—historically, the Roman goddess of love; a succubus and incubus associated with abnormal sex desire, false love, and lesbianism; under Witchcraft; a constrictor, this serpent spirit is also associated with pain in the veins and carpal tunnel syndrome.

violence—a function of spirits including Abaddon, Absalom, Alvaizeitan (alcohol addiction and murder), Asmodaus (violence, suicide, and killing), Asmodawn (vengeance), Baalbalieth (blackness, murder, and satanic power), Baalberiath (blasphemy and murder), Babel (sexual violence), Carvar (spiritual destruction, under the demon called Lucifer), Druler, Evil Eye, Gehazi, Goratus, Karate (violence and murder), Kelton, Lexel, Meamerana (destructive violence), Orbiton (with anger), P. Verde, Waldridrianumco, and Yaba. See Abaddon, Absalom, and Yaba.

Virgo—Its works include religious control; manifested as an eel shocking the emotions; gained permission through witchcraft and the veneration of St. Bernadette.

vows—a function of Bethumet, a blessing robber that has gained access through oaths to a labor union.

Vulcan—territorial spirit over Africa; manifested as a snake.

vulgarity—Associated demons include Ike, Ishtar, McKreg, and Rathcon. See Ishtar.

W

wandering—a function of Gypsy, Jarthor, and Nomad. See Nomad.

warts—Spirits associated with this issue include Ghoolagosh (a ruler of warts), Jeremiah, Dana (causes genital warts), Higbiggler (causes genital warts), and Redelic (causes genital warts).

Watcher—a spy for the territorial spirits; gathers information for the witches; associated with a G, or maybe Agee (a ruling prince and watcher that has manifested as a blue dragon); located on the outside of the body; gained permission from a Wiccan curse; also associated with Beton (manifested as an eagle).

weakness—a function of Marlo (causes candida), Seala, Sula, Titan, and Wangleesa (linked to heart disease).

Wearer of Gold—a general in the demonic kingdom; its works include division and distraction through addictions; during deliverance he kept pointing to his crown, which fell when exposed to the crown of righteousness belonging to Christ Jesus; works with the territorial spirits Traveler and the Great Warrior.

Wicca—Its works include thyroid problems, cold feet, embarrassment, humiliation, sexual perversion, occultism, tarot card reading, mediums, fatigue, guilt, shame, hopelessness, and depression. Setia is a Wiccan spirit of fear.

witchcraft—a function of Ambilflin, Charlotte, Clarex (puts a hex on car drivers to cause them to drive off the road), Diana, Keeshba, Rosemary, Mojo (entered from a voodoo curse), Moletha, Tobetha, Jezebel (its works include manipulation and female dominance; it manipulates to control people), Evil Eye, Third Eye, Ra, Attuor, Horus (causes injury and harm and is associated with jealousy, witchcraft, and mind control), and Venus (its works include witchcraft, supernatural sex desires, and false love). See Horus, Jezebel, and Ra.

Wormwood—Its functions include bitterness, grief, conniving, anxiety, depression, suicide, confusion, anger, fear, arthritis, and fibromyalgia; causes the root of bitterness to grow deep and become entangled; a parasite in the joints; gained permission from hatred in ancestry; manifested as a baboon.

Woteige—A ruling spirit, its works include gluttony, body illness, digestive disorders, self-hatred, weight gain, fatigue, diabetes, frustration, idleness, self-reward, listlessness, giving up, retreating, lust, pride, anger, nearsightedness, hypertension, self-pity, and compulsive eating; manifested as an octopus in the eye muscles; is an octopus over the diabetes kingdom; when asked who's in charge, it said, "Who's got more legs?"; associated with Fells (linked to gluttony and may be related to fear of disapproval) and Felix (whose works include self-pity); causes weakened hearts; permission was granted by a word curse when the person said, "I wish I could wear glasses."

Wu Toga—territorial spirit over Kenya and Morocco; said, "I rank seventh in the heavenlies"; destroys health and causes diabetes (by attacking the pancreas); said, "You've never seen anything like me. I'm one of a kind; Leviathan has nothing on me"; has seven heads that spew fire, as well as wings and a tail that stings.

X

Xanthan—known for bringing a totality of affliction; equal to Baath; its works include bringing total darkness and complete void, rebellion, cancerous cells in moles, depression, hopelessness, suicide, migraines, cancer, and endometriosis; has manifested as a large X and cloaked in a red cape; a friend of Samhain (whose functions include cancer and fear of abandonment). See Baath and Samhain.

Xeniah (or Zeniah)—an incubus whose works include hate, torment, discord, disgust, and distrust; of Irish background; responded in an Irish accent during a deliverance session.

Xerxes—a destroyer of belief that makes one sleepy; a fire of fear; under Argon; linked with Hermes under the territorial prince Darius; said, "I'm the king of rejection!"; permission gained through astrology involvement. Historically, Darius became king of Persia after the death of his father, Darius the Great, in 485, at a time when his father was preparing a new expedition against Greece. The Persian King Xerxes is depicted by the Greek historian Herodotus as a superstitious fool and a bloodthirsty tyrant.

Xzen—a thought-disruption, witchcraft spirit from "pocket monsters" also linked to fibromyalgia; manifested as a vulture in the head; linked to Druid worship. See Pokémon.

Y

Yaba—Its functions include alcohol addiction, violence, and destruction; works with Abaddon.

YaYa—Its works include confusion, distraction, and ADD; has manifested as a chicken.

yoga—associated with Kundalini (a spirit that manifested at the base of the spine whose works include guilt/shame), and Tibetan (a spirit that causes deception and false worship whose permission was participation in yoga and transcendental meditation).

Z

Zaba—Its works include rejection, self-pity, death, and destruction; associated with Winton (which brings bipolar spirits) and Bacheen (a demonic prince of fear that causes bipolar disorder, mood swings, a whirlwind of thoughts, depression, sadness with fear, anger, and rage).

Zaccariee—Its works include fear and nightmares; manifested as a man-shaped lizard.

Zachafarius—linked to voodoo and witchcraft, particularly in Africa.

Zelot—Its works include criminal activity and sexual perversion; manifested as a debonair male; caused sex abuse.

Zelsum—Its functions include doubt and unbelief; has manifested as an eagle in the mind.

Zelt—Its works include food addiction; located in the fat/flesh of arms and legs; has manifested as a rooster.

Zeltec—a vulture in the chest whose works include gluttony.

Zelzebarr—a scorpion soldier in the mind whose works include fear and depression.

Zen—Its works include sickness, oppression through torment/ nightmares, and thought disruption; manifested as a wolf; entered through child molestation.

Zephyr—Greek god of the west wind who said, "I blew in on winds of opportunity"; its works include bipolar disorder, havoc in the mind, dysfunction, confusion, depression, fatigue, rejection, perversion, hypertension, stress overload, and chemical imbalance in the brain; a holder of curses; has manifested as a green dragon, a fish, an aardvark in the left arm, a bullfrog, and a snake with the venom of confusion; permission gained through Buddhism and alcohol abuse.

Zeus—territorial spirit whose works include distress, torment, hopelessness, lust, sleep disorders, migraines, poverty, disaster, fear, rejection, family trauma/disorder, and impatience; manifested as a hammer and a constrictor in the throat; exaggerates/chokes the truth; a serpent spirit that steals from people; permission gained from occult practices in ancestry.

Zilon—a serpent spirit with the venom of disruption in the central nervous system; a health robber whose works include neuropathy; manifested as a Japanese beetle; gained permission from trauma.

Zippulus—a ram that brings lies and deceit; linked to addiction to prescription drugs, and bulimia.

Zombie—a person whose behavior or responses are mechanical and automatic as if they are in a trance or spell; described as dead men walking; often stems from a voodoo curse or involvement.

Zor—the ancient god of Tyre; linked to Freemasonry and Baal Zor, the Phoenician god of Tyre; a consuming fire whose works include rebellion, control/manipulation, anger, and addiction. See Baal, Beelzebub, and Molech/Moloch.

Zora—assigned to the heart; its works include arterial sclerosis, rejection, torment, and heart disease.

Zoraster—linked to sexual perversion; has manifested as a vulture with a long beak.

Zorca—a serpent spirit in the central nervous system.

Zorca the Great—considered a king, ruler, and master that robs people of health and brings mental disorders, neuropathy, and fragile X syndrome; has manifested as a Japanese beetle.

Zoroaster—a ruling prince of deception over a large kingdom; called for territorial spirits; permission gained from an ancestral oath of Freemasonry; associated with Reginald, Alistar, Rasheed, and Tank (a blocker outside the body).

Zucum—Its works include the opposite of gluttony, gluten intolerance, and a ripping/tearing in the nervous system; manifested as a devouring vulture; gained permission from a Druid curse.

CONCLUSION

WALKING IN AUTHORITY

SOMEONE REMARKED TO me recently that they were told in a Bible study group that it is not wise to venture into deliverance ministry. They said, "We were told that we must have a huge prayer covering before attempting deliverance." Interesting!

Where does the Word say that? Of course, I would always prefer to have many people praying for me, but the disciples didn't have that covering—they had a commission. Jesus sent them to people. He sent the twelve disciples and He sent seventy rookie disciples out, and there was no large prayer covering; they went in Jesus' name, and that has not changed today.

The name of Jesus is sufficient.

You can't act in Jesus' authority unless that authority has first been exercised in your own life. You can't cast from others what you entertain yourself. But at the same time, I say with great boldness, know who you are in Christ. Know what has been given to you in Christ. Take everything that is yours! We are heirs of God and joint heirs with Jesus Christ—and He knew His power was superior to every other power!

DID JESUS PICK A FIGHT?

Caesarea Philippi, an ancient Roman city, lies twenty-five miles northeast of the Sea of Galilee at the base of Mount Hermon. Known for its abundant spring, one of the largest sources of the Jordan River, the area is lush and scenic. This spring once emerged from a large cave, which became a focal point for pagan worship beginning in the third century BC. Worshippers cast sacrifices into the cave as offerings to Pan, the half-man, half-goat god associated with nature and capable of instilling "panic." The city was initially called Panias in his honor, a name that later evolved into Banias in Arabic. In 2 BC, Herod the Great's son Philip renamed it Caesarea to honor Emperor Augustus, distinguishing it as Caesarea Philippi to set it apart from Caesarea Maritima on the Mediterranean coast.

The cave and spring were believed to be the birthplace of Pan, and a sanctuary was built there. Ancient followers saw the cave as a gate to the underworld (Hades), where they believed fertility gods resided during winter, spurring people to commit abhorrent acts in worship of these false gods. In the Old Testament, this region is referred to as Baal-gad, after a god of fortune who may later have been equated with Pan.

In the New Testament, Caesarea Philippi marks the northernmost point of Jesus' ministry, a place where He could retreat beyond the reach of Herod Antipas, ruler of Galilee. It was here that Jesus asked His disciples, "Who do you say that I am?" (Matt. 16:15, NKJV). In a region steeped in paganism, dotted with the temples of Baal and other gods, Jesus chose this symbolic setting—what some called the "gates of hell"—to pose this profound question. It almost seems that Jesus picked a fight with the so-called gods of this world, asking to be compared with them.

Jesus asked, "Who do men say that I am?" His disciples replied, "Some say John the Baptist, some say Elijah." Jesus pressed them: "But who do you say that I am?" Jesus was speaking to Peter, who boldly replied, "You are the Christ, the Son of the living God" (Matt. 16:16, NKJV). What a tremendous statement of faith!

Jesus responds: "Blessed are you, Simon Bar-Jonah, for flesh and blood has not revealed this to you, but My Father who is in heaven. And I also say to you that you are Peter, and on this rock I will build My church, and the gates of Hades shall not prevail against it" (Matt. 16:17–18, NKJV). They were at the so-called entrance to the gates of hell, possibly an allusion to the cave!

Not even the revered gods of the Syrians, Greeks, or Romans could compare to the Christ. His divinity, power, and authority were real, eternal, and unstoppable. And Jesus is still Lord of heaven and earth. Then Jesus said, "And that's not all. You will have complete and free access to God's kingdom, keys to open any and every door: no more barriers between heaven and earth, earth and heaven. A yes on earth is yes in heaven. A no on earth is no in heaven" (v. 19, MSG).

Jesus declared victory right in the face of all demons and false gods at the very gates of hell. It was His only trip to that demonic city on the northernmost edge of Israel.

In Caesarea Philippi, Jesus declared war on false religion and gave us authority in His name to not fear the enemies of the gospel but rather to stand when the war is raging.

WE ALWAYS WIN!

As believers, we have been given authority over "all the power of the enemy" (Luke 10:19). Jesus holds the keys of death and hell, but He also took the keys of the prison (bondage to the kingdom of darkness) and gave them to the church. God wants His people free, and He has commissioned us to act in the name of Jesus Christ. Demons still bow and retreat in His mighty name.

When Jesus walked this earth, He conquered disease, demons, and death and demonstrated His authority that would soon be given unto believers. He revealed His authority over wind and waves, He walked on water and calmed seas, He spoke a curse to a tree and it died, and He spoke to Lazarus and he lived. He said:

> Have faith in God. For verily I say unto you, That whosoever shall say to this mountain, Be thou removed, and be thou cast into the sea; and shall not doubt in his heart, but shall believe that those things which he saith shall come to pass; he shall have whatsoever he saith.
>
> —MARK 11:22–23

What awesome words He spoke. Have faith in God. If you can believe, you can receive. Please note that the *whosoever* in verse 22 is the same *whosoever* that calls men to Christ. It includes any believer, not just "special" believers. It includes you.

When the seventy had returned from their appointed, anointed mission in Luke 10:1–7, they marveled. These were not the twelve disciples, nor were they their relatives. They were *whosoevers*, representative of the church today, and He gave them authority. You have that same authority.

Do not dismiss this; do not try to keep yourself within the restrictions of a church doctrine. The church is living beneath the oppressing power of the enemy, but it is time for the truth to come out. Jesus told us, "I give you the authority to trample on serpents and scorpions, and over all the power of the enemy, and nothing shall by any means hurt you....The spirits are subject to you" (Luke 10:19–20, NKJV). Receive this wonderful truth and be part of freeing God's people from bondage.

The church should be free! Jesus paid for our freedom. Demons have intimidated our preachers and Christian leaders. We must take back what is ours. The blood of Jesus Christ has not lost any power, nor will it. The name of Jesus Christ still causes demons to tremble and retreat. The gates of hell will never prevail against the church of the Lord Jesus. I tell people all the time, "We always win!"

SCRIPTURES RELATED TO DELIVERANCE

Matthew 4:24: "And his fame went throughout all Syria: and they brought unto him all sick people that were taken with divers diseases and torments, and those which were possessed with devils, and those which were lunatick, and those that had the palsy; and he healed them."

Matthew 7:22: "Many will say to me in that day, Lord, Lord, have we not prophesied in thy name? and in thy name have cast out devils? and in thy name done many wonderful works?"

Matthew 8:16: "When the even was come, they brought unto him many that were possessed with devils: and he cast out the spirits with his word, and healed all that were sick."

Matthew 8:28: "And when he was come to the other side into the country of the Gergesenes, there met him two possessed with devils, coming out of the tombs, exceeding fierce, so that no man might pass by that way."

Matthew 8:31: "So the devils besought him, saying, If thou cast us out, suffer us to go away into the herd of swine."

Matthew 8:33: "And they that kept them fled, and went their ways into the city, and told every thing, and what was befallen to the possessed of the devils."

Matthew 9:34: "But the Pharisees said, He casteth out devils through the prince of the devils."

Matthew 10:8: "Heal the sick, cleanse the lepers, raise the dead, cast out devils: freely ye have received, freely give."

Matthew 12:24: "But when the Pharisees heard it, they said, This fellow doth not cast out devils, but by Beelzebub the prince of the devils."

Matthew 12:27: "And if I by Beelzebub cast out devils, by whom do your children cast them out? therefore they shall be your judges."

Matthew 12:28: "But if I cast out devils by the Spirit of God, then the kingdom of God is come unto you."

Mark 1:32: "And at even, when the sun did set, they brought unto him all that were diseased, and them that were possessed with devils."

Mark 1:33: "And he healed many that were sick of divers diseases, and cast out many devils; and suffered not the devils to speak, because they knew him."

Mark 1:39: "And he preached in their synagogues throughout all Galilee, and cast out devils."

Mark 3:15: "And to have power to heal sicknesses, and to cast out devils."

Mark 3:22: "And the scribes which came down from Jerusalem said, He hath Beelzebub, and by the prince of the devils casteth he out devils."

Mark 5:12: "The devils besought him, saying, Send us into the swine, that we may enter into them."

Mark 6:13: "They cast out many devils, and anointed with oil many that were sick, and healed them."

Mark 9:38: "And John answered him, saying, Master, we saw one casting out devils in thy name, and he followeth not us: and we forbad him, because he followeth not us."

Mark 7:26: "The woman was a Greek, a Syrophenician by nation; and she besought him that he would cast forth the devil out of her daughter."

Mark 7:29: "And he said unto her, For this saying go thy way; the devil is gone out of thy daughter. And when she was come to her house, she found the devil gone out, and her daughter laid upon the bed."

Mark 16:17: "And these signs shall follow them that believe; in my name shall they cast out devils; they shall speak with new tongues."

Luke 4:33–35, NKJV: "Now in the synagogue there was a man who had a spirit of an unclean demon. And he cried out with a loud voice....But Jesus rebuked him, saying, 'Be quiet, and come out of him!' And when the demon had thrown him in their midst, it came out of him and did not hurt him."

Luke 4:41, NKJV: "And demons also came out of many, crying out and saying, 'You are the Christ, the Son of God!' And He, rebuking them, did not allow them to speak, for they knew that He was the Christ."

Luke 8:2: "And certain women, which had been healed of evil spirits and infirmities, Mary called Magdalene, out of whom went seven devils."

Luke 8:27: "And when he went forth to land, there met him out of the city a certain man, which had devils long time, and ware no clothes, neither abode in any house, but in the tombs."

Luke 8:29–30: "(For he had commanded the unclean spirit to come out of the man. For oftentimes it had caught him: and he was kept bound with chains and in fetters; and he brake the bands, and was driven of the devil into the wilderness.) And Jesus asked him, saying, What is thy name? And he said, Legion: because many devils were entered into him."

Luke 8:32–33, NKJV: "Now a herd of many swine was feeding there on the mountain. So they begged Him that He would permit them to enter them. And He permitted them. Then the demons went out of the man and entered the swine, and the herd ran violently down the steep place into the lake and drowned."

Luke 8:35: "Then they went out to see what had happened, and came to Jesus, and found the man from whom the demons had departed, sitting at the feet of Jesus, clothed and in his right mind. And they were afraid."

Luke 8:36: "They also which saw it told them by what means he that was possessed of the devils was healed."

Luke 8:38–39: "Now the man out of whom the devils were departed besought him that he might be with him: but Jesus sent him away, saying, Return to thine own house, and shew how great things God hath done unto thee."

Luke 9:1: "Then he called his twelve disciples together, and gave them power and authority over all devils, and to cure diseases."

Luke 9:42, NIV: "Even while the boy was coming, the demon threw him to the ground in a convulsion. But Jesus rebuked the impure spirit, healed the boy and gave him back to his father."

Luke 9:49: "And John answered and said, Master, we saw one casting out devils in thy name; and we forbad him, because he followeth not with us."

Luke 10:17: "And the seventy returned again with joy, saying, Lord, even the devils are subject unto us through thy name."

Luke 11:14, NIV: "Jesus was driving out a demon that was mute. When the demon left, the man who had been mute spoke, and the crowd was amazed."

Luke 11:15: "But some of them said, He casteth out devils through Beelzebub the chief of the devils."

Luke 11:18: "If Satan also be divided against himself, how shall his kingdom stand? because ye say that I cast out devils through Beelzebub."

Luke 11:19: "And if I by Beelzebub cast out devils, by whom do your sons cast them out? therefore shall they be your judges."

Luke 11:20: "But if I with the finger of God cast out devils, no doubt the kingdom of God is come upon you."

Luke 13:32: "And he said unto them, Go ye, and tell that fox, Behold, I cast out devils, and I do cures to day and to morrow, and the third day I shall be perfected."

John 10:21, NKJV: "Others said, 'These are not the words of one who has a demon. Can a demon open the eyes of the blind?'"

Acts 19:15–16, NKJV: "And the evil spirit answered and said, 'Jesus I know, and Paul I know; but who are you?' Then the man in whom the evil spirit was leaped on them, overpowered them, and prevailed against them, so that they fled out of that house naked and wounded."

1 Corinthians 10:20–21: "But I say, that the things which the Gentiles sacrifice, they sacrifice to devils, and not to God: and I would not that ye should have fellowship with devils. Ye cannot drink the cup of the Lord, and the cup of devils: ye cannot be partakers of the Lord's table, and of the table of devils."

1 Timothy 4:1: "Now the Spirit speaketh expressly, that in the latter times some shall depart from the faith, giving heed to seducing spirits, and doctrines of devils."

James 2:19: "Thou believest that there is one God; thou doest well: the devils also believe, and tremble."

Revelation 9:20, NKJV: "But the rest of mankind, who were not killed by these plagues, did not repent of the works of their hands, that they should not worship demons, and idols of gold, silver, brass, stone, and wood, which can neither see nor hear nor walk."

Revelation 16:14, NKJV: "For they are spirits of demons, performing signs, which go out to the kings of the earth and of the whole world."

Revelation 18:2: "And he cried mightily with a strong voice, saying, Babylon the great is fallen, is fallen, and is become the habitation of devils, and the hold of every foul spirit, and a cage of every unclean and hateful bird."

NOTES

CHAPTER 2

1. Marcela Zapata-Meza and Rosaura Sanz-Rincón, "Excavating Mary Magdalene's Hometown," May/June 2017, Biblical Archaeology Society Library, https://library.biblicalarchaeology.org/article/excavating-mary-magdalenes-hometown.
2. Zapata-Meza and Sanz-Rincón, "Excavating Mary Magdalene's Hometown," emphasis added.

CHAPTER 3

1. James Wesser, "Why Geese Are So Aggressive and Mean," KXAN, May 1, 2023, https://www.kxan.com/news/national-news/why-are-geese-so-aggressive-and-mean/.

CHAPTER 4

1. Tommy Thomas, "Emily Mann Testimony with Don Dickerman," YouTube, accessed November 27, 2024, https://www.youtube.com/watch?v=qya-pqx5pIk.
2. Thomas, "Emily Mann Testimony with Don Dickerman."
3. Thomas, "Emily Mann Testimony with Don Dickerman."
4. Thomas, "Emily Mann Testimony with Don Dickerman."

CHAPTER 5

1. Greg Locke, *Cast It Out* (Charisma House, 2023).
2. "Matthew 12 Bible Commentary," Christianity.com, accessed November 21, 2024, https://www.christianity.com/bible/commentary/matthew-henry-complete/matthew/12.
3. "Matthew 12 Bible Commentary," Christianity.com.

CHAPTER 8

1. Blue Letter Bible, s.v. "*archē*," accessed October 23, 2024, https://www.blueletterbible.org/lexicon/g746/kjv/tr/0-1/.
2. Blue Letter Bible, s.v. "*exousia*," accessed October 23, 2024, https://www.blueletterbible.org/lexicon/g1849/kjv/tr/0-1/.

3. Blue Letter Bible, s.v. *"kosmokratōr,"* accessed October 23, 2024, https://www.blueletterbible.org/lexicon/g2888/kjv/tr/0-1/.
4. Blue Letter Bible, s.v. *"epouranios,"* accessed October 23, 2024, https://www.blueletterbible.org/lexicon/g2032/kjv/tr/0-1/.
5. *Vine's Expository Dictionary of New Testament Words,* s.v. "ruler," accessed October 23, 2024, https://studybible.info/vines/Ruler.

CHAPTER 9

1. *Concise Oxford English Dictionary,* s.v. "paranoia," (OUP Oxford, 2011), https://www.google.com/books/edition/Concise_Oxford_English_Dictionary/4XycAQAAQBAJ?hl=en&gbpv=0.

CHAPTER 10

1. Blue Letter Bible, s.v. *"agalliaō,"* accessed October 23, 2024, https://www.blueletterbible.org/lexicon/g21/kjv/tr/0-1/.
2. *Concise Oxford English Dictionary,* s.v. "exult."

CHAPTER 11

1. "Anubis," *Encyclopaedia Britannica,* last updated November 4, 2024, https://www.britannica.com/topic/Anubis.
2. "2 Timothy 3:8," *Jamieson-Fausset-Brown Bible Commentary,* BibleHub, accessed November 23, 2024, https://biblehub.com/commentaries/2_timothy/3-8.htm.
3. "Ketev Meriri," Halacha Yomit, July 5, 2021, https://halachayomit.co.il/en/default.aspx?HalachaID=2641.
4. Wikipedia, s.v. "Rahab (term)," last updated October 25, 2024, https://en.wikipedia.org/wiki/Rahab_(term).
5. "Lilith," *Encyclopaedia Britannica,* November 8, 2024, https://www.britannica.com/topic/Lilith-Jewish-folklore.
6. "York Rite Honorary Bodies," ooCities.org, accessed November 26, 2024, https://www.oocities.org/athens/forum/6255/Allied.html.
7. "Superior Mesenteric Vein," Cleveland Clinic, accessed November 26, 2024, https://my.clevelandclinic.org/health/body/25169-superior-mesenteric-vein.
8. Wikipedia, s.v. "Rahab (term)."
9. "Arachne," *Encyclopaedia Britannica,* last updated October 28, 2024, https://www.britannica.com/topic/Arachne.

ABOUT THE AUTHOR

A TEXAS NATIVE, DON Dickerman played college basketball at
the University of Texas at Arlington and semi-pro baseball
until a call to ministry led him to seminary. He graduated valedic-
torian from Trinity Valley Seminary and received a Doctor of Theology from Phoenix University of Theology.

Having served as a pastor and associate pastor, in 1974 he birthed
one of the largest prison ministries in the world, preaching in
more than 850 different prisons around the world. He also ministered at two executions. In 1987, Dickerman received a very special
anointing for deliverance and healing.

He and his late wife, Peggy, have two sons, Don Jr. and Rob, who
are the pride of his life.